MR. KNOW-IT-ALL

MR. KNOW-IT-ALL

The Tarnished
Wisdom
of a
Filth Elder

JOHN WATERS

FARRAR, STRAUS AND GIROUX

NEW YORK

Farrar, Straus and Giroux
120 Broadway, New York 10271

Parts of chapter 12, "Delayed," appeared in a different form in *The Wall Street Journal* under a different title. Parts of chapter 9, "I Got Rhythm," and chapter 15, "One-Track Mind," also appeared in different forms in *W* magazine under a different title.

Library of Congress Cataloging-in-Publication Data
Names: Waters, John, 1946– author.
Title: Mr. know-it-all : the tarnished wisdom of a filth elder / John Waters.
Description: First edition. | New York : Farrar, Straus and Giroux, 2019.
Identifiers: LCCN 2018057165 | ISBN 9780374214968 (hardcover)
Subjects: LCSH: Waters, John, 1946– | Motion picture producers and
    directors—United States—Biography. | Aging—Anecdotes.
Classification: LCC PN1998.3.W38 A3 2019 | DDC 814/.54—dc23
LC record available at https://lccn.loc.gov/2018057165

Designed by Abby Kagan

Our books may be purchased in bulk for promotional, educational, or business use. Please contact your local bookseller or the Macmillan Corporate and Premium Sales Department at 1-800-221-7945, extension 5442, or by e-mail at MacmillanSpecialMarkets@macmillan.com.

www.fsgbooks.com
www.twitter.com/fsgbooks • www.facebook.com/fsgbooks

1   3   5   7   9   10   8   6   4   2

He knows . . .

CONTENTS

ILLUSTRATIONS

MR. KNOW-IT-ALL

Somehow I became respectable. I don't know how, the last film I directed got some terrible reviews and was rated NC-17. Six people in my personal phone book have been sentenced to life in prison. I did an art piece called *Twelve Assholes and a Dirty Foot*, which is composed of close-ups from porn films, yet a museum now has it in their permanent collection and nobody got mad. What the hell has happened?

I used to be despised but now I'm asked to give commencement addresses at prestigious colleges, attend career retrospectives at both the Film Society of Lincoln Center and the British Film Institute, and I even got a medal from the French government for "furthering the arts in France." This cockeyed maturity is driving me crazy!

Suddenly the worst thing that can happen to a creative person has happened to me. I am accepted. How can I "struggle" when my onetime underground movies are now easily available?—even *Multiple Maniacs* was rehabilitated music-rights-wise and is back in theatrical release from Janus Films, the original distributor of Godard and Truffaut movies, for God's sake. *Pink Flamingos* has played on television! How can I whine about my films being hard to see when Warner Bros. now handles many of my titles and Criterion, the classiest of all DVD distributors, is restoring some of my rudest celluloid atrocities? Even the Museum of Modern Art now has in their collection the elements of my earliest 8mm movies that have never been formally released, and, jeez, seven of the books I've written are still in print and two of them became *New York Times* bestsellers. How could that be? How?

I can't even impersonate a damaged artist anymore. I have actually had friends for *fifty* years and some of my dinner dates are *not* tax-deductible for business—the sign of really having a successful personal life. Knock on wood, I'm in good health. Good Lord, I'm seventy-three years old and my dreams have come true. Couldn't you just puke?

Success is not the enemy you may think it is when you're young, but if it comes too quickly it can be a high-class problem. Yes, you should feel slightly panicked if your insane early work is taken seriously without any initial resistance, but know that being a starving artist is an outdated concept. There's nothing wrong with making money from doing something you love. You can be happy and fucked-up and still triumph, I promise you.

But suppose you're still failing, struggling unsuccessfully to find your voice? You should ask yourself, am I the only person in the world who thinks what I'm doing is important? If yes, well, you're in trouble. You need *two* people to think your work is good—yourself and somebody else (not your mother). Once you have a following, no matter how limited, your career can be born, and if you make enough noise, those doors will begin to open, and then, and only then, can you soar to lunatic superiority. Mr. Know-It-All is here to tell you exactly how to live your life from that day forward.

I'm never wrong—just ask Joan Rivers—well, you can't,

because she's dead, but when she was alive, I introduced her to a date after we watched her perform in Provincetown and she said to him, "Are you with John?" When he replied yes, she advised, "Just do everything he tells you to do." Joan knew I was infallible. She knew it raw.

First of all, accept that something is wrong with you. It's a good start. Something has always been wrong with me, too. We're in a club of sorts, the lunatic fringe who are proud to band together. There's a joyous road to ruin out there, and if you let me be your garbage guru, I'll teach you how to succeed in insanity and take control of your low self-esteem. Personality disorders are a terrible thing to waste.

Being crazy in a happy creative way begins and ends with your family. No matter how hard you try, as you get older, you turn into a twisted version of your mom and dad. No, it's not fair. But too bad, you can't choose the house you want to be born in, so just look at fate like a bingo card: sometimes you get a winner, other times you have to improvise, switch cards, and even cheat to not lose. That's just how it goes.

Children can't demand good parenting any more than their parents can expect to be made proud. I was lucky. My mom and dad encouraged my dreams right from the beginning even though they must have been scared of their firstborn, who arrived six weeks too early—a preemie. A teacup baby. A little boy slightly miswired, already not following the rules, ahead of his birth time and ready to roll. Maybe I was baptized too often, stripped of my inner coating of original sin. There's only one thing wrong with the Waters baby—It's Alive!

All I know is I was born with a screw loose. I realize now how hard it must have been for my parents to understand my early eccentricities. As a child in kindergarten I always used to come home from school and tell my mother about the twisted little boy in my class who'd only draw with black crayons and never talked to the other kids. I yakked about this unnamed friend so much that my mother eventually mentioned him to my teacher, who looked confused and then blurted, "But that's your son!" I was creating characters early for myself and you should let your kids do the same. Having multiple personalities when you're young is mandatory for a happy childhood.

A few years later, every morning I would slink down the steps of our family home on the way to school pretending I was the *Nude Descending a Staircase* painting I had read about in *Life* magazine. "What's the matter with you, boy?" my dad would sputter, confused for good reason. "Haven't you heard of Duchamp, fool?" I'd haughtily think without ever explaining out loud the roots of my fantasy behavior. My parents didn't overreact; they just took a deep breath and opened their minds a little wider.

But suppose your mom and dad *did* freak? That doesn't mean you have to punish yourself by repeating their humiliations for the rest of your life. Realize all childhoods are treacherous, followed by teenage years of further torture. Being an adult should finally be a relief. Don't waste time spinning your wheels for the rest of your life trying to get back at your parents. Marvel at how they were even more neurotic then than you are now. It takes two to do an ass-backward tango, so why not dance?

Let's be fair. Maybe you got on your parents' nerves, too. After adolescence, stop trying to shock them. Haven't they had enough? You've learned early how to push their buttons because you grew up with them pushing yours. But it's a losing battle. Your parents' fucked-upness came first.

Let's say, for example, that you're a gay "bear" and they've not only accepted your sexual preference but also the homo subculture you live in. You're an overweight, hairy gay man who's about to make an honest "husbear" out of your "significant otter" and your parents have agreed to come to the hirsute wedding ceremony in your hometown during the annual "Bearquake" celebration. Leave it at that. Don't tell the relatives that the bridesmaids are all bear "blouses" (feminine tops). Let them figure that out for themselves. No need for them to know the best man identifies as a "dolphin" bear, a onetime fat hairball who tired of his faux-masculine role, shaved his entire body, and then started acting nelly while fluttering his arms like Flipper himself . . . or was that herself?

Radical kids forget to feel sorry for their liberal parents. They've tried to understand the ever-changing sexual politics of the young but sometimes they're just plain flummoxed. These well-intentioned left-leaning folks spent a fortune to send their children to fancy private colleges, and they accept that there are no report cards given and one can actually major in "Folk Dancing in New Guinea." When their daughter comes home on spring break sporting a full Gabby Hayes beard, announces she's been taking male hormones, has cut off her breasts, demands to be called Fred, and needs $25,000 for a down payment on the first step of "bottom surgery," well, they panic.

I tell these overwhelmed moms and dads, moms and moms, dads and dads, that they don't get a choice these days. The proper response to "Do you have boys or girls?" is "Ever changing." Two children might really be four if you count their sexual reassigned identities. He or she or "they" could then "come out" as gay in their new sexual being, change their mind and "come in" again to be straight, get a sex change, and end up being gay all over again.

The next minority? The few transgender souls who feel they've made an irrational decision once they've completed their gender switch and demand new surgery to go back to their original plumbing. Is "reluctant pussy" a new way to rebel? Can "dislocated dick" suddenly be the new frontier? Of course it can, and it's bound to happen. Sooner than you think. There's no such thing as boys or girls anymore. Get used to it.

So what is a real man today? A heterosexual male should realize (even if he was once a woman) that Freud was wrong about only one thing: men have penis envy, not women. Or at least they should. Envy of all penises that stand up for strong women without shrinking in fear or going soft at the first mention of any female "asking for it." Jealous of all penises that have learned to own the male gaze with humor, lust, even dominance, as long as they are ready to turn the tables sexually and let any woman do the same invasive thing to them in return. Any self-respecting pubic unit should envy the more intellectually developed penises of others who have considered and tried to understand all erotic behavior as long as it's between enthusiastic consenting adults.

Gay men must accept that there really *is* such a thing as a completely heterosexual man and that he shouldn't have to put up with endless lewd cruising just because it's coming from another male. Straight guys can mean "no," too, just as a woman can, but at least they will now get how their girlfriends must feel every day of their lives walking the streets of any big city. Hip young queers appreciate how you modern hetero dudes sometimes experiment with us homos but need to understand that many straight guys just can't hack performing fellatio, no matter how well intended, and feel much like the late actor/performance artist Spalding Gray, who, after trying to give a first-time blow job on a one-night stand in Greece just to see what it was like, wrote in his journal, "I find that I'm choking on what felt like a disconnected piece of rubber hose."

But hetero guys, by the same token, don't expect your straight girlfriends to be fake lesbians for your voyeuristic sexual arousal, either. And your penis is definitely *not* what Sapphos "need" or they wouldn't be gay in the first place, would they? Would you like it if your lady love requested you to give your straight frat-guy roommate a "bro-job" for her watch-queen pleasure? Probably not. And listen, if you always expect blow jobs from your "old lady," be prepared to embrace cunnilingus on demand with the same enthusiasm you expect from her.

Ladies, I understand your fury. We should all love women who hate men and hate men who hate women and then we'd be perfectly balanced radical feminists. Read Andrea Dworkin, one of the angriest women's liberationists, who writes that heterosexual sex itself is the "pure, sterile, formal expression of men's contempt for women." "Intercourse," she continues, communicates to woman "her own inferior status, impressing it on her, burning it into her by shoving it into her, over and over, pushing and thrusting until she gives up and gives in—which is called *surrender* in the male lexicon." Should you believe what Dworkin suggests: that all penetration by heterosexual men is basically rape? Of course not! We, the enlightened, know that a woman can be fingered and free, but we must revel in all extreme sexual liberation movements, no matter how insane, to fully understand the human condition. We hold these truths *and* nontruths to be self-evident. We really do.

Aging gracefully is the toughest thing for a rebel. As the years pile on, you have two choices: being fat or gaunt. You should choose gaunt. People think I'm skinny, but after quitting smoking 5,965 days ago (I write it down every day), I'm really not. I have to watch what I eat and so should you. Eat sensibly on weekdays and irresponsibly on weekends. Weigh yourself every Friday morning when you'll weigh the least and never on Monday mornings when you'll weigh the most and keep a diary to follow your skinny progress. Then you can *"Eat Your Way to Happiness,"* as the hilarious title of that cheap paper-back book I keep displayed in my Baltimore kitchen proudly proclaims. If diet fails, I've also figured out that if you wear something weird on your face (mustache) and feet (pointy-toe purple tennis shoes), nobody will look at the middle, where every ounce of my excess weight seems to end up.

Cooking Light should have been your bible. I always made every meal (even for company) out of this magazine, and, no, I was never paid to say that. I'm actually mad they didn't hire me to be their advertising spokesperson. Was I too fat-friendly because of *Hairspray* and therefore suspect to readers who were trying to slim down? I would have told these future Twiggys-trapped-in-Tracy-Turnblad bodies that *Cooking Light* really worked—I never gained weight if I only ate meals made from their recipes. But now my favorite culinary magazine has sud-denly gone out of business, so it's too late. I could have saved them if they'd only given me a chance.

OK, here's another thing I know. Nora Ephron was right to "feel bad about [her] neck," as the title of her book admitted, and so should you as you mature. That is why turtlenecks were invented, and this article of clothing should be a staple of the wardrobe of anybody who isn't a teenager. A T-shirt on any man over forty only makes him look fifty. I've recently seen photos of myself wearing this type of garment and I wanted to scream. Avoid the T-shirt look even if the temperature outside is ninety degrees. Even if you're in the privacy of your own home. Bruce Springsteen may be the exception to this rule, but you're not him, are you? Skinny jeans on anyone over twenty years old are also a no-no—you look like a loser in a Ramones Halloween cos-tume. Shorts and no socks worn in winter are not youthful or butch, they're just as dumb as the term "windchill factor."

There's no such thing as good plastic surgery if you notice it. "Good" would mean *no one* noticed and that is rare except in Switzerland, where "understated" has always been a national trait. In Los Angeles, pretty soon, everybody will look exactly the same: not old, just part fish, part android—desperate and surprised.

Nothing shouts midlife crisis louder than driving a convertible. All sensible old people know a breeze is your hair's enemy no matter how much of it you have left. "Windswept" and "aging gracefully" definitely do *not* go hand in hand. Dyed hair on a man never fools anyone. No human has that dead single-color tone that Just For Men produces. Some males have been known to dye their beards with this same product, to match, which is doubly unfortunate. The thought of pubic dying is too atrocious to imagine but I've heard it's been done. And of course a toupee is the ultimate violation. Every single person who sees you instantly spots your rug, knows it's fake, and laughs at you behind your back. Worse yet, you can develop W.O. (wig odor), the nauseating smell of sweat and glue mixed together. Ewwww!

OK, I've given you pointers on family, parenthood, sexual identity, diet, beauty, and aging. You are now headed on the right path to some kind of newfangled serenity, but still, no matter what your age, you'll need guidance on matters of the heart. Falling in love is a full-time job with little security. There's no such thing as romantic unemployment. "One always loves the other more in a relationship," my friend Pat Moran always warned, "so never let your partner know which one you are!" It is good advice but hard to follow. Blurting out "I love you" is always problematic because it demands an answer. A word of advice: never say "I love you" out loud to the person you do unless they are sleeping. It takes the pressure off. You can't get an answer you don't want. They *hear* you, subliminally. And when they wake, they'll have absorbed it. They feel your love without pressure, control, or imbalance and they can love you back. And if the same thing is said to you while you are sleeping, you'll realize it without knowing, wake up in a better mood, confident of well-being, aroused from the subconscious commitment, oddly emotionally satisfied, and yes . . . dare I say it? Content. It might only last one second and then vanish, but so what? A lot of people never get that one second. Go ahead. Whisper "I love you" tonight, very, very softly. But whatever you do, don't let them hear you.

BYE-BYE,
UNDERGROUND

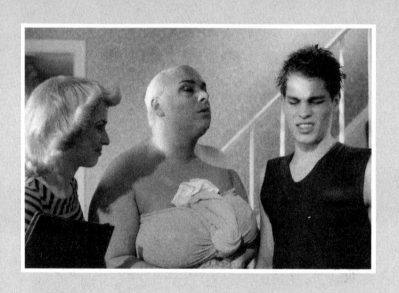

The press always used to ask me, "Did you ever imagine that one day you'd be making Hollywood movies?" "Well . . . yes," I'd think, vaguely annoyed, "I'm not some kind of idiot savant. Didn't I have a successful puppet-show career at twelve years old?" I'd want to bellow. "Read *Variety* at fourteen? Make my first underground movie at seventeen? I was no slacker," I yearned to shriek. My whole being was throbbing with unhinged ambition, ready to claw my way to the top.

You should feel the same. If you have to ask "How do I become successful in show business?" you never will be. The question is not "How?" but always "When?" The damaged and the driven like you and me are so determined that we don't take no for an answer. Believe your own grandiosity and go wrong to make your career go right, just as I did.

In the introduction to a later edition of the first memoir I ever wrote, I explained, "*Shock Value* ends before I made *Polyester* and one day I'll continue that tale with another book." But haven't I already exploited every detail of the making of those later films since, in press interviews and DVD commentaries? Looking back is so exhausting (I know. I sorted through hundreds of boxes of press clippings and business letters at my archive at Wesleyan University), yet the hindsight gained from doing so can be startling. You never make much money on the projects you think up when you're young—the ones that are the most original, the ones that get you noticed. No. You cash in later, once you've made a name for yourself and begin to fail.

I always wanted to be "commercial," and that doesn't have to be a dirty word, if you do it with a twist. Making money shouldn't be your first goal—surprising the world should be—but selling tickets must come in second. We're not in a country such as France or Germany or even Canada where the government steps in and helps finance the most shocking art films. Here in America, even if your idea is foreign to the film-going public, you have to think of a way to make it sound like a potential hit to get funding. And then a certain number of people have to pay to see it.

After *Desperate Living* tanked at the box office in 1977, I knew I needed a new business plan. Videos were just coming out, and suddenly nobody wanted to go see weird movies in a theater at midnight anymore. People wanted to see them at any time, at *their* house, with *their* friends, and smoke *their* pot that they didn't have to hide from nosy ushers. Better yet, they could jerk off while watching—the real reason home videos became so big.

As a young smart-ass movie director with a few . . . well, one box office hit behind me (*Pink Flamingos*), I could never get out of my mind the show tune "You Gotta Get a Gimmick," the stripper anthem from *Gypsy*. Story arcs, surprise endings, marketing, even movie stars themselves—they're *all* gimmicks, and if you use them in real life, the final lyrics to the song, "And you too can be a star," will come true. Everybody needs a gimmick. Get one now.

Archer Winsten, the now almost completely forgotten one time film critic for the *New York Post*, always rose to the bait of underground or midnight movies, and mine were no exception. He wrote after seeing one of my films, "If you ever see Waters' name on the marquee, walk on the other side of the street and hold your nose." Now, *there's* a bad review. I've never trusted directors who say they never read their own notices; you should always read all your reviews—the good ones twice, the bad ones once, then put them all away and never look at them again. But in this case, the write-up was *so* negative that I defied my own rules, read it *three* times, and was instantly inspired to make a movie that really *did* stink. Maybe I could strike it rich.

None of the "smell" movies of the past that I had read about had been successful at the box office, though. *Scent of Mystery*, that 1960 Smell-O-Vision travelogue, bombed because the smell machine hissed and misfired, and audiences complained about odors reaching their noses way before the action on-screen referenced them. With no way to clear the air between showtimes, the entire theater became a stink bomb of failed ballyhoo by the end of each day.

No one I ever met actually saw or smelled *Behind the Great Wall*, the documentary that was released in AromaRama, but I met the guy who claimed to own the rights to this complicated process and would "sell it to me cheap." I realized right away that the real problem with these odorous ideas of showmanship was not the technology itself. The problem was that all the smells were *good*. I had a hunch that bad smells were the road to an olfactional hit. I would reinvent the smellploitation picture and get the whole world to pay me money to smell dirty tennis shoes.

I wrote the script as an homage to both *Father Knows Best* and Douglas Sirk, a parody melodrama about an alcoholic housewife driven crazy by life's odors. I knew I had to change all my acting troupes' images this time. Divine played against type: instead of the woman-monster we had created in the past, he portrayed the victim, the sad one, the well-meaning but tragic wife and mother. Mink Stole, our resident character actress, became the sex bomb, a deluded Bo Derek who lured away Divine's character's porn-theater-owner husband. Mary Vivian Pearce, who played Cotton in *Pink Flamingos*, played a nun, for Christ's sake. Even Edith Massey (sadly in her last role before she died) was reimagined, as a goofy debutante—about as far away from her real-life gap-toothed thrift-shop owner's persona as possible.

But who would finance such a picture? Bob Shaye had overseen the distribution of *Pink Flamingos* and *Female Trouble* through his company, New Line Cinema, but was having second thoughts about my climb up from the underground after doing the same for *Desperate Living* in 1977. He thought I had taken a step backward with that movie. I *was* gross, but suddenly I couldn't gross. "Come on, John," Bob griped impatiently, "make a movie that can play everywhere. Let's make some money!"

"OK," I thought, "here's my big chance." I had read that Larry Flynt's *Hustler* magazine had already featured a center spread with a scratch-and-sniff vagina (lavender smell). I also knew about children's books that celebrated disgusting smells using the same technology. Doing a little research with the help of Bob's head honcho, Sara Risher, a New Line executive I loved and had traveled with extensively promoting my earlier titles, we found out the 3M Company pretty much had a monopoly on smell-related ventures. Their "library of smells" was inspirational. Along with the script, I pitched the scratch-and-sniff movie idea ("Ladies and Gentlemen—*This is Odorama!*") to Bob and he said yes! Oh my God, a $300,000 budget, an unheard-of amount to me at the time. Finally I could shoot in 35mm. No more grainy, weirdly framed blowups from 16mm. A real movie!

Of course there were strings. New Line put up half the budget, and Bob got Michael White, one of the producers of *The Rocky Horror Picture Show*, to put up more, but I had to raise $50,000 of it myself. "OK, that's fair," I thought, "I have no pride; I'm used to asking rich friends for cash."

Learning to raise money in nontraditional ways is one of the most valuable lessons I can teach you here. Today there's Kickstarter, but public begging is not only embarrassing, it often doesn't work. Discreet private lunatic investors are not always available. Sometimes you really have to think out of the box to raise money. When I was forming limited partnerships for one of my earlier films, I had run into a counselor who had me as a camper when I was about fourteen years old. I remember him because he used to jerk me off under the covers in our group cabin as he was telling us ghost stories before we went to sleep. I didn't mind. It wasn't traumatic. Actually, I was thrilled and had been looking for this kind of action for a while but didn't know where to find it. As I got older, though, I realized this was hardly appropriate on his part. He seemed happy to see me but a little nervous. "What have you been up to?" he asked, as I eyed the much-too-young boy who was with him. I figured now was the time to turn straw into gold. "I'm making a movie and I need money for the budget," I said with a slight edge in my voice. He gave me $30,000. I paid him back, too. You learn early in independent film financing to work with whatever you've got.

Odorama wasn't enough. We needed a star. A bankable one. A *Hollywood* star to play the male lead, Todd Tomorrow. One with a name that theater owners knew, one they'd never imagine working with the "filthiest people alive," as we were still referred to in some circles. Tab Hunter fit the bill perfectly. He was still handsome, could act, had fifties movie-star baggage, and carried a hint of tabloid notoriety. Better yet, he didn't have an agent at the time to talk him out of it.

I had read that Tab loved riding horses, so I nosed around the few connections I had with the old-money Maryland horsey set and found his home phone number. I just called him cold, and when he answered himself, I started my motormouth pitch for the film, hoping he wouldn't hang up on me. Tab may have been startled to hear the ridiculous plot and the details of Odorama, but he just laughed good-naturedly when I mentioned his leading lady would be a man named Divine and they had an on-screen love scene together.

Luckily, he had never seen *Pink Flamingos*. I explained I only needed him for one week and could shoot the rest of the film around him. "Sure," Tab said with a chuckle, "I'll consider it. Send me the script." I couldn't believe my ears.

Make sure when you submit your material to a star that it looks extremely presentable; good cover page with a possible early attempt at an ad campaign, even a high-concept one-paragraph pitch for agents who don't have time to read more than the first few pages (what gets a film greenlit) or the last few (what makes a film a hit). More important, develop a good-luck, hoodoo-voodoo ritual you go through right before shipping.

I raced home, boxed up Tab's script, and, as always, licked the package several times, getting it wet with my saliva to remove any "curse" of show business rejection before dropping it in the mailbox. Even if I'm not physically present, my staff knows that they, too, must lick all parcels of anything we send out for consideration. After all, if the recipient says no, their jobs could be in peril just like mine.

It must have worked because Tab said yes. I offered him the

most money I had ever paid anyone to be in my movies, and he accepted probably the lowest amount he ever received. When we hung up, I let out a scream of happiness. Tab Hunter was going to be in my film! Hot damn! My production company just got reinvented! Dreamland Part Two was about to begin.

I actually hate the making of a film even if it goes well. As the director and writer you are in a state of constant anxiety whether you'll "make your day" (and you never *do* have time for all the camera setups you need). Talk about bad hours! If you are awake, then you're at work. No one from production ever stops asking questions. If it's low budget, you don't get to eat because there is no food, and if it's big budget, your whole lunch hour is spent doing press that is required by the studio. One thing all future auteurs must learn—you will never have time to defecate while directing a movie.

You should always do *one* more rewrite before the shoot begins. The third act of *Polyester* is so preposterous that even Divine muttered, "Totally unbelievable," before we filmed the climactic scene where her character catches Tab Hunter having an affair with the elderly grandmother. Who knows, if I had been able to fix this dubious plot point, *Polyester* might have gone on to be a TV series today.

Try to scope out your locations for troublemaking neighbors early on. I learned this the hard way. We rented an empty suburban house for *Polyester* and basically just moved in and started shooting twenty-four hours a day with no thoughts that the generator noise, night scenes, and general anarchy of a low-budget movie crew might disturb anyone. Except for a few (who became extras), most of the neighbors hated us. It took them a while to figure out that the overweight man who showed up unshaven and dressed in a one-piece garbageman work suit early in the day and the one who later came running out the front door in a dress screaming "Help me!" was one and the same person: Divine. Tab wasn't due on the set until the end of the shoot, and even though we used his name to try to impress the local naysayers, I don't think they believed he was coming since I couldn't announce him to the press yet because my movie was nonunion. I had told Tab this potentially deal-breaking reality before he got there, but he hadn't realized that as a Screen Actors Guild member he was violating their rules by even setting foot on my set (and was later fined when the film was released). It was a good thing Christine Jorgensen, the first transgender woman I had ever read about as a kid and loved, had politely turned down the role of Divine's mother in the film. Imagine what the neighbors would have thought of *that* addition to the cast!

The sight of the punk rocker Stiv Bators on the set seemed to cause further alarm in the little cul-de-sac of suburbia we had taken hostage. Even though he was a total pro and a gentleman at all times, his skinny appearance and snarling on-screen demeanor didn't cross over to the culture of our neighbors' families. I wonder if any of these contempt-before-investigation *Polyester* oppositionists followed his career after the movie was released. Did they ever know Stiv later dropped the final *s* of his last name, was hit by a car in Paris, and died shortly thereafter from the injuries? Had they read that he was cremated and his girlfriend at the time snorted his ashes? I hope at least one of them knows now what a good guy Stiv Bator really was and how their chance encounter with him was special, happily tarnished, and fleetingly historical.

Our new discovery, Ken King, didn't go over any better in the neighborhood. Sharon Niesp, Cookie Mueller's girlfriend and Dreamland actress, and I had found him in a bar on the Lower East Side of New York at the last minute right before shooting began in Baltimore, and unlike Lana Turner, perched on that stool in Hollywood's Schwab's drugstore, waiting to be found, he was just sitting there minding his own business, an acting career the furthest thing from his brain. We practically kidnapped him, and three days later there he was on set playing Divine's son, Dexter (named before the TV show was developed), aka the Baltimore Foot Stomper, a character based on a real-life luna- tic who had been convicted more than forty times for stomping on the feet of unsuspecting females he followed on the street. Kenny barely knew what hit him, but he seemed to inhabit his role immediately. Was he a Method actor without even realizing it? All I know is that once I said "Action" and the neighbors got a load of him staggering up their peaceful street, snorting poppers and rubbing his crotch, they recoiled in fear, and when he stomped on Divine's foot in a scene, moaned in sexual pleasure, and then laughed maniacally in fetishistic afterglow, the entire community realized this was certainly not a normal movie they'd ever pay to see. I don't know why they didn't warm to Kenny King. Everybody on *Polyester* (including Divine, Mink, and me) fell a little in love with him—why couldn't they?

To make matters worse, right in the middle of our shoot- ing schedule, the local papers printed a big article about how the Maryland Censor Board had banned *Multiple Maniacs*, a movie I had made ten years earlier, because it was finally getting a commercial run at a local art theater and therefore needed an official seal of approval. "Even the garbage can was too good for it," Mary Avara, the head of the censors and my arch- enemy from the beginning of my career, ranted after a judge declared it was "obnoxious but not legally obscene." "The Court's eyes were assaulted," he continued, ". . . horrendous, sickening, revolting." I guess he didn't like it. "I tried to move heaven and earth not to release this film," Mary Avara sputtered in defeat. While I secretly chuckled at the thought of her having to watch the "rosary job" scene, I knew that as we were trying to convince the *Polyester* neighbors that we were making a Hollywood film, this was not the time to debate the socially redeeming reverence of this sacrilege-on-screen sex act between Divine and Mink Stole. We were already causing a stink *without* Odorama.

By the time Tab Hunter arrived, it didn't matter to the local community what a team player he was. They couldn't have cared less how kind he was to Divine, how he calmed him down from nervousness that first day on the set when Divine and he had to slow dance together on film. Nobody but our gang knew how lovely Tab was the day we filmed the love scene when he tenderly moved Divine's face into the proper lighting before falling to the floor and kissing him on the lips (the mouth that had eaten shit, as some later howled).

The final straw was the Sunday morning we shot the car-accident scene where Tab's and Divine's characters "meet cute" when they've both stopped to gawk at the dead, mutilated bodies. For us it was comedy, but for the churchgoers on their way to Sunday services it was a tragedy, and many of the pastors asked their congregations to pray for the victims. They thought it was real. When the word spread after church that it was us, they were furious! Wasted prayers! Tab Hunter was just as bad as Divine in their book. We were all underground scum who had raided their community in the name of filth. They were sort of right.

Pay for your music rights, young directors, and pay for these rights in the beginning of your postproduction—they only get more expensive the longer you wait. If you only knew the headaches and financial heartbreaks I went through on my early films because I ignored these very real legalities, you'd never fantasize about having any tune on your soundtrack again. Budding directors always seem to make the mistake of using one of their favorite songs from their youth in their movie and then imagine they'll just figure out the rights question after they get a little attention at a film festival.

Suppose your movie *does* become the toast of Sundance. The festival audience loved your life-affirming but edgy ending, especially with that great song you used on the soundtrack with the lyrics that fit the plot so perfectly. Distributors are offering big advances, you might even be able to pay back your partners up front. But there's a little detail you haven't revealed: you haven't yet cleared the music. It costs an average of $25,000 a song for each needle drop for worldwide rights, and you have to find and make a deal with both the publisher of the music *and* the writer (*not* the singer). Guess what? You're fucked. Forever.

When Chris Stein and Debbie Harry, then riding high in Blondie, came on board to write the music and lyrics for a lot of the original vocals, I was over the rainbow of retro heaven. Finally the music in one of my films would be legal from the very beginning! Tab had had a few manufactured hits in the fifties ("Young Love"; "Red Sails in the Sunset"), and Debbie told me she had been his biggest fan. So if Tab would sing again and have Debbie doing vocal backups, old wave could meet new wave and listeners just might levitate. Michael Kamen, who was just starting out in his career before going on to compose the scores for monster hits such as *Die Hard* and *Lethal Weapon*, did Bob Shaye a favor by agreeing to contribute soundtrack music, which added a whole new level of professionalism to our crackpot melodrama. When Bill Murray said he'd sing the vocals on one of the more ludicrous love songs ("The Best Thing"), I thought I might finally have a real soundtrack album that could be a hit. But alas, Blondie's record contract forbade them from releasing any music on another label, so, once again, legal snafus kept us off the charts.

Make sure you take good stills when you are shooting your movie to use later for promotion. The unit photographer is an incredibly important position on the crew. As time goes by and the cinema history books are written, audiences don't remember the actual movie, they remember the stills. No one today can recall the plot of *From Here to Eternity*, but everybody remembers the still of Burt Lancaster and Deborah Kerr making out on the beach. That shot of Divine in that fishtail gown pointing the gun from *Pink Flamingos*? It's still the most famous image from any of my movies thanks to Lawrence Irvine, the photographer who was there on the set almost every day when we barely even had a real crew. That posed portrait of Tab Hunter embracing Divine that we had shot separately from the scene was kept secret until after we wrapped and New Line took out the then-traditional "Principal Photography Has Been Completed" ad in *Variety* and used this image. Readers couldn't believe their eyes. Tab Hunter and Divine in love? It couldn't be true!

But it was and the movie was a hit. A modest one. It started off great. The first screening with the Odorama cards took place at the Hof International Film Festival in the upper-Bavarian section of Germany, and the audience went nuts. I was there and I wanted to shout out the character Dr. Quackenshaw's on-screen dialogue along with him when he explains to the viewers at the beginning of the film how to scratch and sniff the cards. "It works," he happily shouts after the crowd smells a rose, "by God, it actually works!" And "work" it did. Moviegoers would hear the sound of a fart, see *#2* flash on the screen, and even though every person in the world knew that they would smell the manufactured odor of flatulence, they'd still eagerly scratch and sniff the card and howl in group repulsion. The urge to smell a fart is universal. Remember that.

When New Line took *Polyester* to the marketplace of the Cannes Film Festival in 1980, I was so proud. The main industry hangout at the time was still the terrace of the Carlton Hotel, and we had the only billboard above it. There it was for the world to see—that same great photo of Divine and Tab in love blown up, and I was sitting there under it being oh so international. So many people came to the screening that there was a mini-riot and the glass doors of the theater were shattered by pushing cinemaniacs. Foreign rights were snapped up ("I don't have to see your films," the old-school sales agent groused to me, "I just have to sell them"), and Bob Shaye, Sara Risher, and I all came home excited and ready for the U.S. release.

Polyester opened aboveground in America in real first-run movie houses that even had matinees! We had never before been seen in the light of day, and I thank Tab Hunter's name for making that possible. At first the movie did well in the big cities. Reviews were pretty good, too, even though some of my early supporters felt I had sold out. Ha! I wish. Once New Line tried to widen the release to midsize hubs in the heartland, *Polyester* stalled quickly. Should I have been amazed that my film about a porn-theater owner, his alcoholic fat wife, and their abortion-loving teenage daughter and foot-fetishist son had gotten as far as it did, or should I have been disappointed that a love story between a drag queen and the movie star Tab Hunter with the smell of natural gas and pizza mixed in hadn't ripped it up at the box office in Peoria? Another problem: theater owners never paid the distributor their Odorama bills, and those little muvvas didn't come cheap. But what could we do about it? Odorama repo men? No such thing. And our threat, "If you don't pay up on your Odorama bill, we'll never give you any more for your next smell picture," hardly worked. They laughed in our faces.

Over the years, *Polyester* has gone on to have a life of its own. It even made a little money ("How do you always manage to make friends with New Line's accountant?" Bob Shaye once griped). Years after its initial theatrical release, the DVD came out and included a smaller version of the Odorama card, and in France the movie was broadcast on TV and you could pick up your card at local 7-Eleven-type convenience stores. More ludicrously, a *Rugrats* Hollywood sequel copied my scratch-and-sniff card idea in 2003 but made it worse by using the Odorama name and the exact same logo after New Line had forgotten to renew the trademark. I was horrified to see that, in some sort of product-placement deal, the studio was giving the cards away at Burger King! Those fuckers! When I complained, the offending marketing team said, "We did it as a tribute to you!" Oh, come on! Everybody in Hollywood knows a "tribute" means money. Oh, well, maybe imitation *is* the sincerest form of flattery. Just recently, new Odorama cards were developed and *Polyester* was again rereleased commercially in movie theaters. It goes to show: You can't keep a smelly girl down.

ACCIDENTALLY
COMMERCIAL

All you need is *one* really good idea. And, boy, a fat white girl fighting for racial integration was it! The miracle of *Hairspray* is a gift that keeps on giving. First came my original movie in 1988, based on my exaggerated memories of *The Buddy Deane Show*, a local TV dance party only broadcast in Baltimore. *Hairspray* was a dance movie, not a musical. None of those crazy-gimmick rhythm-and-blues songs you heard on the soundtrack (except the great title song by Rachel Sweet) were written for the film. They were hidden away in my record collection just waiting to be listened to again in a brand-new way.

Even though I didn't yet have any kind of agent, I tried to go Hollywood when my L.A. friend Jeff Buhai, suddenly hot with his hit movie *Revenge of the Nerds*, offered to take me around to the studios to pitch my new movie idea. I didn't even know what a pitch was, but Jeff taught me. He explained how you go into a producer's office and basically do a stand-up routine: a fifteen-minute song and dance about your imagined movie; why it will be good, make money, and bring coolness to the studio. I figured with all my experience being on the road and hyping my past "trash epics," this new vaudeville routine might be a snap.

We went everywhere: Geffen, Fox, Paramount, Columbia, David Madden, Laurie MacDonald, Dale Pollock—they all turned us down. Even though I hadn't written the script yet, I did have the entire movie in my head right down to some of the more obscure dance steps, which I performed live right in their offices. Nobody went for it. Not one nibble. I had a past that could scare away even the most adventuresome executive. Yes, they respected what I'd done—Odorama had been a marketing coup and most of them had seen *Pink Flamingos* at midnight somewhere in their youth, but that didn't mean they were willing to risk their jobs by backing my next production. I was still unsafe.

OK, no development deal. I had to write the script on spec, but since I had already thought up the pitch in such detail, it wasn't that hard a job. Larry "Ratso" Sloman, the editor at *National Lampoon*, who had been publishing some essays that ended up in my book *Crackpot*, suggested I contact a friend of his, the New York producer Stanley Buchthal, who might be able to get me the budget for *Hairspray* after New Line had been non-committal. Bucky, as he was known, never did get anyone to invest, but he talked a good game, and the chance of his possibly taking over the project bluffed Bob Shaye into stepping up to the plate and including Bucky in the deal.

We talked New Line into a real budget of $2.7 million, and I remember holding my breath before having the nerve to ask Bob Shaye for $100,000 to write and direct *plus* a share of the profits (the film took twenty-one years to break even according to reports I still receive). When he didn't blink and said yes to my demands, I almost collapsed. We went Screen Actors Guild, too, something I had always needlessly feared and shouldn't have, because they worked with me to give us a good deal since we hired so many African American actors. I stupidly *didn't* join the Directors Guild of America or the Writers Guild, which was so naive of me. Always join the unions! You later get royalties on DVDs, foreign levies, and TV sales without the expenses deducted as on usual studio paperwork. Even if your film was a big bomb! If I had been in the Writers Guild when I made *Hairspray*, my deal on the musical with New Line would automatically have been more lucrative. The biggest perk of all in the unions? Guild members must be flown first-class by the studios when out on a promotional tour. I still was flying coach! But who's complaining? I was about to film a Hollywood movie!

Making *Hairspray* was one of the happiest times in my life. The shoot went miraculously well even though that summer the dreaded invasion of the seventeen-year locusts was in full force. These ugly cicadas ruined sound takes with their infernal buzzing and smashed their disgusting little bodies into the camera lens by the hundreds. Ricki Lake wasn't fazed; she *was* Tracy Turnblad for real, and even though only a handful of fat girls showed up to audition in 1987 (there was a line of a thousand Tracy wannabes outside the NBC studios when they announced open casting for that role for the 2016 version), no one has ever topped Ricki's performance, in my book. She deserves every bit of the success she's had since. I haven't spoken to the original Link Larkin, Michael St. Gerard, for decades but I do know where he is. This onetime Elvis look-alike was for a while a Christian minister in Harlem, and Ricki's still in touch with him. Colleen Fitzpatrick (Amber) went on to be the pop star Vitamin C, and Clayton Prince (Seaweed) later was high up in the Guardian Angels, the real ones—not the movie version. Jerry Stiller (Wilbur) is alive and well and went on to *Seinfeld* and lots of other TV and film hits. Leslie Ann Powers (Penny) seemed missing in action until recently, when she stepped out of her self-imposed Hairspray Witness Protection Program and showed up at the thirtieth-anniversary screening at the IFC in New York City, coming up onstage with me to do a Q&A. Sadly, Ruth Brown is no longer with us, but, wow, what a legend, what a career. Sonny Bono was killed in that tragic skiing accident, and the only real time I ever met Cher, she thanked me for the nice things I said about him on Ted Koppel's show right after the news broke. Debbie Harry is more than still working, she's a living legend, and I was first in line to buy tickets for her cabaret act at the Café Carlyle in New York. We're still buddies and sometimes even go out on "dates" to premieres. She "puts out" in the glamour department big-time.

Pia Zadora was brave to make *Hairspray* with me at the pinnacle of her screen notoriety. I'm proud that I got her good reviews for her performance as a beatnik chick. Allen Ginsberg seemed offended when I asked him for permission for Pia's character to read "Howl" out loud in the movie. Lighten up, Allen; I wasn't making fun of the poem *or* Pia. Both were always iconic without irony in my book. Did I bring up your unrepentant membership in NAMBLA, the long-term pedophile's rights group? No, I did not. Don't be so judgmental. Pia never was.

I got my first taste of Hollywood marketing hell when New Line decided to give *Hairspray* test screenings in California before it opened nationally. Obviously, I had never tested my earlier films (imagine the forced reshoots that would have resulted for *Pink Flamingos*; Divine would have eaten gummy bear worms at the end!), so I didn't fear the results as much as I should have. Mercifully, I wasn't there in Long Beach, but I did hear about it soon after. Of the 293 recruited audience members, 55 walked out. Overall the film received "below average" ratings. Males liked Ricki Lake much better than females did. Fifty-seven percent described *Hairspray* as "corny," and 23 percent said it was "unbelievable." Amber's throwing up on the amusement park ride was singled out as a "least favorite scene." Duh.

When the MPAA gave the film a PG rating, I, at first, thought I'd never work again, and New Line was nervous, too, suggesting I dub in the word "shit" somewhere on the soundtrack so we'd get a PG-13. But then I realized maybe a family-friendly rating *was* the shock I needed to turn my career around forever. I didn't know it yet but *Hairspray* was a Trojan horse. It had the power to sneak into middle-class homes and espouse gay marriage and teenage race mixing without anybody noticing. We were soon to find out that the test results were wrong. Even racists loved *Hairspray*!

But New Line was still anxious about marketing a John Waters film for mainstream moviegoers. Instead of visually showing our fat teenage heroine or her drag queen mother in the ads, they shot a generic photo of two sets of dancing legs vaguely dressed in sixties fashion and used that for the poster. No members of the cast were shown at all. I had thought up an ad line, "Their Hair Was Perfect but the World Was a Mess," but I guess that didn't test well either because it wasn't used until much later, in the U.K. release.

None of this mattered once the reviews came out. Except for *The Baltimore Sun*'s Lou Cedrone ("Admittedly doing a comedy about racism isn't that easy, so maybe we can blame it on that. Waters is obviously aiming for camp but it doesn't quite work") and Rex Reed ("disgusting"), all the notices were spectacular. Divine was especially pleased when Pauline Kael praised his performance. My favorite good review, in *Rolling Stone*, was by David Edelstein, who described *Hairspray* as a "family movie that both the Bradys and Mansons could love." The grosses were good, too—the first week we averaged $10,000 a screen and it opened wider the next week and continued doing well. "Could play here forever," *Variety* trumpeted of the grosses at the Waverly Theater in Greenwich Village (now the IFC). Finally it seemed I had a real aboveground hit.

And then Divine died. I'm still shocked to this day that he's gone. He was only forty-two years old. My friends' *children* are older than that today. *Hairspray* had been in the theater for just two weeks. The last time I saw Divine was when we met for dinner at Odeon Restaurant (last table on the right on the southern wall) in New York City. He arrived in a limo (God knows who paid for that) and we ate alone and marveled happily at our new success. After, I walked him to his car, kissed him on the cheek, and said goodbye. The next time I saw him was in his open coffin.

I was home in my old apartment by Druid Hill Park in Baltimore when I got the call. Divine died in his sleep from a heart attack in the morning hours at the Regency Plaza Suites Hotel in Hollywood, the day before he was supposed to start shooting *Married with Children*, in which he was to play a light-in-the-loafer uncle, one of the first gay parts ever on a hit TV show. It could have been a real game changer in his career. Divine had been out to dinner with the photographer Greg Gorman, and after Greg dropped him at his hotel, Divine had come out onto the balcony of his room and sung "Arrivederci Roma" to Greg as he walked back to his car. When Greg heard of Divine's death that next morning, he called his buddy, "Coroner to the Stars" Thomas Noguchi, who made sure Divine's body was taken away out of view of the awaiting paparazzi. To this day, Greg Gorman remains one of my best friends.

Pat Moran was the next to call, and she had heard, too, and was frozen in shock and grief. I told her to come over with her husband, Chuck. The phone started ringing and never stopped. The answering machine couldn't keep up with the calls coming in on both lines. The press arrived outside my apartment building, and one local TV crew left the message that they wouldn't leave until I came down. We were way too stunned to reply. It was like a sad off-Broadway play, *The Day Divine Died*, only no one wanted to be in it. We just sat there in disbelief and listened to hundreds of phone messages of sympathy as they came in. I don't think I ever picked up.

The press agents for the film convinced me to answer questions from the media in a hotel a few days later, but I bolted from the lectern and ran off halfway through. The funeral home handled the crowds well, and Divine was laid out in an open coffin dressed in an expensive suit as the proud man he had become. You could see his big stomach sticking up and it reminded many mourners of Alfred Hitchcock. No charities were mentioned in the funeral announcement and flowers were encouraged (daffodils or gardenias were recommended in the press as Divine's favorites). So many arrangements were delivered that the florists themselves sent flowers to thank the deceased for the business. Stars' accompanying sympathy cards were pretty funny. "See what a good review will do?" Whoopi Goldberg's read. "Why didn't you just tell us you didn't want to do the show?" *Married with Children*'s asked.

Everybody we ever knew showed up, including Divine's mother and aunts. But our favorite blast from the past was a friend named Diane none of us had seen for decades. She had the dubious distinction of being David Lochary's "girlfriend," whatever that meant since David was so gay that even the police had snarkily given him the fictitious middle name Gaylord on his arrest report when we'd been busted for conspiring to commit indecent exposure for *Mondo Trasho*. Diane was remembered fondly by all of us for her extreme look. She always wore her shoulder-length hair teased straight up in the air, heavily sprayed and never even slightly combed out; black stretch slacks; pointy-toe red tennis shoes flopping open without laces; and an ever-present swab of Nair hair-remover cream above her upper lip. She also seemed to get into car accidents almost every day of her life. She arrived at the funeral home in an ambulance on a day pass from a mental institution. God, I hope she's alive and well today!

At the funeral service before the burial, I gave a eulogy, calling Divine "a lifelong friend, a business partner, a confidant, a coconspirator, and an actor who could say the words I wrote better than anybody." Divine's family's minister from their local church, the Reverend Leland Higginbotham, tried to explain to the grievers how hard it had been for Glenn (his real name I hadn't uttered in years) to go from "the boy who was always sensitive to the feelings of others to Divine, the cult movie star" that most of the mourners knew. "He and his parents spent many hours with me trying to figure out what was going on," the reverend confessed. "It was an agonized period and I, as a pastor, felt totally inadequate to help in any way." Even *I* could understand how hard it would be for *any* parent to be proud their son had been in a movie dressed in drag eating a real dog turd. "But although Glenn took the painful road to find himself," Rev. Higginbotham continued as Divine's mom listened on, "at least there was reconciliation." He noted, "The tragedy was that Divine was cut off at the point of becoming who he really was, and the world will never see how that flower could have unfolded."

The burial at Prospect Hill Cemetery in Towson, Maryland, was a mob scene. Here in the little graveyard where Divine used to steal flowers because he couldn't afford his own for dinner parties, here where we used to meet up as teenagers with other suburban delinquents and drink beer on school nights, here in the little town that we had finally escaped, was Divine's final resting place. His last public appearance brought to a standstill by a traffic jam of grieving fans, friends, and family. Here we were, right where we started. Even his parents had understood their son at the end. They put the name Divine right on the gravestone along with his real one. There could be no better acceptance, could there?

Divine would have been pleased at the melodramatic atmosphere of that day. I can't remember much about the actual burial except the paparazzi on the hill with their long-lens cameras; Divine's mom watching the whole thing from inside her limo; Pat Moran dressed all in black with a giant picture hat complete with veil covering her whole face, sobbing by the gravestone like Kim Stanley in *The Goddess*; and my own mother arriving alone and looking both scared and very, very sad.

Death is not always a good career move. It was hard for me to care much about the box office after Divine's final exit. At the time I was too shocked to realize that the tragedy had hurt *Hairspray*'s chances of crossing over to mid-America any further than it had. Even though the press coverage of his passing was huge (cover of both the *New York Post* and the New York *Daily News*) and respectful (big obits in *The New York Times* and the *Los Angeles Times*), who wants to go laugh at a comedy when the star died the day before? Practically every TV station in the country had photos of Divine and me happily promoting the movie, and now they were cutting to footage of me carrying the coffin with other pallbearers.

New Line tried to continue *Hairspray*'s successful momentum, but after opening wider in 227 theaters right after Divine's death, we faltered a little, and the next week it stalled even further. The fun was gone. *Hairspray* ended up grossing $8,266,397 on a budget of $2.7 million plus prints and advertising. Nobody got rich and nobody lost money. Everybody was too stunned and saddened to complain.

It took decades for me to finally experience the euphoria *Hairspray* should have brought originally, but even up to then there had been detours: a TV series based on my movie was originally developed by New Line, but I had little to do with it and it went nowhere. In 1990, Scott Rudin, the brilliant and risk-taking producer, optioned *Hairspray* to turn it into a Broadway musical, but that, too, never happened.

Then a miracle did. The producer Margo Lion, a Baltimore native I had never met who had left her hometown decades ago and never looked back, had had the flu and watched a VHS of *Hairspray* in bed in New York and got the same bright idea Scott Rudin had—to turn my old movie into a Broadway musical. Only she actually did it.

Sometimes you just have to trust people in show business, and I know that's hard. But every once in a while the road to heaven *is* paved with good intentions. When Margo came to me with her pitch for the stage, she had already optioned the rights from New Line and hired Marc Shaiman and Scott Whitman to write a couple of songs on spec. Guess who sang Divine's part in the first demo tape before Harvey Fierstein was brilliantly cast? Nathan Lane, that's who.

Margo told me she wanted to keep my original voice intact in her production and have me involved from the very first read through. I owe Margo, Marc, and Scott a shitload of gratitude. *Hairspray*, the musical, went on to be a smash success, won eight Tony Awards, and made me more money on any one project than anything else I ever did in my life. My parents could finally say, "We loved it," without their noses growing like Pinocchio's. The show has played all over the world and is still being done by high schools everywhere. I've even seen it with a cast of mentally challenged teenagers and it worked. Wasn't that the ultimate test of crossover potential?

Of course there were some problems. South Korea put black-face on actors, and when we howled, they argued at first, "Well, we don't have any black people here." "So, use another minority," we demanded, and they eventually did. In Texas, a high school had white kids playing all the black parts, and when the local press complained, the school defended themselves by saying that at first no black kid had auditioned, and after a few finally did, they dropped out. So the Seaweed character sings, "The blacker the berry, the sweeter the juice," yet he's white? The thought of Motormouth Maybelle played by a white girl in a curly blond wig singing, "I know where I've been," is blasphemy to my ears and should be to yours, too. No wonder the black kids dropped out. They probably ran for their lives.

I'm also usually the lone holdout on the fat-suit debate, always against casting a skinny Tracy and putting her in one. Isn't a fat suit the blackface of insult to overweight girls? There's plenty of fat talent in the United States. Everybody's fat! Find a *real* fat girl that can sing and dance. A skinny Tracy is like a white L'il Inez or a female Edna. It's just not right.

But maybe I'm old-fashioned. Since writing in *The New York Times* in 2002 that "finally the fat girl and drag queen will get the parts" in high school productions, I have been proven dead wrong over and over. Trigger warning. Because of political correctness, public-school drama teachers now can't cast by weight or race, so I've seen the reverse of the all-white Texas high school casting—a skinny black girl playing Tracy. Somehow I didn't mind. It may not make much sense—how can Tracy sing about the injustices of not letting black kids dance on the all-white TV show when she *is* on the show and she *is* black, but who cares? It's theater of the absurd all over again—right where I started. Let's go further—why not switch all races when casting *Hairspray*? Genders, too! The ultimate insanely politically correct diverse *Hairspray*. For the people, by the people, with a color-blind, gender-fluid cast for all!

New Line then remade the musical as a big-budget Hollywood movie, and I actually loved that, too. I even play the Flasher in the opening number. Some of my longtime fans, out of misplaced loyalty, complained about the slickness of Adam Shankman's version, but I think he did the right thing—he changed *Hairspray* again. This time my little independent movie was big, brassy, and filled with A-list Hollywood stars; I mean, John Travolta played Edna. That's why it worked. The movie versions of *Rent* and *The Producers* didn't work because they just filmed the stage musical exactly the way it was on Broadway. Remember when you are trying to cash in on a successful previous work, the concept must change or the Xerox copy gets weaker and weaker until you can't read it at all.

This third *Hairspray* wasn't even filmed in Baltimore, and as much as I wanted to scream, "You'll never make Toronto look like Baltimore!" they did just that. *Hairspray* was big-time yet the flavor of my original was still there *and* they paid me again! Who was I to look a gift horse in the mouth? I hopped back on the *Hairspray* train and hoped to never get off.

I didn't have to, either. Craig Zadan and Neil Meron, the producers of the Shankman version, then hired me to write a sequel to both the musical and my original movie that would be yet another cinematic version of *Hairspray*. *White Lipstick*, I called it, and already had the ad line thought up when I turned in the treatment: "When the Color Lines Blurred, Things Got Hairy." "It's 1965," I wrote, "and the mod revolution has already hit. Big hair is out and the Beatles have made Motown music old hat." "*The Corny Collins Show* is still on the air and is integrated but the ratings are down and the black kids want their own all-black show with Motormouth Maybelle as the host." Tracy has flat hair. Penny is a Weatherman lefty, Seaweed a Black Muslim, and L'il Inez a Black Panther. Edna has gone on a diet and is actually thin, and Wilbur has invented novelty eyeglasses for his joke shop that enable you to see through clothes. Link is obsessed with the British Invasion, and underneath his mop-top hairdo are pimples that sing to him like the Chipmunks. There are hairdo riots, sea-nettle attacks, bad LSD trips, and actual miracles, all built around musical numbers with titles such as "Grinding My Love," "Purple Bone," "Bedhead," "Contact High," and the finale, "Hairdo Paradise." I don't know. Maybe I went too far. I thought it could work. They didn't.

Move on, I always say. Don't get stuck. Projects live and die quickly in show business. But *Hairspray* development deals kept on a-comin' over the years and I hope they never stop. I was hired by Warner Bros. Television in 2010 to write a pilot script and "bible" for a series based on my original movie, not the musical, but it never got made. In this version, Tracy becomes fed up with Mr. Pinky's increasingly exploitative and "fattist" commercials that he expects her to do on air, and suddenly the show's management wants her gone. Edna has become a pushy stage mother obsessed with Tracy's career, while Wilbur tries to get his wife back on a politically active path. Penny is finally accepted on the Council after she crashes the auditions and wows the remaining skeptics with a torrid version of "The Ubangi Stomp," but then scandalizes even her supporters by immediately trying to unionize the teen dancers on the show. Seaweed once and for all integrates *Corny Collins* by disguising himself as a popular soul singer who is allowed to lip-synch his hit rhythm-and-blues song on the air in front of the all-white teen Council members, until he can reveal his true Baltimore Negro self in front of the cameras. There's even a spy from Dick Clark's *American Bandstand* lurking beneath all the teen melodrama, but neither Corny Collins nor the movie militant Motormouth Maybelle even notice. "Here We Go Again!" my teaser ad line read, but alas, we went nowhere.

But in 2015, like a vampire who can't be kept dead, the idea for a "new TV event," *Hairspray 2: The Separate but Equal Sequel*, was pitched to HBO and they paid me to write yet another new script, one that moved *Hairspray* further into the future. OK, I'm always game! I've been living with these characters for thirty-one years—I know them better than my own siblings and am always ready to bring out the file folders of old notes, put on some music, and let Tracy and gang dance up a storm.

This time, *The Corny Collins Show* was already integrated. Seaweed and Penny are both Council members, but there's only one other black kid on the show and she's the squarest person of color the management could find. Worse yet, Penny and Seaweed are forbidden to dance on the air together. While all the earlier *Hairspray* scripts concentrated on integration, *Hairspray 2* is about mixed-race prejudice, "checkerboard" couples and their fight for freedom. There's also an important new character named Lotta Wishbone, and her very existence is a threat to Tracy's mantle of fame *and* her happy love life with Link. Come on, don't you want to see what happens? HBO didn't. Oh, well. They treated me fairly *and* paid me.

But it *still* wasn't over. The day my *Hairspray* sequel bit the dust, NBC announced a live version of *Hairspray* the musical would join other TV musical specials that were ripping up the ratings: *The Sound of Music*, *The Wiz*, *Peter Pan*, *Grease*, and now us. Nobody from the network ever contacted me about this version. Not once did anybody ask me about casting, writing, or promoting the show. I even had to contact the press office myself to ask them how I should handle calls I was getting about the project. Their publicist didn't seem to know but arranged a hurried meeting between the new Tracy and me when they were doing some casting in Baltimore (as a stunt, if you ask me) without hiring Pat Moran, my longtime casting agent, who has cast many, many Hollywood movies and TV shows whenever they shoot in Baltimore. Oh, well, I got a nice free dinner. And a onetime nominal fee.

The NBC TV *Hairspray Live!* was OK—but the weakest of all the productions, in my humble opinion. You can't ruin these characters, but why oh why would you make Motormouth Maybelle thin with Vegas-type showgirl breasts? The gym teacher is now *not* a lesbian and Rosie O'Donnell plays her? I guess I could live with all those dubious decisions, but the one blasphemy I couldn't handle was that during the live "breaks" on the air they went to Philadelphia to talk with original dancers on Dick Clark's *American Bandstand*. Heresy! That show never aired in Baltimore—only *Buddy Deane* did. But did NBC talk to any of the local Committee Members, as they were really called here, the ones who actually taught Ricki Lake to do some of the dance steps in the movie? Hell no! You gotta be kidding me.

But you can't kill *Hairspray*! I used to joke on TV that I wanted *Hairspray on Ice*, but then real ice-show producers took me seriously and wanted to do it. *Hairspray in Space*, a friend suggested recently. Why not? It could be a reality one day in the not-too-distant future. I guess the only thing left then would be the porn version: *Pubic Hairspray*. Come to think of it, what a perfect way to end it.

GOING HOLLYWOOD

Young filmmakers, go Hollywood whenever you can. It's *not* lonely at the top, I promise you. The chance to rake it in doesn't last long, so seize the moment, as Bobby Seale used to say. My *Hairspray* wasn't a big hit at the box office but it felt like one, and that's all that counts out there. The perception of a hit is all you need—a vague suggestion of a new kind of success, even if it didn't exactly happen. Suddenly, I was hot. Well, hot-ish. It was time to try pitching again.

But this time I needed an agent. You need one for two reasons: first, you cannot blow your own trumpet, someone else has to brag about your brilliance; and, second, you yourself cannot say out loud the astronomical fees you are now asking for your services. My old pal Jeff Buhai, still shocked he hadn't been able to get me a development deal for *Hairspray*, recommended his agent friend Bill Block, who agreed to handle me because he knew of my past and had heard the *Hairspray* buzz. Bill was so "Hollywood insider": handsome, edgy, nuts like me, and prone to yell things to executives like "Come on, I fuck on the first date!"—which, he patiently explained, means "Make us a big offer now and we won't go to your competition." More important, Bill hooked me up with entertainment lawyer Tom Hansen, the best in the business in my opinion—well liked, powerful, straight but super gay friendly, sexy in an ex-biker way, and tough without appearing so. Tom is still my lawyer today and has handled some of the baddest boys working— David Lynch, Robert Downey, Jr., Charlie Sheen, Al Pacino, and Mel Gibson. What I like best about Tom is that no matter how urgent the legal call, he starts off the conversation on a personal note; good-naturedly gossiping, catching up on how you're doing, asking what movies you've liked recently, all before getting to the meat of the matter. With a lawyer like Tom, the position of "manager" is redundant.

A Hollywood pitch is like turning in the ultimate homework assignment to strict teachers. Public speaking is one of the few things I was ever taught in school that I actually used later in life. And the Boy Scouts of America *were* right about one thing—be prepared. You can't bullshit an exec in a pitch meeting. You have to know the *whole* story, especially the end. Come up with an ad campaign, too, just to let the studio know you realize they must market your film to the whole wide world. And if you really want some brownie points, pick up the restaurant tab at the follow-up meeting and say, "We're all in this together." Believe me, they've never heard this before and the reward is much better than in school. Instead of an A-plus you can get a six-figure advance. You don't even have to give the money back if they decide not to make your movie. Let's make a deal, indeed!

After *Hairspray* every studio in town wanted to hear my pitch for *Cry-Baby*, a musical comedy about juvenile delinquents in the early fifties before rock and roll was born. And this time they weren't scared. Executives went for it big-time (little did they know that all the visuals I used to sell this project were gay soft-core male pinups from Athletic Model Guild, Bob Mizer's pioneering little studio of beefcake). When a bidding war started, Bill Block and I were in a dream situation. Even Dawn Steel, the notoriously explosive producer, wanted it for Disney, which was astounding, considering my past tawdry cinematic reputation. Paramount finally won out, and after writing the script and a year of executive shuffle and turnaround, I happily ended up with a green light from Brian Grazer and Ron Howard's Imagine Films shingle at Universal. For more money than I'd ever dared imagine. You can't get much more Hollywood than that. Finally I could hire an assistant. And buy a house.

I owe it all to Johnny Depp, because his agreeing to star in *Cry-Baby* clinched the deal. I realized how powerful he was when Brian Grazer, definitely a healthy, in-shape type of L.A. guy, allowed Johnny and me to chain-smoke cigarettes in his office whenever we'd meet to discuss the project. Johnny was at the height of his teen idol phase, starring in the original *21 Jump Street* TV show. He hated being the Justin Bieber of his time and figured making a movie with me was a surefire way to haywire that image, and that's exactly what he did by making fun of his "dreamboat" status in *Cry-Baby*. Traci Lords, fresh from escaping the porn world and causing an adult-film-industry scandal by revealing she had been underage while shooting all but one of her hit videos, did the same thing with me. By making fun of being a bad girl by playing one on-screen, she was no longer one in real life. Patty Hearst had started her own rehabilitation by serving her time for bank robbery (what a travesty) after being kidnapped by the SLA and was finally sick of being a famous victim. Who wanted to be, as I called her, the "Lindbergh baby who lived"? She wrote a book, called *Every*

Secret Thing, that retold her kidnapping saga from her point of view, hoping that would be it and she could move on. When Paul Schrader bought the rights and made a great movie out of it, called *Patty Hearst*, it premiered at the Cannes Film Festival in 1988 and I was there doing press for the international distributors who were buying the rights to *Hairspray*. My best friend in Europe, Matthias Brunner, who almost went to jail for screening *Pink Flamingos* in Switzerland in the seventies, smuggled me into the after-screening dinner, and seated me right next to her. We hit it off despite my blundering introduction ("I loved the movie. It made me think you weren't guilty for the first time"). "Thanks a lot," she huffed with a sense of humor I could see bubbling under the weariness of having to relive her lurid story once again with this film, no matter how sympathetic her portrayal, "I was in prison because of people like you." I asked Patty to be in my next movie. She thought I was kidding. I wasn't.

Patty's own family was appalled when she agreed to be in *Cry-Baby* ("*Why* would you want to attract more attention to yourself after what you've been through?" a sister argued), and her father offered to pay her not to take the part. But Patty understood why she wanted to do it. She was famous for something she didn't want to be famous for. She was sick of being a crime headline. Why not have a little fun with this notoriety that was hanging around her neck like an iron weight? Once she lampooned her supposed criminal conversion, they could never use it against her again. Doing a movie was certainly a much safer way to rebel. Besides, she could act. Hadn't she been performing with the SLA all that time so as to stay alive? This time, at least she'd have on-set catering.

The rest of the cast were the nutcases! Maybe I helped invent that term "stunt casting," yet I never put anyone in my films who I thought was so bad they were good. No, *Cry-Baby*'s cast was so great they were perfect, like a dinner party in a celebrity mental institution of my choice. The amazing Iggy Pop came to us freshly sober and serious about being an actor, and to this day I thank him for setting that tone on the set. I felt bad that his on-screen costar Susan Tyrrell, who played his wife and was beside him in almost every shot, was constantly drunk throughout the movie. Su-Su, as she demanded to be called (I refused), would say to each cast and crew member she was introduced to, "Hi. I have the pussy of a ten-year-old." She was a character all right, but the alcoholic harridan she won an Oscar nomination for portraying in *Fat City* was not too far away from her real self. Sometimes she'd be so loaded she couldn't even focus on me directing her before a take. Once she told me in the middle of our filming that her mother had died, which turned out to be a lie; she just wanted off when she had a hangover. Her "friends" visited the set and actually stole the script supervisor's jacket right off her chair. I never saw Susan after the shoot, but other cast members kept in touch and told me about the one-woman show she performed with her dead stuffed dog in her lap called *My Rotten Life*. When she later had her legs amputated in 2000 from some rare blood disease, *Cry-Baby* alums would visit her in the hospital and she'd greet them with "Want to fuck an amputee?" She died in 2012, happy at last, I heard. She had talent, yes, but, God, was she exhausting.

Joey Heatherton was another one for the books. "Hiring her in this condition verges on exploitation," Polly Bergen, ever the lady, accused me as she played poker with the Teamsters on the set between takes. Maybe Polly had a point. Right before I cast Joey to play the religious-fanatic wife of one of the *Cry-Baby* girl gang's fathers, Joey had been arrested for assaulting a passport clerk in the New York immigration office after a dispute over exact change. The clerk claimed (even though Miss Heatherton was eventually acquitted) that the temperamental star "reached over the counter, grabbed her hair, slammed her head into the plastic partition and then slapped her." Oh, well, we all have bad days.

At the audition, Joey spoke in tongues convincingly as the script called for, but seemed to be unable to stop after I told her the read through was over. As the casting assistant gently led her to the elevator, Joey was *still* speaking in tongues even though I had told her she'd got the part. Maybe she's never stopped.

When Joey arrived on location in Baltimore, she was *very* thin, yet sweet and cooperative even though the AD told me our day player had been taping up the tiny cracks in her dressing room wall and talking to herself. When Joey was brought to set to shoot the courtroom scene with her on-screen husband, Joe D'Allesandro (thrilled to be cast against type as a homophobic, fully clothed minister), Joey seemed overly protective of her real-life pocketbook, which she refused to leave behind in her changing area. It seemed as if she hid notes to herself inside the bag. Chris Mason, our immensely talented butch-lesbian hairdresser (who sadly died of cervical cancer in 1999), was much loved by our gang but at first feared by the Hollywood types, seemed scared herself dealing with Joey and reported back that she had seen Joey *talking* to her handbag as if to a person. When we were ready to shoot the first take, Joey refused to hand over her bag to the assistant costumer, but we finally reached a compromise. He would stand directly outside the frame line, and when I called "Action," Joey would hand over the purse, say her lines, and the second after I yelled "Cut," the pocketbook would be safely placed right back in her arms. Fair enough. Whatever it takes to get the shot.

I never saw Joey again after that day on the set, but she must have gotten better for a while because she appeared nude in *Playboy* magazine seven years later, and believe me, that wouldn't have been possible if she was in the same physical condition she'd been in with us. Then all was quiet. I didn't hear a peep about her in the press until 2014, when she got nailed again. It seems Joey's upstairs neighbor in Sherman Oaks, California, had a blender that she repeatedly used every morning even though Joey had warned her it made a *brrrrrrrrr-ing* noise that got on Joey's nerves. She complained. She banged on the ceiling. Yet the neighbor *still* used it. "God damn it!" Joey must have thought. She warned her, didn't she? Yet there was that noise again and her complaints were obviously being ignored. Finally reaching her limit, Joey waited outside the lobby of her building, and when Miss Noisy Homemaker exited, Joey attacked her with a high-heeled shoe. Sound familiar? I'd used a high-heeled shoe as a murder weapon in my earlier film *Desperate Living*. Does this mean I'm psychic?

The most shocking casting coup for me in *Cry-Baby* was David Nelson from the *Ozzie and Harriet* show. I grew up in the fifties watching David and his incredibly cute brother, Ricky, on that TV show, and both their images were singed into my memory. And there he was (thanks to Kathy Nelson, his cousin by marriage and head of Universal Studio's music department, who I'm sure talked him into it) right in my living room rehearsing to play a lunatic version of the same part his dad played on the TV show, but instead of having Harriet Nelson as his wife, she was played by Patty Hearst and Traci Lords was cast as their daughter! O happy day! How could this even be possible?

Troy Donahue was thrilled to be asked to portray Mink Stole's character's husband because, for once, I wanted him to look bad, not like the long-gone fifties teenage-pinup-boy image he by now detested. At one point he'd supposedly been homeless, living on a park bench in New York City, but what did we care? The cast had their own mental issues—we didn't judge. Like the rest of the *Cry-Baby* actors, Troy was a team player and always good-naturedly reminded his fellow cast members, "I'm the straight one," to distinguish himself from Tab Hunter, the "gay one," whom he knew I had already worked with.

Ricki Lake was back with us, as the "knocked-up" Pepper, Cry-Baby's juvenile delinquent sister, and adapted well to playing a supporting role rather than the leading one as she'd had in *Hairspray*. Her only complaint was that the tabloids now used photos of her dressed in costume with a fake pregnant stomach as proof that she'd gained an enormous amount of weight in real life, which was total bullshit. Also coming along for the ride was Norman Mailer's son Stephen, who played the villainous Baldwin, Johnny Depp's "square" nemesis. I knew the whole Mailer family a little from Provincetown, where Norman and his wife, Norris, lived, but Stephen got the part because he was, by far, the best actor who auditioned.

Rounding out the younger members of the cast was Kim McGuire as Hatchet-Face, a girl with "an alarming face and a great body," as the casting office tactfully put it. We meant ugly. When sad girls with physical deformities began showing up to audition, I feared we'd never find our girl, until Paula Herald, who worked alongside Pat Moran, spotted a head shot sent in for an extra's part in another production. Kim wasn't exactly ugly but she had a startling look—albino chic almost—and we knew that with the help of Van Smith (our ugly expert), she might be the one. We had no idea how old Kim really was when she came to us to read for the part, but she knew how to sell the role and gleefully agreed to let us turn her into the happy teenage monster. Kim later went on to work with David Lynch and then became a lawyer in California in 1997 before going back to the South and literally getting swept away by Hurricane Katrina and rebuilding her entire life afterward (she wrote a book about it titled *Flashback Katrina 10 Years After*). I was startled to see her interviewed on the bonus features of the Director's Cut of *Cry-Baby* released in 2005. She looked completely unrecognizable from the Kim McGuire I knew. Not bad, just normal and nice. Is it possible to get a head transplant? Sadly Kim died of cardiac arrest in 2016. I didn't even get to say goodbye.

I may be the only director who turned down Brad Pitt in a casting session. Completely unknown at the time, he came in to read for the role of Milton. We all knew somebody this handsome couldn't be cast as Johnny Depp's goofy sidekick—we needed a guy with a quirkier look (Darren Burrows got the part). When Brad walked out of the audition room without being picked, everyone agreed, "Whoever that was, he's gonna be a huge movie star." The few times I've seen Brad since at industry events over the years, he has been totally lovely to me. Maybe because I'm the only director who ever said no to Brad Pitt.

You wouldn't believe some of the big stars who came in to read for *Cry-Baby*. Carol Channing wanted to play Ramona Rickettes—Cry-Baby's hillbilly grandmother—and even though I knew she was dead wrong (Susan Tyrrell and her ten-year-old pussy got the part), I agreed to listen to Miss Channing's perplexing proposal that she should play the role as a Native American Indian woman. Huh? "Cyd Charisse herself" (as Divine called Ricki Lake in *Hairspray*) came in, too, elegantly overdressed and completely misled by her agent, who confided to me he wanted to reinvent her image by casting her against type. She had absolutely no idea who any of us were, what the project was, or why she was there, but I was gentle and respectful. Cyd Charisse herself! I couldn't stop saying it!

In hindsight, the saddest story was that of Amy Locane, the lovely seventeen-year-old actress who played Allison, Cry-Baby's square teenage princess, who eventually goes "bad" for his love. Cast while still in high school, she had to get permission to finish her senior year early so she could come to Baltimore and begin shooting. She didn't even get to go to her prom.

Amy arrived with her mother for the first day of rehearsal in my living room and had to kiss Johnny Depp in front of the other cast members. She actually fainted and I don't blame her. She was innocent, too young to hang out with her hell-raising costars in bars, but we soon found out she was not only a first-rate lip-synching pro, she was a really good actress, too. We used to play a game on set by asking everyone involved, "Have you ever been arrested?" It seemed Amy was the only one who said no. She was so naive that she confided to Patty Hearst, whom she'd never heard of, "You're the only normal one here." I felt bad Amy had no one to befriend on set.

Amy went on to have a career in Hollywood, played for a while in *Melrose Place*, but eventually gave it all up and moved back to her hometown in New Jersey, got married, and had two daughters. Unfortunately, this is where she caught up with the rest of the cast of *Cry-Baby* and got arrested, only for something more tragic—a DUI accident where she killed a woman and injured the woman's husband while driving drunk. To make matters worse (for me), a dear friend of mine knew both the woman Amy killed and her family.

As awful and terrible as that was, couldn't it have been you or me, dear reader? Hasn't everybody driven while legally drunk one time in his or her life? And couldn't it also have been us being *hit* by a drunk driver one day driving home from anywhere? Life is never fair, a lottery always stacked against us in the long run. I hadn't been in touch with Amy for twenty-five years but I wrote her once I read she had been sentenced to prison and was supportive of her new sobriety, honest sorrow, and shame-filled repentance. When the worst thing that can happen to you does, I try to be a friend.

Amy got out on parole after serving three years, and I met her for lunch near my apartment in Manhattan. She was quite nervous to be in the big city again, but she looked stunning, and we finally, as adults, had the chance to bond. I hope Amy gets back to acting one day—she's really good—but I understand that after what happened she'd probably be more comfortable with a lower profile. It isn't very pretty what a town without pity can do.

Not everybody had good memories of being in *Cry-Baby*. When I was doing *This Filthy World*—my spoken-word act— at Sweet Briar College in Virginia (both my mother *and* two sisters graduated from there), a young woman came up to me after the question-and-answer period and said, "I used to be against you because once I was the little baby that Ricki Lake gave birth to in the backseat of the car during the chicken drag-race scene in *Cry-Baby*. For many years, I harshly judged my parents for putting me in that situation when I obviously had no say in the matter." I guess I looked at her in confusion because she quickly added, "But after hearing you speak tonight, I forgive them." Wow. I'm happy my words of filth brought this family back together again. You never know, do you?

The *Cry-Baby* shoot went fairly well despite endless days of rain that made us go a little over budget. Rachel Talalay, a young producer from Baltimore who had also coproduced *Hairspray* for New Line Cinema, had a huge cast and crew to supervise and a director (me) who had never experienced union rules

(WGA, DGA, Teamsters); cumbersome company moves of trucks, lighting rigs, and trailers; and studio executives on set watching the clock. Of course, there was drama. Johnny Depp (who always called me Mr. Walters and didn't flinch when I referred to him as Cry-Rimmer) was constantly battling paparazzi or wild girl groupies who would leave notes at his hotel reading, "I'd like to suck your dick through a garden hose." One pack of teenage lovelies even approached crew members and offered to pay top dollar for the sewage under Johnny Depp's trailer. The Feds raided the set and served Traci Lords with papers trying to force her to return to L.A. to testify against the mob for distributing all her underage porn films. I'll never forget Patty Hearst, maybe in character, comforting offscreen her sobbing on-screen "daughter" with a hug.

Susan Tyrrell had a wild fling with one of the most volatile Teamsters, and they walked around the set cooing and making out like a teenage David and Lisa. The Universal Studios press agent assigned to our film, who had his hands full keeping the cast's troubles out of the newspapers, was himself busted in the middle of the shoot for copping heroin on the streets of Baltimore between call times. My best friend, Pat Moran, who was busy casting the film and helping out in all departments, dealt well with the fact that her son, Brook Yeaton (the prop master working with Vincent Peranio), was now an item with Traci Lords. They were eventually married (and divorced). Both Brook and Traci have happily remarried wonderful non-showbiz spouses and now have one child each. Katherine, Brook's daughter, didn't fall far from the family tree; she played the role of Cotton at ten years of age in 2015, when I shot my art video *Kiddie Flamingos*, where I rewrote the script of *Pink Flamingos* G-rated and filmed the all-children cast giving a costumed table read.

Ricki Lake lost her virginity halfway through the shoot on *Cry-Baby* and seemed gung ho in her new position as a woman of the world. I had an affair with an insanely cute hipster who walked into the Club Charles in Baltimore with a female date in the middle of a wild cast night out on the town. He looked at me, I looked at him, and he said, "Let's go," and we did. To Washington, D.C., to a hotel room. What the hell was I thinking? I don't know what happened to his date. As the shoot went on and I continued to see him, my great friend Henny Garfunkel, the female unit photographer, nervously confided, "You know, John, that boyfriend of yours. Well, he keeps making obscene phone calls to me. I know it's him, I recognize his voice, but I don't know how to handle it." "Oh, just hang up," I advised.

For the first time in my career I had to cut the whole movie in L.A. I bonded immediately with my editor, Janice Hampton, and her assistant, Erica Huggins (who went on to produce many movies at Imagine Films), but it took a bit of adjustment to actually *live* there. One thing I learned is that your tastes can change. Things you'd never wear in real life begin to look attractive in L.A. until you get back home to Baltimore and see yourself in the mirror. Good God! I bought that? I still have a pair of hideous yellow suede loafers that I picked up in Beverly Hills that prove this point.

The test screening this time was even more stressful, but that's only natural. The more money the suits give you, the more they're going to have to say. It's a simple mathematical formula. If you don't want "notes," focus groups, or forced reshoots, make a film on your cell phone for no money and nobody will bother you. But they gave me six figures to write and direct *Cry-Baby* so I was prepared to earn that salary. If you want to deposit big checks in showbiz, be prepared to weep. It comes with the territory.

Brian and Ron treated me fairly. The first test screening of *Cry-Baby* was at Universal Studios in Los Angeles, and the recruited Johnny Depp fans responded beautifully—they screamed every time he came on the screen like at Elvis movies in the fifties. The problem was, that never happened again. Each time we tested the film farther and farther away from Hollywood, the result got worse. His fans correctly smelled a rat. Me. We were making fun of Johnny's teen celebrity, and while his TV audience didn't exactly get it at first, they subconsciously realized we were making fun of them, too. Never having seen an Elvis movie, they missed the satire on that level also. After yet another test screening of *Cry-Baby*, the head of National Research Group asked me honestly, "What is the norm we test you against?"—admitting the futility of his company's entire purpose. As soon as you cut out the extremes of my film (always picked as "least" or "most" favorite by test audiences), then *nobody* likes it, not even the dumb ones too cowardly to have an opinion of their own.

But I played the game—read the preview cards that detailed the reactions of the focus ("fuck-us") groups and agreed with Brian and Ron to do reshoots to clarify some of the plot points that confused audiences. In turn, they allowed me to keep in one of my favorite shots, where the Allison character (Amy Locane) guzzles down a big gulp of her own tears she has saved in a jar, even though audiences had either been confused or repulsed by this scene. Did any of this tinkering work? Was it worth the millions of dollars it cost to bring back the whole cast from Baltimore and New York to Los Angeles, build sets, *plus* go on location just to make deeply suburban audiences who had never seen my previous films "like" it on the preview cards? Once we edited in all the new footage, the movie tested just the same!

There are so many different cuts of *Cry-Baby* that even I get them confused: the theatrical version (a little short), the U.K. DVD (not sure I ever actually saw it), network TV (the worst one—whole "lifts" of cut scenes put back in without our input to pad the running time), cable TV (fine), and finally the DVD U.S. Director's Cut (I guess my favorite but a little lengthy). Maybe they're all the same in the long run.

The world premiere was in my hometown at the Senator Theatre and the proceeds went to AIDS Action Baltimore, my favorite charity. All the stars showed up, including Johnny, with Winona Ryder, who had become his girlfriend while we shot the film. Photos of them together that night still show up in the tabloids whenever editors try to dig up dirt about these two's past. Before we wrapped, Johnny's lawyers had done the paperwork to get me ordained as a minister in the Universal Life Church because the couple wanted me to perform the marriage ceremony, but I gently talked them out of it because Winona was so young. Her parents thanked me.

After screening at the Cannes Film Festival, followed by an always welcome, but often misleading, standing ovation, we opened wide in America. Big billboard on Sunset Strip. Another on Times Square. In 1,229 theaters. National publicity for weeks. And we tanked. Reviews ran from great ("*Cry-Baby* has true madness; it's like an epic teen opera by some mutant pop Berlioz," Jack Kroll, *Newsweek*) to mixed ("brilliant but exhausting," David Denby, *New York* magazine) to awful ("it may be time he got out of Baltimore and started redefining the cutting edge," Owen Gleiberman, *Entertainment Weekly*). We did some good business in the big cities, but as far as crossover to the multiplexes, well, you could hear the crickets. Opening weekend was just $3 million with a $2,445 per screen average. *Cry-Baby* was thought of as *Hairspray*'s weak little brother, a reputation it only partially shed years later after new fans saw it all over the world on television because of Johnny Depp.

Then in 2008, *Cry-Baby* flopped all over again on Broadway. After *Hairspray*'s huge success on the Great White Way, it was only a matter of time before theatrical producers were interested in turning my only *real* musical film into another show-tune extravaganza. I loved what this whole team did with it. *Cry-Baby* on Broadway was actually closer to the tone of my films than *Hairspray*, but that was the problem. It was the sexiest Broadway musical for the whole family. Male frontal nudity. A French-kissing chorus singing "Girl, Can I Kiss You with Tongue?" A great number about schizophrenia, called "Screw Loose," mixed together with a polio-shot dance routine and a power ballad titled "I'm Infected," added up to a magical night in the theater to me. But alas, the *New York Times* critic Ben Brantley didn't agree, and even though we got four big Tony nominations (Best Musical, Best Book, Best Choreography, and Best Score), we won none and closed soon after. At least the original-cast album was finally recorded and released in 2015, seven years later. Listen to it; you missed a good one.

But after all these years I have come to realize why *Cry-Baby* was never as popular as *Hairspray*, and it's my fault. The character Allison. I wrote her as a traditional ingenue, and no matter how well acted the part, this was a flaw. My heroes and heroines should never fall in love with a traditional anything! Cry-Baby should have fallen in love with Hatchet-Face. Then we would have had a hit.

Can failure sometimes be welcome? It certainly can. You'll take two steps back in the Chutes and Ladders board game known as show business, yet you'll have time to breathe, a moment to accept you're not the wizard you thought you were. No agents will call, but isn't it time for a little quiet? You fantasize the grosses might go up in the second week but they never do. If you are lucky enough to have "real" friends not in the movie business, they'll feel thankful to have you back in the fold without all the hubbub. David Lynch once wished in an interview, "It would be fantastic to make movies and never put them out. I love getting to where they are all really right for me—that part is just beautiful. When it's time to release them, the heartache begins." Once you flop, take a deep breath and accept that sometimes a turkey is good for your mental health.

Floundering is like treading water: you have to learn how to do it before you swim. Right after the failure of *Cry-Baby* the movie, I came up with an idea for another film that was the opposite of nostalgia: "*Glamourpuss*, an irreverent 'whitesploitation' picture that satirizes the sexual, racial, and economic sacred cows of today." Did I actually think Hollywood would go for Trent Marlowe, a new kind of homeboy (this was five years before Eminem) who is mistakenly gay-bashed by a band of skinhead trendzoid Nazis and rescued by a cliché-busting gang of gay militants led by the rapping African American fashion goddess known underground as Glamourpuss? "She doesn't need a man anymore," I'd announce in the most trailer-friendly voice I could muster to any backer who would listen. "She fucks the system!"

I actually pitched this story to every studio head in Hollywood who would take a meeting. "When a white yo-boy and a black fag hag team up, look out!" I'd bellow. "This glamourpussy means business, and her all-rapping new breed of sexually confused fashion-conscious outsiders want the nineties all to themselves. *And* they want it now!" Development executives looked at me blankly when I was done. One said, "John, if I didn't know you, I'd think you were insane." I thought to myself, "You *don't* know me." I think he meant no.

But a no is free so I didn't let rejection stop me. I raced back home in 1991 and thought up a whole new project: *Raving Beauty*, the searing comic melodrama about a female movie star shooting a film on location in Baltimore who is driven crazy by stalking fans, rabid tabloid reporters, her controlling megalomaniacal director, a vengeful ex-husband, a Tourette's-syndrome-suffering personal assistant, a teenage daughter who is only sexually attracted to the homeless, and her radical ACT UP gay son who relentlessly cruises the Teamsters on set. "When mental despair almost takes her over, our diva heroine suddenly finds love in the arms of a handsome sewage worker (from the I.O.U.A#2 Sanitation company) who is hired to empty the toilet underneath her movie star trailer." And oh, yes, he believes he's an extraterrestrial. And I thought this was commercial?!

You know what? I was right. David Kirkpatrick from Paramount Pictures bought my idea for $300,000 and I was back in the "development" business. But by the time I had written the full shooting script and turned it in, this green-lighting executive was long gone and no one there still in power shared in my excitement over the project. *Raving Beauty* wasn't going to get made, yet I still got to keep the writing money. In Hollywood, being fired is a good job. I'd apply if I were you.

CLAWING MY WAY

HIGHER

My mom always said *Serial Mom* was the best film I ever made and I think she's right. It also was the only one where I had enough money to make it look Hollywood. New producers, new director of photography, and, yep, Kathleen Turner. So many people in the biz blanched when I told them she had been cast: "She's extremely difficult," "She drinks," "She's a ball-breaker," they warned. But I found none of this to be true. She was a total pro, a team player, and the performances of everybody else in the film went up a notch from being around her. By now, my directorial advice was much more low-key and natural—no more characters screaming the way I used to love in my early midnight movies. Just watch Mink in *Serial Mom*— so realistic, so underplayed, so funny. I think it's her best performance with me. The scene where Kathleen and Mink cuss each other out on the phone in split screen is just perfect in my book. "Is this the Cocksucker residence?" snarls Kathleen, playing the devious mom Beverly Sutphin, before Mink Stole, as the snotty neighbor Dottie Hinkle, barks back, "God damn you!" Imagine my delight when, years later, Boy George gave me his cell phone number and, when I called him and got his voice mail, the first thing I heard was Kathleen's voice from *Serial Mom* snarling, "Cocksucker residence." My dialogue had become a state of mind.

Sure, Kathleen liked a cocktail, but she never drank while we were working. I'd join her for a beverage on our day off, and one of my favorite sights and sounds is seeing Kathleen take her first sip of a martini and then letting out a ferocious growl of "Ahhhhhh" after it goes down. Difficult? Not with me. Movie stars *want* to be directed. The worst thing I could ever have said to Kathleen as we approached a new scene together would have been "What do you think, Kathleen?" Also, never leave a leading lady alone once she's in costume and has been delivered to the set. She is *why* you got your movie made in the first place. Idle time for major talent can only lead to shit-stirring from the ignored and famous. Pay attention to your stars as if your life depended on it. It does.

At first, dealing with the Hollywood studio system on *Serial Mom* was a dream come true. When I pitched "the true-crime parody told in a mock-serious docudrama style about a lovable, sweet serial killer that could be your mom," the execs' ears perked up. "This is a 'true' story about 'real people' set right up the street from where you live," I continued. "Not the usual John Waters movie about crazy people in a crazy world but a movie about a normal person in a realistic world doing the craziest thing of all as the audience cheers her on!"

As my producer John Fiedler and I left one such pitch session at Columbia Pictures with Barry Josephson (rumored to be the inspiration for the studio-exec character in *Swimming with Sharks*), we waited outside his office for the elevator. Suddenly Barry came rushing out into the hall and said, "Come back in here right now, please." We did. Then the ultimate fantasy of any writer-director came true. "OK, we'll give you the development deal if you don't go anywhere else today to pitch and don't fuck with us!" I couldn't believe my ears. *Serial Mom* was going to happen. Instantly. We were "fucking on the first date."

But that was the only good thing that happened within the Hollywood system on this film. Naturally Barry had also moved on to another studio by the time the script was finished, and even though I was lucky enough to get the film picked up in turn-around by Savoy Pictures, it was a nightmare experience from then on.

Not the shoot—that went fairly smoothly. Vince Peranio, for once, had the budget to build handsome interior sets, and Van Smith proved he could do "real" clothes with just as much style and wit as he could do "insane." Bobby Stevens' cinematography added a gorgeous sheen to the look of the film, which is exactly what I wanted. We found the perfect location for the Serial Mom's family house, and the elderly male owner even let us continue filming when his wife died in the middle of the shoot. Towson High School (where Divine had been ridiculed by teachers and beaten up by bully students) let us film the murder of an uppity teacher who was judgmental about Serial Mom's son because he was a horror-film buff. Poetic justice? We paid a fortune to get the rights to the song "Tomorrow" from the musical *Annie* to use over one of the most gruesome murders in the film (Kathleen even beats the victim with a leg of lamb *in time* with the music), and I learned the on-screen trick of how to get any dog to lick human feet on cue. It's simple. Just put butter on the toes and the dog will "shrimp," take after take after take.

Kathleen Turner bonded well with what was left of Dreamland, and Pat Moran and Paula Herold came up with some great new casting choices, especially Matthew Lillard, who, after playing Serial Mom's son, Chip, went on to a big career that included the *Scooby-Doo* series. Sam Waterston, yes, *that* Sam

Waterston, shocked us all by agreeing to play Kathleen's clueless husband and added a touch of true class to the production. Patty Hearst joined us again and proved she was not only a talented comedian but a stunt performer supreme as well. "Nobody could take a hit as convincingly as Patty Hearst," marveled Kathleen after filming the scene where Serial Mom slugs one of the jury for wearing white shoes after Labor Day (a capital fashion offense I still believe in no matter who says different—and that means you, Anna Wintour). Suzanne Somers good-naturedly made fun of her own TV image by agreeing to play a fictionalized version of herself in the courtroom scene. Brigid Berlin, the Warhol superstar, made the first of her appearances in my films in the small role of a trial groupie but surprised the transportation coordinator when he was trying to book her travel. Instead of a round-trip train ticket from New York, Brigid preferred to take a taxi! And she did. Whether he kept the meter running I don't know. She agreed to pay the fare herself. Both ways.

L7, an all-female punk-rock group I loved, was hired to play Camel Lips, an even more aggressive fictional riot-grrrl act who wore tight white trousers with padded vaginal lips outlined in the crotch. "This is too much," fumed an initially outraged Mary Ellen Woods, my AD, when she saw them on the set before eventually calming down. I asked L7 to cowrite a song with me, called "Gas Chamber," and at first it seemed as if they were hesitating. Were they pro–death penalty? I never found out, but no matter what their capital-punishment politics were, the song they helped dream up was great (I still get royalties as cowriter), and the scene where they perform their catchy little number with Sam Waterston bodysurfing into the crowd of slam-dancing extras in the now long-gone Baltimore club Hammerjacks is one of the highlights of the film.

Joan Rivers also played a skewered version of herself on her own talk show doing the interview "Serial Hags: Women Who Love Men Who Mutilate." I didn't even go to New York the day she was filmed on the set as I was in Baltimore directing another scene, but I think Joan understood creative film budgeting. Later in the editing room, I could hear her howling between takes, "The lowest form of show business—the director's not even here!"

But when the studio screened the rough cut, the shit hit the fan. They were completely horrified. "You can't show Serial Mom setting a teenage friend of her son on fire!" one sputtered, red in the face, spittle flying. "That scene is in the script you approved exactly as we shot it," I argued, amazed at his outrage. One thing I've learned: this argument *never* works. Most of the execs assigned to your picture weren't even there when it was greenlit and never read the script in the first place, just "coverage" by their assistants.

When Savoy canceled the first test screening scheduled somewhere outside L.A., I begged, "Let's just have an informal screening at the Directors Guild of America in Hollywood for a recruited audience of people who like my films, not an official NRG [National Research Group] one." "OK," they agreed, "but it won't count."

Of course that audience cheered, laughed, and applauded at the end, but that only pissed off the studio more. "Meaningless," they groused, "this audience knew you directed the film." Huh? "Why did you hire me, then?" I tried to argue with a straight face, not hearing a word back acknowledging how well *Serial Mom* had just played. They immediately scheduled an "official" test screening for later in the week in some deep-suburban neighborhood miles outside Hollywood, probably where Rodney King's jurors lived. And while recruiting the audience, they eliminated any moviegoer who admitted to knowing who I was!

The studio got their wish. This audience hated it. The Savoy executives actually looked happy when they told me the results. I was shocked to read in *The Wall Street Journal* just three months later an article that claimed the NRG testing group sometimes doctored the results negatively to help justify the changes the studios demanded from their directors. God! Even in my worst dreams I never imagined that!

The battle escalated. The studio wanted to have a new editor come in (over my dead body! I had bonded heavily with Janice Hampton as we cut our second picture together) and without our involvement recut the film so *Serial Mom* would be convicted at the end, not set free as the script always read. The test audience in Mongolia, or wherever we had just been, seemed confused on the comment cards—they believed the satirical opening credit of the movie: "This is a true story. The screenplay is based on court testimony, sworn documents, and hundreds of interviews conducted by the filmmakers. Some of the innocent characters' names have been changed in the interest of a larger truth." Ha! "No one involved in the crimes received any form of compensation" (except me, the cast, and the crew). I guess the closing card of the movie (which I wrote and rewrote many times to get it just right)—"Beverly Sutphin refused to cooperate with the making of this film"—was the final straw. The test audience wanted her strapped to the electric chair.

I brought my agent, Bill Block, with me to the showdown meeting, which pissed the execs off because they wanted to bully me alone. I said no. They basically countered with "You'll never work in this town again." And I said, "If I do the version of the film you want, it will be so bad I'll never work in this town anyway, so what do I have to lose?"

In fairness, I *did* listen to some of their notes. I tried different structures in the editing room, but since I rejected their "happy ending," rewrite ideas all seemed impossible. The script just wasn't written that way. Besides, no matter what we tried, some people would love it, some people would hate it. We were never going to appease the middle. The story of my life. The worst possible scenario in Tinseltown.

I quickly retreated to Salt Lake City, where we recorded *Serial Mom*'s beautiful classical score by Basil Poledouris, played by the Utah Symphony, making sure we provided just the sheet music, not the violent visuals that went along with it, in case there were any extremist Mormon members. Halfway through the session, I got the frantic phone call alerting me that Liz Smith, then the most powerful syndicated gossip columnist in the country, had headlined her column that day "Leave Serial Mom Alone." I had told Kathleen the whole nightmare that was happening with the executives, and without telling me, she blabbed the whole story to her friend Liz. Thank God! It worked. The studio executives were now the bad guys trying to wreck a dark comedy that cool preview audiences loved. Thank you, Liz! Thank you, Kathleen, for this great sneak attack against Hollywood interference. Savoy was furious. Studio heads ranting! Executives screaming mad! Threatening me. Yet they couldn't take it out on Kathleen because they had paid her millions to do the picture (well deserved) and needed her to promote the film internationally (which she did, even demanding a Mercedes truck from a German TV show, which she eventually got after rejecting their offer of a sedan). My executive blamed me personally, but since the studio now believed mid-America would hate the film (later tests in Garden City, New York, also reported "below average" results, with focus groups complaining the film "was in poor taste"), the marketing department figured they better keep me around for whatever audiences were left.

I guess the studio was right. Even though we had a great

official, out-of-competition screening at the Cannes Film Festival ("Boy, this beats the Oscars," Kathleen whispered to me as we paraded up the steps of the Palais to greet the festival president, Gilles Jacob—always a huge supporter of my films), *Serial Mom* flopped when it opened wide in America on the first beautiful spring day of 1994. After a long, tough winter, nobody went to see *any* movies that weekend; they all went outside to become one with nature. Even a lovely review in *The New York Times* couldn't save us. We lasted about five more weeks in the theaters and finally grossed a total of $7,820,000 on a budget of $13 million plus prints and advertising.

"But my pictures are like backlist book titles," I always argue in damage control. "They don't fade away. They last way past their sell-by dates." "*Serial Mom*, which in hindsight predicted the O.J. madness, always gets screened on television on Mother's Day," I like to point out, adding, "I even get a free laugh today when the movie is screened in revival houses and one of the potential victims says, 'I *love* Bill Cosby pictures,' way before his recent sexual assault conviction. Another reason for Serial Mom to kill her." But studios don't care. A cult film is the last thing they want, and I don't blame them. "Cult" means three smart people liked it and nobody paid to see it. I didn't want a cult film, either!

Do I feel bad that Savoy Pictures lost money on *Serial Mom*? I would have felt guilty if the friends I had borrowed money from to make my earlier trash epics hadn't gotten their money back, but Hollywood studios' entire business is based on a gamble. I *did* make the exact film I wrote and they approved. Instead of trying to make the audiences who didn't like the film like it, they should have plotted how to make the ones who would like it love it more. But I have to admit they were doing their job. If one of the movies they greenlit loses money, they lose their job. That's why I never name the suits who gave me such creative trouble. They gave me a lot of money to write and direct *Serial Mom* (even if I did have to threaten lawsuits to get the final payment). I cashed all the checks, didn't I? All's fair in love and war, I guess, once the show business dust has settled. Savoy Pictures went out of business three years later. I didn't. But my real Hollywood days were over. I may have clawed my way to the top, but now it was time to learn how to slide back down to the bottom.

TEPID APPLAUSE

rom here on in, none of the movies I made turned a profit. But do you think that stopped me? Midcareer is the time to realize that failing upward is the only way to go, but it's a tricky thing to pull off. Show business never takes place in reality; it combusts in the heat of the moment, so turn up the gas, light a match, and make your reputation explode. You have to love the press. Read it every day. Make tabloid news stories your personal soap operas. Pretend you're on a talk show when you're just home in your apartment. Try speaking in only sound bites for one whole day on your job. Once you understand how the media works, then you both can use each other—one for free material, the other for unpaid advertisements. It's a dance of mutual exploitation where both partners win. If you make as much noise as you can in the media and still keep a sense of humor about yourself, both the public *and* future investors will look the other way at your box office disappointments. You'd think the powers that be would know better at this stage of the game, but luckily for us, they never do.

Pecker, my "nice" movie, got made mainly because Japanese teenage girls loved Edward Furlong and he had agreed to star in the title role. Eddie was young, hairless, and androgynous; just what they line up for at the box office in that country. He was so hot in Japan that a record label talked Eddie into recording a rock-and-roll album that was only distributed there. He told me he was mortified at the final product, but I made him give me a copy and it still sits on my office shelf, unopened but worshipped.

In 1997, foreign sales still mattered. Well, they still matter now but only the Chinese ones. I hold China responsible for wrecking the worldwide independent film business as I once knew it. Chinese movie producers don't want comedy anymore, they don't want pesky movie stars whose salaries eat up profits, and more important, they don't want wit. They want $100 million comic-book/video-game/sci-fi tentpoles that celebrate one thing—special effects. They want science projects.

Cam Galano at New Line Cinema, who helped run the foreign sales division there, is solely responsible for getting *Pecker* made. I was back at the Cannes Film Festival with the whole New Line gang hawking international sales of the twenty-fifth anniversary director's cut of *Pink Flamingos*. In the heat of the festival wheeling and dealing (*always* the best time to get overpaid), Cam talked a Japanese distributor into committing to part of *Pecker*'s budget, and once they came aboard, other countries fell into line and Bob Shaye, bless his grouchy soul, agreed to finance it for America. We even signed some deal memos on a napkin at the terrace of the Majestic Hotel. Yes, movie business clichés *are* true, and when they happen to you, it can be a beautiful thing!

Before we even started shooting there was trouble. The Motion Picture Association of America rejected our attempt to register the title *Pecker* as soon as New Line tried, calling it "obscene, profane or salacious." We immediately fired back that

Pecker was not pornographic in any way and that the title referred to the main character's nickname, which he received, as explained in the script, "because he never ate properly as a child—always pecked at his food."

When the big day of arbitration finally happened at a hearing in Los Angeles at MPAA headquarters, I was there as the star witness. I couldn't believe it. Here I was, a grown man appearing in court over my right to use the word "pecker": I was well prepared. "No angry child carves the word 'pecker' in his school desk," I argued. "No misogynist men demand that women 'suck their 'pecker,'" I shouted like Clarence Darrow to the stupefied faces of the humor-impaired arbitrators. "And what about all the other filthy double-entendre titles you have approved in the past?" I challenged, like an outraged Perry Mason. "How about *Shaft? Octopussy? Spaceballs? In and Out?* Even Barbra Streisand's *Nuts!*" I shouted as if I were making the closing statement of a capital case.

And you know what? We won! The only time I ever defeated the censorious MPAA, who agreed "by unanimous decision" to overturn the rejection of my title. John Waters' *Pecker* was ready for the marquees.

Critics always thought that *Pecker,* "a rags-to-riches tale of a goofy, cute eighteen-year-old blue-collar kid who works in a Baltimore sandwich shop and takes photos of his loving but peculiar family and friends on the side and accidentally gets turned into a star in the New York art world," was autobiographical, but it wasn't. I wasn't naive. Pecker was. I wanted New York to discover my early works; they just never did until way later. I wasn't blue-collar either, even though I wished I were. True, there once was rumbling from my core acting troupe that I was getting rich from my movies and they weren't (the way Pecker was from his photographs), so the main eight people who

were the most involved in those first productions banded together and decided who should benefit, and I agreed to give them
25 percent of the profits to split. Today they, or their heirs, *still*
get 3 percent each of the titles up to and including *Female
Trouble* and Divine's estate gets 4 percent. I believe in the long
run they did better with me than they would have if they had
Screen Actors Guild residuals.

Pecker was really inspired by the lives of Diane Arbus and
Nan Goldin. How did that little kid holding the hand grenade
in that Arbus photo feel when he saw the six-figure auction price
of that fleeting moment in his young life that day in Washington Square Park? Proud, it turns out. I knew there had been a
lot of complaining from Nan Goldin's subjects years later about
her success with their portraits showing raging alcoholism, drug
addiction, even suicide, but I always pointed out that Nan had
picked up the tab of their restaurant dinners for years, gave
many of them prints of their portraits that would today be worth
a fortune, and received little back in return.

Yet in a way, I knew how they felt. One year I invited Nan
to my Baltimore house for breakfast the day after my annual
Christmas party, and she showed up with her camera. "Oh,
no, you don't." I blocked her. "I have no desire to see a picture
of myself with a bad hangover hanging in Matthew Marks
Gallery next year no matter how artful it may be." She seemed
to understand.

The Japan Times later called *Pecker* "a Disney film for perverts" and I guess that's pretty accurate. We had a wonderful
cast: Christina Ricci, Martha Plimpton, Brendan Sexton III,
Mary Kay Place, and Lili Taylor. Before Eddie, I had tried to
cast Beck, who was just beginning his musical career, as Pecker,
but he seemed amused and mystified about why I wanted him

for the role since he had never before acted, and he turned me down nicely.

As soon as we went into rehearsal, I realized Eddie was depressed in real life. He had made his name in the business by playing mopey, damaged young men, and while he was a great actor, comedy did not come easily to him. Directing Eddie Furlong was like doing auteur push-ups. Each take I had to build his energy level up to a normal actor's before I could yell, "Action." He was still with his girlfriend Jackie, who had started her affair with him when he was sixteen and she was his thirty-two-year-old on-set schoolteacher. "They tried to put me in jail," she once complained on set, and even though Pat Moran mouthed "No wonder" behind her back, I didn't judge. I liked Jackie. She got Eddie to set on time and made him promote the film during production, activities I'm not sure he would have been capable of on his own. All that really counts is the final performance, not how it was achieved. Eddie Furlong *was* Pecker! Nothing else mattered.

Almost the entire film was shot in the Hampden neighborhood of Baltimore. Once a white working-class community notorious for racist housing segregation, today it is hipster central and is fast becoming our own Brooklyn, New York. Almost none of the original locations in *Pecker* are still there except for the sub shop where Pecker was supposed to have worked. Pecker's Place, the redneck bar that became the rage for visiting uppity New Yorkers in the script, is long gone. Originally known as B-J's, it was a semi-notorious redneck dive where I used to hang out in real life, and which I later wrote about in *Role Models*, but it's torn down now and was replaced by an H&R Block. Pecker's family home in the movie burned to the ground after the owner mom's son accidentally set it on fire while she was getting her hair done. Is there a more Baltimore story than that?! The Spin n' Grin Laundromat is now a hair salon, and the Fudge Palace, actually the Atlantis, the onetime male strip club located right next to the prison, is now Scores, a supposedly high-end gentleman's titty bar.

I do, however, still have the talking Virgin Mother statue in my attic, the one that Pecker's grandmother (played by the late and great Jean Schertler) believed talked to her. Sometimes I think I hear her mumbling "Full of grace" upstairs the way she did in the film, but then I realize I'm just hearing things.

One thing I've learned—you can be *too* budget conscious once you're back making nonstudio films. *Pecker*'s 1998 cost was $6 million, which seems like a lot today, but at the time (before fucking China) was a fairly routine budget for an independent movie. One of the overly thrifty producers of *Pecker* said toward the end of the shoot that we didn't have enough money left to film the interior of the bus for the credit sequence, so we never got to show Pecker photographing the two black girls with the amazing hairdos or the white lady shaving her legs on board. About a week after production had wrapped, Janice, my editor, horrified me by announcing she had just completed putting together the rough assemblage of the film and it was only eighty-three minutes long—even before we had cut out a single frame. A nightmare! I panicked and frantically alerted the producer, who wasn't even still in Baltimore. He never informed New Line but took postproduction money he was hoarding and brought Eddie Furlong back to Baltimore. We cast the bus-riding extras, hired the same crew, and shot the entire scene with New Line none the wiser.

Another joke we had never had the time to get because of the overly threadbare shooting schedule was of Little Chrissy, Pecker's sugar-addicted younger sister who turns rabid vegetarian, snorting a pea through a straw off a plate like cocaine. I begged the producer to let me go back to the location and get that shot, too, and he OK'd it. When the film was released, this gag got the biggest laugh in the entire movie. Coming in under budget on a film, I learned from this experience, is a stupid thing to do.

We kept other secrets from New Line, too. During the shoot I had an "art attack" myself, just like Pecker. I noticed right from the first day that the key grips and camera assistant were drawing a picture for me every time they put down gaffer tape marks on the floor for the actors to hit so they'd stay in focus. Realizing that these hurried gestures, color coded for each character, would be ripped up and immediately destroyed after the shot was completed, I started photographing the involuntary blueprints in context. Now I could document the only thing left on set that is never supposed to be seen in a movie still—the actors' tape marks. I was celebrating an abstract sense of passive directorial control that couldn't be put to market testing. Maybe I was just being paranoid over the movie's chances at the box office. If you didn't buy a ticket in a theater, maybe you'd be moved to buy one of my "anti-stills" and want to hang one up on your wall. When the same producer who later pulled off the reshoot finally figured out what I was doing art-career-wise midshoot, he asked half-jokingly, "Since you are taking these photos on company time, do I get a percentage of the sales if you later show them in an art gallery?" Luckily I said no right away, so when I *did* have a show years later at Gavin Brown's gallery in New York (arranged by my art dealer, Colin de Land), nobody from production showed up trying to collect.

Even though *Pecker* was the only one of my later films to be rejected by Gilles Jacob for official selection by the Cannes Film Festival, for being "not offensive enough like your other usual stuff," the movie did have its fair share of sex scenes. "Tea-bagging" became the newest rude sex act I could introduce to the public. It involves dropping your balls on a partner's forehead as sexual foreplay. Yes, it's a fleeting moment, but it's safe, you can't get pregnant, and it's more common than you'd initially think. After all, aren't many women accidentally tea-bagged when their husbands climb over them nude in the morning to get out of bed? In the U.K., tea-bagging means dipping the testicles into the mouth of your partner like in a cup of tea, but I went for the more family-friendly R-rated American version. Once the Republicans started their far-right spin-off groups known as tea-baggers, it became obvious to the news media that these conservatives were unaware of what tea-bag meant to a small but more sexually advanced minority of members of the Democratic Party. Rachel Maddow on MSNBC tried to explain on her show, but she started breaking up and you could hear her crew behind her laughing on set right on the air.

Sex scenes can be complicated to film, especially animal ones. In *Pecker* there's a scene where our title character discovers two rats fucking and takes their photograph for "art." But how do you get a rat to fuck on camera in real life? Do you try to make the rats horny by showing them *Willard* or *Ben*? If they hear Michael Jackson singing "Ben, . . . you've got a friend in me" on the soundtrack, will that get your rodents' erotic juices flowing?

I hired an animal trainer for the scene, but in the long run that was a waste of money. Animal trainers *always* say they can get the animals to do whatever the script calls for, but they're often unsuccessful. He tried everything to get the rats going, but even putting peanut butter on their sex parts didn't work because I wanted the missionary position, not rat fellatio or cunnilingus. I was stationed on the other side of the interior

trash-can set near the video monitor so I could see on camera
what it would look like on film, if and when the rats started
humping. I could hear the trainer off camera trying to coax
them, but I couldn't see him. Since we were filming MOS (without sound), so I could later dub in fictitious rat panting, I could
talk out loud without ruining the take. Just to lighten the mood,
as we tediously waited for the rats to feel the urge, I started talking "rat dirty" in a last-ditch effort to inspire them to mate: "Oh,
fuck me, rat hog! Eat that cheese, bitch! Fuck my dirty rat hole!"
I growled in my best sex voice. No one on set laughed, which
seemed odd. Leaving my director's chair to see what the matter
was, I was mortified to realize that the trainer, on the other side,
had brought his child along with him to witness how a movie
was made. She had heard every filthy rat-porn-talk-dirty thing
I'd said. Brook Yeaton, my prop master supreme, knew it was
time for drastic action. He grabbed both rats by the back of
their necks, put one on top of the other, told me to frame up cutting off his hands at the bottom, and began shaking the little
critters violently. It looked on camera exactly as if the rats were
fucking, and it gets a big laugh every time that scene comes up
on-screen. I guess I still paid the animal trainer. In a similar
situation, I would advise you to do the same.

Pecker's real theme was the elimination of irony. I once said,
"Nothing's so bad it's good if you're poor," but a critic pointed
out that this was an elitist, ironic statement in itself. But is it?
Is anything camp if you're hungry? Do boat people crack jokes
about their dire situation? Is anything a laff riot for Syrian ref-
ugees? I guess it is ironic that I'm toasting "the end of irony"
in the finale of Pecker since all my life I've made a living from
just that. I'm practically an irony dealer, but Pecker isn't ironic
in the final analysis. Once Pecker is dubbed by the press in the
movie "a teenage Weegee whose paintbrush is the broken-down

camera he found in a thrift shop," irony ruins his loving relationship with his newly so-called culturally challenged friends
and family. His mom and dad are suddenly humiliated by the
national attention, his friends become self-conscious, and his
blue-collar girlfriend who runs a Laundromat immediately feels
inadequate when she compares herself to her New York City
counterparts. When she yells for the whole world to hear "I hate
contemporary photography," we may laugh at this ludicrous line
of dialogue, yet who couldn't understand exactly how she feels?
The tagline I dreamed up for the ads says it all: "He's poor. He's
white. But he sure ain't trash. All he wanted was to take your
picture."

Pecker opened "softly." That's the polite word the distributor
uses when they call you the Sunday night of the opening weekend to tell you that you flopped. We got decidedly mixed reviews
(though a nice one in *The New York Times*), and some of my
hard-core fans were distressed at the movie's basic sweetness.
A few even thought it sentimental. Yet others, and they were a
definite minority, liked it the best of all my films, and over time
Pecker found a wider audience on television, where it seemed
to play better. I like *Pecker* just fine. And oh, yeah, it *was* a hit
in Japan. But I knew we'd never break even when the porn parody was released soon after. Its title? *Pecker.*

SLIDING BACK DOWN

ecil B. Demented is one of my favorite films I've directed, but few agree. I always choose it when I appear at a college and am asked what movie of mine I'd like them to show first. I guess all directors have a soft spot for one of their films that did the worst at the box office, the way a parent sticks up for a mentally or physically challenged child. I stole the name Cecil B. Demented from a headline in the gay magazine *The Advocate*, which ran over an interview with me conducted by Lance Loud, arguably America's first reality TV star. *Cecil* is another of my movies that critics assumed was autobiographical, but it's really not. Demented is a cult-film director and shoots on the run. My cinematic posse and I did the same thing in the old days, but I hope I had a sense of humor about my own importance even then. Cecil does not. Like all fascists, Cecil B. Demented, the character, is humor-impaired about his deluded directorial vision.

I pitched *Cecil* everywhere in Hollywood as an "R-rated action thriller about a young lunatic film director and his gang of film cultists who kidnap a real-life Hollywood movie goddess and force her to act in their own Super 8 underground movie." Even Bob Shaye at New Line said no to this one, so I imitated all the white American rockabilly singers who went overseas in the sixties after their fifties careers died and found new fans and sources of funding. If the original Drifters can all be dead yet still tour in Europe today as they do without anyone being the wiser, you, too, can impersonate a misunderstood, eccentric film director whom the stupid Hollywood system almost destroyed. Across the pond, European producers pretend to care only about art, so perk up your wardrobe, buy a plane ticket, and start being the highfalutin salesman whose product can only be fathomed on "the Continent," where cinema is really respected.

I sold my *Cecil* pitch to the big French distributor Canal+, who had a reputation at the time for financing the work of American crackpot auteurs I love such as David Lynch and Jim Jarmusch. I remember well that meeting in Cannes with all the Gallic movie executives. "Lots of kids dream of making a movie," I enthused between bites of the elegant lunch buffet, "but only the ones willing to die for it succeed." "Oui," they said. I didn't need subtitles to realize that meant a green light. I was so excited to finally be a real foreign film director! Oh, yeah, I got a million dollars to write and direct. I'm not kidding. Talk about failing upward. Boy, those were the days.

Stephen Dorff had always been my first choice to play Cecil, and at the time he was "bankable," a ridiculous concept that is still in use today. So was Alicia Witt, who was cast as Cherish, Cecil's porn star girlfriend whose career highlight was a film called *Rear Entry*, where she inserted a live gerbil named Pellet up her ass for erotic voyeuristic enjoyment. I'm telling you, these actors were brave! Melanie Griffith threw caution to the wind, too, and signed up to play the role of the spoiled movie-star victim Honey Whitlock. Audiences don't know how hard it is to play a bad actress without being one, and I think Melanie pulled it off spectacularly. At the time, Melanie was freshly in love with Antonio Banderas, who had made his name in the early films of Pedro Almodóvar, and I think Antonio was the one who encouraged Melanie to take a chance with me.

The rest of the cast was just as good. The Sprocket Holes were Cecil's band of cinema terrorists who each had somewhere on his or her body a tattoo of the name of their favorite director (Kenneth Anger, William Castle, Sam Peckinpah). I always thought that in real life the mandatory tattooing of directorial idols on every single unmarried citizen would, in the long run, make dating much easier. Me? I'd ink JOSEPH LOSEY right on my chest.

Kerry Barden, the casting agent who worked on the film with Pat in Baltimore, brought to the table some new names that were almost unknown at the time to the public but went on to become stars (Maggie Gyllenhaal, Adrian Grenier, Michael Shannon). Larry Gilliard, Jr., graduated to *The Wire* and *The Deuce* and countless other movies and TV shows, and Harriet Dodge (as she was known then before she transitioned to Harry) became a nationally celebrated visual artist later in life. I learned so much from Harriet, who despite her female name at the time wore a full beard. She explained how traumatic it was for her to put on the dress I wanted her to wear in the film to show off her character's hairy legs. It's not easy being a movie star when you work with me. I'm so glad he's Harry now. He always was.

Mink Stole had a smaller part than she was used to in my films, and I don't think that sat well with her at the time, but Ricki Lake did, too, and they both shine in *Cecil* in my opinion.

Audiences know how good Mink is, but Ricki's talk show success overshadows the fact that underneath that bubbly personality is a really good actress just waiting to be let out again.

Mary Vivian Pearce was still recovering from a brain-tumor operation but she's in there, too, as is Roseanne Barr (a liberal when I knew her) and Eric Roberts doing celebrity cameos that added even more Hollywood lunacy. Eric Barry, an unknown actor who went on to play the Domino's Pizza boy in national commercials, was cast as Fidget, the least committed of Cecil's gang, who can't stop playing pocket pool. He looked exactly like the young man who was the first love of my life, and Pat Moran knew I'd pick him as soon as he walked in to audition as long as he could act, and thank God, he could. Fidget gets to say my favorite line in the movie. As Cecil and his gang of kidnappers sneak their movie-star victim into the drive-in movies to disrupt her past commercial screen success, he whispers to her, "We're beyond the critics' reach now." Ha! We weren't but I could fantasize, couldn't I? But wait, maybe there's another line I like just as much. Michael Shannon plays Petie, the Sprocket Hole terrorist who wishes he were gay but isn't, and demands Melanie, the kidnap victim, to "tell me about Mel Gibson's dick and balls." I don't know which line I like better. I guess it's a tie.

The most outrageous bit of casting was Patricia Hearst (as she prefers to be called today, rather than Patty, even if she knows deep down that's a losing battle) playing the mother of a kidnapper. The final fuck-you to her supposedly criminal past? "Did my mother say those exact same words?" she asked me on set after a first take that included dialogue about her on-screen son turning revolutionary. "Of course not!" I told her. "That would have been asking you to do something in *really* bad taste."

The shoot went fine even though the endless nights spent

on the roof of the concession stand at the Bengies Drive-In filming the finale seemed especially long and tortuous. Stephen Dorff
understood the character of Cecil perfectly and never winked
to the audience—he played him with just the right mixture of
Jim Jones, Charles Manson, and Otto Preminger. Sometimes
today I put on the spiky Warholish wig that Cecil disguised
himself with in the film and jump out and scare my partner
right before we have sex. He always laughs.

God knows Melanie Griffith was game. She confided to me
between camera setups that the only time she felt "safe" was
on a movie set. I guess she meant she was protected from the
real world there? Not me. I never feel safe on a movie set if I'm
the director. Do I have enough coverage? Do the takes match
for editing? Is a meal penalty for the unions coming up? Danger lurks every second. Making a movie is a quicksand pit just
hoping you fall in.

Early in the shoot when we were filming the big opening
scene where Melanie is kidnapped by Cecil at a movie premiere,
Melanie fell in her dressing room at lunch and cut her face
badly. I never asked her how or why, but it was a big problem.
We had completed all the shots of her we needed except the last
one, where Cecil drags her out of the theater as the extras erupt
in panic. Since she now had a big gash in her face, we couldn't
shoot her from the front, so David Davenport from the costume
department thought fast, grabbed a skinny-boy extra from the
crowd who was roughly Melanie's height, put him in Melanie's
costume, and we filmed the scene showing "Melanie" from
behind. You can't tell it's not her. Always let the talent know that
nobody's irreplaceable in independent cinema.

Even if you hate *Cecil B. Demented*, the credit sequence is
now locally historical because it's a montage of the marquees of
many of Baltimore's last standing movie theaters. Some are now

abandoned; many were destroyed or, worse yet, turned into churches. I got Moby to compose a mix of front-title music made up of distorted, scratchy, soundalike cliché movie themes, and I think his parody score only added to the foreboding predictions of my script: sequelitis, tentpole flops, wrongheaded dubbing of foreign classics, and the worst title you could ever see on a marquee—FOR RENT.

I added a lot of punk rock and noise music (The Locust, Meat Joy) to the score and further mixed up genres by including an unknown Liberace song ("Ciao") that he recorded for a perfume ad that was never released. And move over, Jay-Z, I co-wrote a couple of rap tunes ("Bankable Bitch," "No Budget"). I'm always amazed when I receive royalties from BMI (again, join the unions!) for these obscure lyrics—$2.83 from airplay in New Zealand, three cents for TV in Brazil. It can add up. If I can make over $1,000 a year in music royalties, just think what the Beatles make!

Cecil premiered at the Cannes Film Festival and, of course, Stephen Dorff was there, Melanie, too, and she was showing off her brand-new ANTONIO tattoo, which made the paparazzi go wild. He didn't come, though. Melanie's date was Donatella Versace, and they walked up those famous red-carpeted steps to the Palais with Stephen, me, and my date, Pat Moran. Donatella seemed just like a Baltimore girl in real life, all peroxided up, raunchy, unapologetic, unpretentious, and a little trashy. I liked her.

The film received a standing ovation at the end, but believe me, that was the last one it got. The reviews, once it opened in the United States, were pretty grim. *Entertainment Weekly* said Cecil's terrorists were "a cross between the Symbionese Liberation Army and the staff of *Film Comment*," which was OK by me, but *The New York Times* called it "less than hilarious," and Rex Reed came through negatively as always with "the genuinely rotten taste of *Cecil B. Demented* makes the Farrelly Brothers look like the Warner Brothers." The bright spots were few and far between. Richard Corliss in *Time* magazine said the film "proves how a dose of smart bad taste can be jolly good fun," and Kevin Thomas, bless his soul, saved us in the *Los Angeles Times* by calling *Cecil* "a fast, furious and funny fusillade of a movie."

The grosses were terrible. We bombed big-time in both America *and* France, pulling in only $2 million on a budget of $10 million! God, it was awful. Last year when I received the Order of Arts and Letters medal from the French Ministry of Culture, I was proud but relieved that my old executives didn't rush into the ceremony and try to grab it from around my neck to offset their losses.

I don't know, I still like *Cecil B. Demented* a lot. Maybe one day others will, too, the way some Tennessee Williams fans eventually revised their opinion on one of his biggest box office flops, *Boom!* Every once in a while, I'll be walking down the street and a fan will pass me by and whisper to me Cecil's militant call to arms, "Demented Forever," and keep on going. It makes me feel all warm and scuzzy inside.

BACK IN THE GUTTER

Maybe my movie career ended where it began— in the gutter. *A Dirty Shame* (2004) was my sexploitation satire and I'm amazed it got made at all. I have one person to thank for that: Bob Shaye at New Line Cinema, which was now owned by Time Warner for God's sake. No matter how much he grumbled, "New Line's not your patron, you know, we run a business here," Bob must have known that this ludicrous comedy about head-injury sufferers who turn into sex addicts was a risk. Maybe Bob just had nostalgia for all the straight and gay S&M bars we used to go to with my gang and even his lovely wife, Eva, back in the seventies. Who knows? But bless his kinky-friendly, damaged little soul for giving us the green light. Even my production team back in Baltimore was shocked.

I violated my own rules when I hired a comedian to star in *A Dirty Shame*. Before, I had always maintained that the talent should just say my lines, no matter how ludicrous, as if they believed every word. I realized dialogue such as "Make a list of all the people you've fucked and apologize to their parents" or "You have what is known as a runaway vagina" might make this task nearly impossible, but I felt a comedian would always bring their own shtick to the material and dilute the punch. Winking at the audience was not necessary if you believed, as I did, that the lines were funny enough on their own.

But suddenly I heard Roseanne Barr was aggressively interested in playing the lead role of Sylvia Stickles, a normal middle-class working mother who ran a convenience store with her husband (eventually played by Chris Isaak, who I knew was a good actor from seeing him in David Lynch's *Twin Peaks: Fire Walk with Me*). While I was in Seattle with *Hairspray* the musical, in previews before its Broadway opening, Roseanne came up and we spent a raucous weekend together discussing the project. I knew she could be reckless and thought maybe that would be good. I had earlier asked Pat for suggestions on "bankable" actresses to approach for the role, and she had thrown up her hands in desperation and suggested Margot Kidder, who had just had a much-publicized nervous breakdown in real life and shown up huddled inside a cardboard box in filthy clothes without her dental work. Nobody but me believed *anyone* would take the role, but Roseanne seemed to understand perfectly the humor in a repressed sex-hating woman suddenly turning by accident into a raging horny vixen. She seemed ready to commit. Then we both went home and I never heard from her again. Did she really have multiple personalities as she has said in TV interviews? Nah. I think what happened is her own children read the script. And that was that.

But then a miracle happened. Tracey Ullman was suggested by one of the producers and I jumped at the chance. Yes, she was a comedian, too, but I had seen her play so many different characters that I knew she could completely lose herself in a role and not let vanity get in the way, something almost impossible to find in a female star over thirty years of age. She told me right at the beginning she "had never been in anything controversial," so I think she was ready to shake up her career a little, and I also knew that her husband, Allan McKeown, the U.K. theatrical impresario who produced the musical based on Jerry Springer's life, encouraged her to take the role.

Tracey was fearless, not at all vain, and seemed ready for anything. The material was so over-the-top that she only had to underplay it a little to be totally believable. She "went for it," as Mink Stole always said when asked about all of our cast's early acceptance of outrageous material when the public just shook their heads in incomprehension. We *all* "went for it" on *A Dirty Shame* and Tracey led the pack from the very first day. Maybe it was the new hands-on but very well-liked producers Christine Vachon and Ted Hope, maybe it was the anything-goes attitude of the ensemble cast. No, it was Tracey. She made the set of *A Dirty Shame* the most relaxed of all my films.

Johnny Knoxville was another big name that got the film financed. He played Ray-Ray, the spiritual leader of all the sex addicts, and he fit in perfectly with not only Tracey but my Baltimore gang, too. I think the *Jackass* movies he starred in were the closest films ever made to my own early cinematic atrocities, but I always tell him, "You did the same thing as we did only you made millions and I made hundreds. *How* did you do that?!" I saw the first *Jackass* in a Baltimore movie theater, and blue-collar dads and their teenage hetero sons were happily bonding while watching male nudity and a hipster daredevil sticking a toy truck up his ass. Again, how could this be possible?

I knew Selma Blair had been in Todd Solondz's *Storytelling*, where her scene was the most controversial, so I figured she might be game for *A Dirty Shame*. I always like to copy Todd in casting choices because he's already broken actors in for trouble from the public. Selma seemed quite comfortable accepting the role of Caprice, Tracey Ullman's character's daughter, who has tits bigger than her head and is on home detention in her bedroom at her parents' house after being convicted of "nude drinking and driving." The giant fake tits were made of silicone by Tony Gardner, who also created the killer Chucky doll of horror movie fame, and much later John Travolta's fat suit for Edna's character in the Hollywood-remake version of the musical *Hairspray.* Those huge fragile tits had to be carefully and seamlessly put on Selma every shooting day. Each time she was filmed "nude" it cost $5,000, $3,000 if there was just cleavage, and $1,000 for everyday under-the-sweater presence. Because of the heat of the movie lights, the latex didn't last long, and at the end of every day of the bosom shoots, the tits would lie on the set floor, shriveled up and ready to be thrown in the trash. But one day the tit rubble was missing. A Teamster had swiped them. I tremble to imagine why.

The last character to be cast was Big Ethel, the frigid sex-hating mother of Tracey's character, who along with Mink Stole as Marge led the "Neuter" revolt against the sex addicts' taking over the neighborhood. Suzanne Shepherd was recommended highly by Kerry Barden, once again casting for us in New York, and both Pat and I loved her audition tape. She was a respected New York actress with a long, impressive résumé and we started shooting in one week. "Hire her," I told Ted Hope, and even though Suzanne had read only one scene (and a rather mild one) he put her on the train to Baltimore for the first day of rehearsal. *On* the train she read the entire script and flipped out. "I can't make this movie!" she ranted as she was led into the production office. "Put me back on the train now! No! I won't do it!" Ted took her aside and explained it was all done for comedy; no explicit sex would be shown, and he begged her to "just go to one rehearsal with John and the cast and see how it goes." She reluctantly agreed, and Johnny, Tracey, Selma,

Mink, and the rest of the sex-addict characters (Ronnie the Rimmer, Fat Fuck Frank, Loose Linda, and Dingy Dave) took over wooing Suzanne to our way of cinematic thinking. On the way over in the Teamster van the cast started shouting out the most hideous lines ("I'm a cunnilingus bottom, but I'm still your mother," "'Sploshing' is the erotic urge to dump food on your private parts," or "I've got a hard-on of gold and my tongue's on fire") and explaining some of the obscene sex lingo in the dialogue ("funch": fucking after lunch), while others shouted out the many referenced slang terms for cunnilingus ("yodeling in the canyon" or "going below Fourteenth Street").

By the time Suzanne got to my living room, the group madness had begun taking effect and she was ready to give it a try. We had a seated read through of the entire script, and when she bellowed out Big Ethel's line "Horndogs are everywhere and pretty soon they'll be living next door," I knew she had found her character's voice. When Mink followed with "It's not safe out. People are shaving their crotches as we speak. There's pubic hair in the air everywhere!" I saw Suzanne laugh out loud. We had her. Suzanne was suddenly full tilt aboard the filth wagon. "We're all Neuters and we're never gonna be not normal again," she shouted with completely believable militancy. In just one hour we had brainwashed her. *Folie en famille* was now complete. "Let's go sexin'!" Johnny Knoxville yelled, echoing the battle cry of his sex-addict gang, and I thought of the catch line I had come up with for the film's advertising campaign, "What happened to Sylvia Stickles . . . was a dirty shame." It had happened to Suzanne, too.

We shot much of the film in the Harford Road area right across the county line, just outside Baltimore. The neighbors were much nicer and more understanding than in any other community where I've worked. None complained when our art department landscaped their lawn with giant bushes shaped like boners or added fake vaginas and anuses to the bark of their trees. One elderly lady who watched us film a sex-addict attack right in front of her house said to me with a straight face, "I don't mind telling you—this is all making me horny." Extras who had never met before had to make out and pump on one another in the background of scenes for hours on end. When I called "Cut," there was a lot of laughter but never one complaint.

Our headquarters was the Holiday House, a heterosexual biker bar that I had hung out in a lot in the early nineties. Right before *Cry-Baby* the movie had opened, I was trying to find a new place to go drinking in Baltimore where I wouldn't have to talk about the movies, so I drove out to Harford Road because I knew it was an uncharted hipster-less neighborhood that housed a lot of supposed bad boys and girls. Every bar I went into I got recognized (I had just been on *Letterman*) and all the patrons gave me the exact same piece of advice: "There's only one bar around here you should *never* go to—the Holiday House." Naturally that's exactly where I went.

I couldn't believe my eyes. At the time, it was like a biker bar in a Roger Corman movie. The Fat Boys! The Pagans! Everybody dressed in "colors." Big fights! Tables thrown through the air like in westerns. All biker action, all the time! They couldn't have been nicer to me, bought me drinks, and laughingly offered me the choice of any biker chick I desired. They knew. They just loved fucking with me.

I kept going back. At first always alone, but then I got my nerve up to bring friends. But they had to be the right kind of friends. "Butch it up," I used to advise any undercover gay males I brought in. One time Paul Reubens came with me. The bikers kept staring at him, and one finally whispered, "John, that's not Pee-wee Herman, is it?" I nodded sheepishly and admitted, "Yep." They couldn't believe it, and neither could Paul once he was surrounded by fawning tough biker dudes. "It's just like the biker bar in your *Pee-wee's Big Adventure* movie," I yelled. "Yes, it is!" he shouted back over the din of adulation. "But I never knew there was a real one!" Every year after, Paul sent the manager of the Holiday House a Christmas card. You can still see them hanging up framed in the back near the men's room, where I once saw graffiti written on a blackboard over the urinal that said BLOW ME, ASSHOLE. I ran home, got my camera, came back, took a photo of it, and later sold it in a New York art gallery for $5,000. Art is everywhere. You just have to notice.

Filming went fairly well . . . considering. Jean Hill, Dreamland's only African American regular, who had her biggest role as the killer maid in *Desperate Living*, was now in poor health. I wanted to put her in the movie somehow—even if it was just a cameo. Now weighing three hundred pounds or so (skinny for her!) and wearing a nasal cannula full-time, she had to be carried to the set (along with her oxygen tank) and up three flights of steps to a fire escape where her character was supposed to catch her on-screen husband luring a horny Tracey Ullman (whose talking vagina in the movie was yelling under her skirt, "Get it! Get it while you can!") for sex and then beat him senseless with a baseball bat. It was not an easy scene to capture on film. Once Jean was in place, I'd yell "Action!" Jean would wheeze her lines out, then gasp for air. I'd say "Cut," and crew members would rush over with her oxygen tubes, she'd huff a few loads, they'd rip them off, I'd say "Action" again, and Jean would do her best. Somehow I got one take I could use. Carrying Jean back down the steps once she'd wrapped was a stunt that movie audiences never got to see.

Susan Allenback, one of my longtime assistants (you might have read about her in my book *Carsick*), had a stunt all her own in *A Dirty Shame*. I knew she was a good actress and had had a long career in show business before she started working with me, so I asked her if she'd play the part of Betty Doggett, one of Ray-Ray's sex-addicted followers. She auditioned for the producers and got the part. The only hitch was that in one scene she had to answer the door full-frontal naked to a dumbfounded Neuter played by Chris Isaak. In real life Susan is a good-looking middle-aged woman, and after asking her grown daughters for approval, she surprised me and said she'd do that scene as written. I have courageous employees. The scene turned out to be as deadpan funny as I'd hoped. If Susan has any regrets today, it's that if you google her full name, the first thing that comes up online is the nude scene on one of those "naked movie stars" websites—not exactly the most dignified starting point when she negotiates a speaking fee for me with a client. Oh, well, she looks swell.

David Hasselhoff was another great addition to our cast lineup. I was amazed when the *Baywatch* star agreed to play himself as a passenger on an airplane who's taking a dump. Maybe it was because his scene was such an important plot point; his turd falls from the plane, mixes with blue ice on its ferocious plunge to earth, and hits Neuter Chris Isaak in the head, causing him to turn into the sex addict who introduces a new form of eroticism (head banging) that signals a sexual resurrection that triggers mass levitations of the populace. Or maybe it was just because he was originally from Baltimore and had a great sense of humor about himself? So great that he didn't even balk when I got up my directorial nerve and asked him on the last take to "strain . . . now grunt" as he sat on the prop toilet of our interior airplane set. What a pro!

My favorite "discovery" from *Hairspray* the musical was Jackie Hoffman, an Imogene Coca–type rubber-faced comedienne who came down from New York between Broadway performance days to play Dora, the militant chronic masturbator who complains on-screen of having a "Swedish headache" (code word for "horny"). "Nothin' the matter with beatin' the bush once in a while," her character reasons to the freshly sexually sober Tracey Ullman. "Ever jerk off when one of your hands is asleep?" Jackie would ask in that brilliant comic timing of hers. "You should try it," Jackie advises with a straight face. "It feels like somebody else is doing it." Ah, we had dialogue then!

George S. Clinton was hired to do the rockabilly score to go along with the double-entendre "party record" dirty tunes ("The Pussycat Song," "Eager Beaver Baby," and "Itchy, Twitchy Spot") I used as source material on the soundtrack. He even composed an end-credit call-to-arms anthem called "Let's Go Sexin'," which I still think works better than Viagra. And of course it was sung by the most talented and handsome man on earth, James Intveld, whose singing voice I dubbed in for Johnny Depp's in *Cry-Baby*. I hadn't seen James since we made that film, but when he came back from Nashville, where he then lived, to L.A. to record for *A Dirty Shame*, I realized he was still such a star, the real-life Cry-Baby in person, that I couldn't look him directly in the eyes when we were both in the same room. James Intveld, I bow down to you.

Once we tested the movie (and New Line was reasonable about how realistic the results could be for a movie this far out of the mainstream), we realized the original ending, where the sex addicts have a second sexual awakening and look up to the treetops as the leaves bud and flower in erotic celebration, just wasn't strong enough. For once I agreed with the focus groups. We needed a fix.

I remember the meeting afterward well. We were in some restaurant in New York City, and Bob Shaye and all the other head suits from New Line were there. Usually the word "reshoot" brings fresh paranoia to the concept of postproduction in my mind, but this time I was enthusiastic and hopefully one step ahead of the game. "Come on, Bob," I begged. "Let's do a new ending where Johnny Knoxville's character levitates higher in the air than we had shot him, yells, 'Let's go sexin' one more time,' and then his head explodes like a penis shooting out sperm and the CGI load speeds back down to earth beautifully and lands with a SPLAT on the camera lens. A cinematic facial for the whole audience."

After a moment of silence, Bob once again said "Yes." I told you he was a great film executive! Many other industry types remember him for his visionary green-lighting of all three *Lord of the Rings* movies to be shot simultaneously. But not me. I remember Bob Shaye for approving my last cum shot. It cost $100,000 to film it. Thank you, Bob.

Oh, but if I only knew the trouble that was about to come. My contract said I had to deliver an R-rated movie, and I believed I had shot one. There was little nudity and the plot was so juvenile that I secretly believed no one *over* seventeen years of age should be admitted.

We sent the film over to the MPAA and waited. And waited. Finally word came back that we had received the NC-17 kiss of death. New Line execs had tried to warn me in their "problem search" report and had wanted me to let the ratings board look at the script *before* we shot. Even though they were right and I was wrong on what was found objectionable, if I *had* agreed, the film would have been canceled before we shot a frame.

I still say never cooperate with the enemy. And believe me, the MPAA *is* the enemy of all radical filmmaking. Letting them preview your hopefully transgressive scenes is like going in front of a judge *before* you rob the bank and asking what your deal will be after you plead guilty. Defense lawyers always say, once arrested, never talk to the cops before you have hired an attorney, and I agree. Commit your cinematically disobedient crimes, try to get away with them, and if you're caught, keep on lying and never admit guilt.

I know of many cases where filmmakers have gone back to the MPAA with a few nips and tucks to the sex scenes in contention and had the rating reclassified without further ado. It's an open secret that putting in a few explicit shots that you know you'll have to cut is a good strategy. That way you can at first act outraged, give in, put your cinematic tail between your legs while complaining about compromising your artistic vision, and pretend to let the powers that be win.

I tried to be cooperative. Joan Graves, the head of the rating board, got on the phone with me and I greeted her politely. "I was surprised by the rating," I told her. "What can I cut?" She sweetly said, "After a while we stopped taking notes." Those seven words sent shivers up my spine. That meant there was nothing to negotiate. I was forever NC-17. Many theaters wouldn't play it. I had just been X-ed out of all chances of commercial success. "Overall content," she explained cheerily like a polite warden talking to a capital-punishment prisoner seconds before she drops the pellet in the gas chamber. "Can't we at least try some trims?" I asked, using the kinder and gentler word for butchery. "Sure," she answered, nice as pie. Liberal censors are the worst kind. They're smart. Dumb ones are easy to defeat, but the educated ones fool you. They're like snakes.

Panic. Recutting a new version where a few of the more extreme (and hilarious if you ask me) reaction shots of Tracey Ullman while Johnny Knoxville goes down on her offscreen disappear. Turning down the volume of ridiculous sexual sound effects. The "thrusting" of the animated squirrels doing their cartoonish sex scenes. But it didn't work. We still got an NC-17 rating. Same reason: "overall content." So it was time to go through the rigmarole of filing an official appeal. I had won once with MPAA over the *Pecker* title, but the outcome here was much less certain.

New Line was panicking. They explained to me it was rare to get the MPAA to change their minds. Expensive, too. I met with lawyers who specialized in these hearings and started preparing my defense. Word had trickled back from a sympathetic mole inside the board that Joan had been especially offended by the use of the word "felching" in the dialogue and had actually gotten an expert to explain that it meant "when two men are having oral sex in sixty-nine position, ejaculating in each other's mouth, and then exchanging the fluids by kissing." Yes, I might concede this was wandering into NC-17 territory, but could the MPAA prove that's what it meant, especially if I took the stand and said, "No, felching is when you fart in the bathtub and bite the bubbles"? Beyond a reasonable doubt? I practiced my much more R-rated-friendly testimony over and over in the mirror. God, I hate censorship.

When I finally "took the stand" on the big day of *A Dirty Shame*'s trial in front of MPAA members who were hardly my peers, with Joan Graves as my chief prosecutor, I got to go first with my arguments. I explained *A Dirty Shame* was a comedy, and a juvenile one at that. No sex was on-screen. The dirty talk was ridiculous, not salacious. I presented touching letters from teenagers who had written me how my films had "saved their lives," made them feel good about being themselves for the first time, given them a place to belong. I introduced into evidence photos I had taken of Los Angeles billboards that read TALK TO

YOUR TEENAGERS ABOUT SEX—EVERYBODY ELSE IS! I went on and on about outsiders, diversity, and the power of humor with teenagers, but I could tell by the blank faces of the board members that I was wasting my time.

The process is rigged. Joan gets to go last and you don't get a final rebuttal. She addressed not one of the issues I brought up and said simply that the rating should remain since the initial vote was unanimous for NC-17. She pointed out to her certainly *not* unbiased jury (she was their boss, after all) that the "no one under seventeen years of age admitted" rating did not prevent college-age kids from seeing the film. And that was that.

I didn't get to argue back that the NC-17 rating was a defective brand just like the unsafe-at-any-speed early sixties Corvair and needed to be recalled. They had an outdated and untuned Edsel on their hands but refused to admit it. The MPAA has highly paid and powerful lobbyists in both Los Angeles and Washington, D.C., who could go out to theater owners and newspaper advertising executives and get them to change their anti-NC-17 policies, but they have never done so. I knew I was doomed.

As we waited for the verdict, Joan's assistant served cookies and warned me, "Do not spill any crumbs on the floor." She didn't seem to be kidding. The results were swift. No hung jury here. We lost. Patty Hearst, on hearing the guilty verdict at her bank robbery trial, had sighed, "I never had a chance." I felt just the same. My whole New Line team and I walked out with a large black cloud hanging over our heads. We were NC-17 (for pervasive sexual content) forever. Those bastards.

Now what? Time Warner owned New Line Cinema at the time, and their policy was never to distribute an NC-17 film. I threw myself at the mercy of Bob Shaye. Couldn't he talk the powers that be into breaking their rule just once for us? Could he explain our shared past, our climb up from the underground to Hollywood respectability? Ha! He said sternly he'd try, but to forget using my tagline of "A Dirty Mind Is a Terrible Thing to Waste" because Dick Parsons, one of the main suits at Time Warner, was involved with the United Negro College Fund and mine was a satire of their famous slogan about "a mind" being "a terrible thing to waste." I immediately agreed. Pick your battles and all that. Ted Hope and Christine Vachon also got involved, and Bob confided to them that Jeff Bewkes and other members of the Time Warner board were having dinner at Bob's house that night and he would try to make the pitch of releasing *A Dirty Shame* as is—*unless* "the mood was wrong." If he was successful, we should play *way* down that this would be the first time Time Warner had allowed an NC-17 film to come out under their banner.

Eureka! They agreed. We were ordered not to gloat, talk about Time Warner policy, or make the NC-17 rating a giant brouhaha. Yes, the movie would be released theatrically with an NC-17 rating and so would the DVD, but I had to agree to cut a special R-rated "Neuter version," no matter how terrible that turned out to be, for the Blockbuster chain. I hope the version you've seen is the NC-17 one, but if you really want to be appalled, watch the R-rated mess. It's the perfect film to view with your whole family if you want to explain to your teenagers what a "plate job" means or how to have consensual sex with a tree. Every other rude line of dialogue or sexual sight gag has been edited out and replaced with the single take of "lite coverage" we had to provide for cable and airline versions. Usually you never use these hastily shot one-takes, but in this case, the whole movie is made up of them.

Some of the "soft versions" of scenes we neutered are predictable: Fat Fuck Frank is now Fat Freak Frank. The graffiti B-O-N-E-R painted on the side of the heroine's convenience store now reads simply B-O-N-E. When Tracey Ullman's character is being orally satisfied by Johnny Knoxville's, her original hilarious moans of pleasure are replaced with giggles and "that tickles" dialogue. Funch is now "fun after lunch." The furious cabdriver no longer complains, "Someone tried to grab my nutsack"—it's now his "knapsack"! The final "cum shot" of Johnny's levitation and head exploding is still shown, but it's not a full "facial" for the viewer as it is in the original.

But what *is* still deemed appropriate for an R-rating is mind-boggling. It's OK for Big Ethel to glare at gay men shopping in her store and complain (just as Anita Bryant did in real life) that "they eat life," meaning sperm. It's fine (with parental guidance one assumes) to explain that a *payday* is "an unflushed turd" in a toilet. The only good thing I can say about the abominable replacement footage I was forced to utilize is that while Tracey Ullman no longer "picks up a bottle with her cooter" as she does under her skirt in the hokeypokey, she *does* do some funny, new lewd dance steps that you can only see in this bowdlerized version. I have no actual remembrance of shooting this footage.

The worst thing about this whole bastardized cut was that by the time the video was released, video stores were on their way out, and the only one left in the neighborhood where we shot almost all of *A Dirty Shame* was Blockbuster. The actual people in the movie, the neighbors who were kept up all night by our shooting schedule and didn't complain, the families who posed good-naturedly for snapshots of themselves with our adult-baby character in costume, the local extras who worked into the wee hours to hit their marks and spell out the word "S-E-X" with their bodies for an overhead shot—those same folks who didn't go downtown to see the movie at an art theater—had to see *A Dirty Shame* the only way they could: from Blockbuster. Neutered. Awful. They went through all *that* for this piece of shit?!

There was even more trouble ahead. Tracey Ullman hadn't seen the film yet, but when word of the NC-17 rating got out, I think it made her nervous. I pestered New Line to give her a private screening and they agreed and, without my knowledge, invited Mink Stole to attend, which was fine, but why they didn't invite the rest of the cast who lived in L.A. never became clear. I know seeing my films without an audience is the worst possible way to view them. The raucous laughter of a crowd of fans is contagious to all audiences, especially to the actors who have gone out on a limb to give me what I wanted on-screen.

I didn't hear a peep from Tracey after she saw it. Worried, I called Mink, who explained that the projectionist showed up late, the sound was terrible, and the projector broke down several times once it began and continued to start up and stop throughout the screening. Mink said she couldn't tell what Tracey thought of it. Uh-oh.

I soon realized from her silence that she must have hated it. I did finally get a polite but, for her, distant e-mail about the film that was noncommittal. Soon her "people" let New Line's "people" know that she would be unable to do interviews on the two upcoming scheduled New York press days or to attend the world premiere at the Toronto Film Festival. I had already accepted that she couldn't make our usual AIDS Action Baltimore benefit premiere in Baltimore, but this new refusal put me in shock. Panic part two. Of course Tracey's publicity rep's spin was that she needed to concentrate on her upcoming role with Carol Burnett in *Once Upon a Mattress*, but I knew that was bullshit.

I wrote Tracey a desperate e-mail imploring her to see the film with an audience (something she has never done to this day as far as I know) and leaked back positive reviews of her performance that were coming in from the first trade screenings ("beyond fabulous," "a comic wonder") and generally threw myself at her feet, pleading for her help in promoting the film.

It worked. A little. Tracey never publicly dished the film, and she did show up for one event (where I, not the film, was being honored) and gave a few phone interviews to the press, and the public never caught on to her dissatisfaction. I'm still crushed and wish she'd seen *A Dirty Shame* with an audience of "our people." I did recently at UCLA, and they went nuts for her. Tracey Ullman was and still is fearless.

Some of the reviews of *A Dirty Shame* were pretty good. J. Hoberman in *The Village Voice* called it my "most radical film in twenty-five years," and the saint of seditious cinema, Kevin Thomas of the *Los Angeles Times*, again came through with a rave, writing "jaw-droppingly hilarious" and "this raucously gritty and high-spirited film could scarcely be bluer in terms of the language but for Waters, it comes as a gust of fresh air."

My favorite review came from the private sector. After my poor eighty-eight-year-old father had to suffer through the Baltimore premiere (with many audience members turning around to gawk at his reaction to the most lurid scenes), he confided to me, "Well, it was pretty funny, but I hope I never have to see it again!" Now that's a blurb for you! Even better was Jeanne Moreau's. I was on the jury of the Cannes Film Festival with her in 1995 and we had gotten along great and remained in touch. How did a weird little boy from Lutherville, Maryland, end up being friends with Jeanne Moreau?! I always asked myself whenever I needed perking up from the despair of show business. I took Jeanne to the Paris premiere along with my usual date, Pat Moran. As the tail credits rolled, I panicked, wondering what on earth the star of *Jules and Jim* and *La Notte* could possibly have thought of my dirty little comedy. Nervously I blurted out to her, "We had a lot of censorship problems." She looked at me kind of blankly and said, "Why? To me, it was poetry." Poetry?! Believe me, nobody else has ever called it that before or since!

Including A. O. Scott from *The New York Times*. Refusing to rise to my bait, he panned the film, ending his review with "I object to *A Dirty Shame* not because it is offensive—to do so would be another way of congratulating Mr. Waters for his bogus daring—but because it is boring." Soon after reading this I was invited to an industry dinner by my good friend Marcus Hu, who co-owns the Strand Releasing company, and inexplicably he seated this critic right next to me. Being the pros both A. O. Scott and I were, we never mentioned the review, and made semi-strained small talk. I don't think an A-list *New York Times* critic should be allowed to mingle. Their restaurant critics never do, and most of their art critics stay way behind the scenes, too. Of course journalists should be allowed to write whatever they want, but meeting up with their prey should be strictly verboten. It's just plain unnatural.

Yup, we bombed again. Was it the NC-17? Was it me? Was it the film? Who knows, but *A Dirty Shame* died at the box office pretty quickly. Maybe it's my last film. Does that depress me? Not really. I'm hardly misunderstood. All my films from *Multiple Maniacs* on up to *A Dirty Shame* are now easily available to the public. Most have even played on cable television, including *Pink Flamingos*—uncut! *That's Entertainment* ain't what it used to be, that's for sure.

Is it perverse that I like my later films better than the early ones that made me "the King of Puke"? They're easier to watch and the acting is better (I directed all the Dreamland crew to scream their lines and overact in the old ones, so don't blame the talent). The bigger-budget ones look like real movies—something I always wanted, just didn't have the money to do. Yet I know the 16mm ones (even blown up to 35mm) appear ruder, scarier, closer to imagined snuff-movie aesthetics, so younger audiences will always like the grain. I'm just happy that all my films are still out there, somehow making the cut and crossing over to the new technology. I don't care *how* you watch my movies these days; I just want you to keep on watching.

Times are tough for independent movies. New Line Cinema, as I knew it, is gone. I would never have had the career in show business I did without its founder Bob Shaye's support, and I'd like to shout that from the rooftops. Never forget the powers that be who helped you. Influence comes and goes in Hollywood but gratitude never should. There used to be ten or fifteen companies I could pitch my movies to, but now there are about three. Art houses are not grossing what they once did. Get used to it. It's just plain over.

On my way up in Hollywood, I started to make a good living, but sliding back down to the bottom is how I really cashed in financially. Was my whole career a scam? Am I a Tinseltown flimflam man? Should I feel guilty that a lot of my films are still in the red? I think not. My promotional tours never end because these days I'm always appearing live for something—an art show, comedy routine, book tour—so I never stop signing those old *and* new DVD copies of my past pictures. Maybe one day my old titles will finally break even for the studios. Then when I die, there'll be one last bump in sales and the movies will finally turn a profit. Sounds fair to me.

I GOT RHYTHM

ou'll need to have really good musical taste to get through life. I'm lucky, I do. That does *not* mean that I dance in public at my present age. The elderly "busting a move" is generally a depressing sight unless you were a teen star on a local televised dance show in the 1950s or 1960s and continue to do without irony the very same dances that made you famous. And no, the hit records of your generation are not better than today's. As soon as you stop listening to new music, your life is over. You are a fart.

Of course, the first music that you loved as a child and your parents hated will remain the overture for the soundtrack of your life. Start making a mixtape of the exact songs that brought rebellion into your youth and play them over and over so you can begin to understand your psychology through music. Even though I may have had a slight memory of deaf Johnnie Ray "crying" his ballads in the very early fifties, it was Elvis, and yes, he still is the king, who made me realize I was gay. Just seeing him twitching and moaning "Heartbreak Hotel" on TV or, better yet, hearing him mumbling, "We're gonna kiss and kiss . . . and we're gonna kiss some more," in "I Don't Care If the Sun Don't Shine" made me masturbate for the first time even though I was only ten and a half years old and puberty hadn't even hit. No one had told me what jerking off even was! Had any other kid done this? I wondered in a panic. Is there anything more rock-and-roll than whacking off the first time to Elvis Presley?

Once I saw hillbilly hepcats, I knew I had a type: the exact opposite of myself. Raised to be preppy and sent to private grade school, I yearned to meet the underclass. All the hip-swiveling, crotch-humping white boy singers I loved (Gene Vincent, Billy Lee Riley, Warren Smith, Buddy Knox, Eddie Cochran) were "common," according to my mother, who reacted in horror to the pinup fan photos of "those creatures" I hung up on my bedroom wall. I first saw real working-class men when my dad took me downtown to see his new company building in the Remington neighborhood in Baltimore. I knew, looking out the car window, that something major was up. I had never seen guys like this! I was beyond excited. There were real rockabillies in the world and I wanted to be around them.

My parents once took me to a bowling alley in Towson, near where we lived. They didn't, at first, realize it was also part pool hall, but after we got there it was too late to leave. Here I saw juvenile delinquents for the first time: boys with their shirt collars turned up, pompadours freshly greased, girls with tight black long skirts, ballet slippers, and head scarves tied around their Debra Paget hairdos. How I longed to be with them! I zeroed in on one particularly sullen guy who was slouched up on the jukebox. I just *knew* he had stolen hubcaps in his young, angry life and I was jealous of his past. He kept playing the same song over and over on the jukebox, "The Joker" by Billy Myles, and was quietly and sexily singing along to the lyrics. Finally my mother noticed. "That *same* song is getting on my nerves," she sniffed. Not mine. I started to memorize the lyrics and sing along myself. "The Joker is what they call me. My friends say I've never seemed so gay," I'd warble along with my new pool hall idol, hoping somehow he might notice. Nobody there, including me, knew the modern definition of the word "gay" at the time, but still, those words burned into my young consciousness forever. "Play it again," I begged him in my mind, and he did exactly that. We were a team! "Can't he play another record?!" my father finally sputtered in frustration. "The Joker is crying over you," Billy Myles continued serenading. He meant me, I just knew it.

And then God created Roddy Jackson, a blond-headed "wild man" white teenager from Fresno, California, who sang with black musicians and recorded his first hit for Sonny Bono (!) way before Cher, when he was an A&R man scouting talent for Specialty Records, Little Richard's first label. Singing in what has been described as a "hamburger throated" voice, Roddy pummeled the piano "like it was a personal threat to his well-being." When I heard him snarl out the lyrics "Sometimes I think . . . ," I'd go nuts dancing around my childhood bedroom like the Mr. Top Ten I was in my mind and then join in with him in the title refrain to his big hit, "I Got My Sights on Someone New." I sure did. Him.

I never wanted to be a drag queen. But if I had to lip-synch to a woman's song even today it wouldn't be Judy, Liza, or Cher. No, it would be Eileen Rodgers. *Who?* you might ask. Well, she was a little-known nightclub singer and onetime understudy for Ethel Merman who had a tiny success in the mid-fifties. Every time I'd hear her sing "The Treasure of Your Love" (not even her biggest hit), I'd get nelly. I'd throw my head high in hauteur and begin belting out the ridiculously earnest unfeminist womanhood lyrics while that god-awful chorus behind her wailed in honky harmony. "The one thing I want, no riches can buy," I'd lip-synch, my mouth perfectly matching her words, "a love that is true and you by my side." I knew other boys probably weren't doing this at the time. Fuck 'em. For a few minutes each day, for a short time in 1958, I *was* Eileen Rodgers. And I was beautiful.

I soon realized that I needed to be funny much more than I needed to be feminine. Dark funny. And Nervous Norvus's "Transfusion" was the first bit of black humor I ever heard. I was always obsessed with car accidents as a child, and this ironically gruesome musical warning about unsafe driving spoke to me like a welcoming stake through my suburban heart. Using the sound effects of automobile brakes squealing, followed by the crash of metal as a chorus, Nervous Norvus's smart-aleck lyrics such as "Slip the blood to me, bud" mocked the anti-juvenile-delinquency propaganda we were fed daily in the fifties. He was my first entrée into sick humor. Lenny Bruce could not have existed without Nervous Norvus coming before him.

Naturally I loved the other car-accident teen novelty records, too, a genre that would be completely impossible today. I learned then that no subject matter was off-limits for music if you did it first. "Teen Angel" was released in 1960 and I'd play it every night before going to sleep, reimagining that stupid girl in the lyrics who was crushed by an oncoming train when she rushed back to her boyfriend's car stalled on the railway tracks to get his high school ring he had given her. "SPLAT!" I'd yell at the musical moment of locomotive impact, picturing her flattened like a pancake.

"Tell Laura I Love Her" by Ray Peterson came next, and the teenage-tragedy genre was cemented forever. When our hero's car flips over and in his last dying breath he begs us to, well, you know, the title, I would revel in the sorrow, the adolescent grief, the unfairness of our teenage lives. I was a drama queen early on, and it will help your musical development if you become one, too.

"Leader of the Pack" took the car-wreck sound-effect teen soap opera to a new level of recorded anguished histrionics. The Shangri-Las were plain bad-girl perfect, and I'll go out on a limb here by saying they were just as tough, if not tougher, than the Ronettes. Their lead singer, Mary Weiss (who, much later, put out an amazing solo CD), was so tongue-in-cheek hard as nails that I always wondered if she hadn't purposely unhooked the brakes of "Jimmy's" motorcycle on that "rainy night." Maybe her cries of "Look out! Look out!" were fake. Maybe she had murdered the leader of the pack!

Whatever the Shangri-Las had done, they inspired what is still probably the most outrageous teen-death novelty song ever recorded, "I Want My Baby Back" by Jimmy Cross. After surviving a terrible auto accident (with the same sound effects as "Leader of the Pack"), our driver sings about his now-dismembered girlfriend ("Over there was my baby . . . over there was my baby . . . and way over there was my baby") and the terrible grief he experienced after the collision. Unable to live without his "baby," he digs up her coffin, climbs in, closes the lid, and sings the final verse, "I've got my baby back," from inside. I was as shocked listening as a teenager as I am shocked today. The only rock-and-roll hit about necrophilia to ever crack *Billboard*'s Top 100 list.

I already had a good start in developing a twisted sense of humor because in 1952 I heard the hit comedy record "It's in the Book" by Johnny Standley on the radio, bought it immediately, and played this comedy monologue over and over in my childhood bedroom. Acting like a persnickety country preacher, Mr. Standley lectured a fake nightclub audience of sophisticates on the logic of the nursery rhyme "Little Bo Peep," and they roared back on the record in overdone canned laughter. I thought his monologue was the funniest thing I ever heard, and still do. His droll, deadpan delivery awakened in me the first stirrings of ridiculously exaggerated comic intellectual superiority that I hopefully still bring to the stage with me when I do my spoken-word shows, *This Filthy World* and *A John Waters Christmas*.

"It says here," Standley sniffed in an arch, theatrical voice, "that Little Bo Peep, who was a little girl, has lost her sheep and doesn't know where to find them." He'd pause here as if everybody in the world but him were a stupid idiot, then continue. "Now that's reasonable, isn't it?" he'd ask haughtily. "It's reasonable to assume if Little Bo Peep had lost her sheep, it's only natural she wouldn't know where to find them!" Deadpan. Hilarious! "Think for a moment, think!" he'd lecture in full condescension to the public listener. "If the sheep were lost and you couldn't find them, you'd have to leave them alone, wouldn't you?" Just as I'd be rolling around the floor laughing in hysteria, he'd yell the title refrain, "It's in the book," and the fake audience would join me in howling approval. To hell with Oscar Wilde, Noël Coward, Oscar Levant; to me, Johnny Standley was the wittiest man on earth and I wanted to be him.

Music had taught me how to develop a sense of humor, but now I had to learn how to "write" with it. Sampling was born in 1956, the day the struggling songwriters Dickie Goodman and Bill Buchanan decided to steal the well-known lyrics from the hits of their time and use those words out of context in a whole new narrative that created what some have called the first rock-and-roll novelty record, "The Flying Saucer, Part One and Part Two." Suppose a spaceship landed on American soil and started a panic à la Orson Welles' *War of the Worlds* and this tale was told through the pirated singing voices of Frankie Lymon, the Platters, or Fats Domino? Once the New York radio station WINS took a big chance and played the finished record for the first time, all hell broke loose. Teenage America understood a unique genre had been born and "The Flying Saucer" became a monster hit. Baltimore was one of the few cities where it went ahead of Elvis Presley's two-sided smash ("Don't Be Cruel" and "Hound Dog") to become Number One.

The soundtracks to all my films, from 1964's *Hag in a Black Leather Jacket* to 2004's *A Dirty Shame*, used the exact same concept of having the music be the narrator and telling the story with the words of other songwriters. Buchanan and Goodman got sued for copyright infringement, and I got sued for not buying the rights to the music I used in my first films. They beat the rap when a judge ruled that what they did was "satire, a parody, a new work," which was a landmark decision that led to the "fair use" defense all documentarians now use to avoid paying for rights to appropriated materials. I, however, lost. I may have shoplifted those early 45 rpm records, but the publishers and writers of those garage-band obscurities sure got their money back when distributors finally paid up decades later to use them legally.

Just like everything else in show business, "bad" can be the key to success. In music, a nasal voice is often a signature that will last for eternity. Shirley of the Shirley and Lee duo seemed to do it first. When I heard her singing "Let the Good Times Roll" in the fifties, I wondered if she had a cold. Was her asthmatic sound the beginning of a trend? When "I Feel Good" became another monster hit for this group soon after, I tried to imitate Shirley's crooning by putting a clothespin on my nose and singing along with the record, but I knew I would never match her nasal joie de vivre.

Years later Rosie of Rosie and the Originals did the same thing when she sang the ballad "Angel Baby." Did she just have a cold or was it purposeful? If she had blown her nose, would the song have gone to Number One as it did? When Kathy Young copied her and sang "A Thousand Stars" in that now-familiar stuffed-up vocal style, did she inspire all future adenoidal singers right on up to and including Rufus Wainwright?

Singing in the falsetto voice has always been a good "bad" gimmick for a man, so if you're a guy trying to start a musical career, I recommend giving it a try. When Lou Christie went beyond the top of the musical scales with his suddenly radically high voice in "Two Faces Have I" in 1963, I thought I was the only teenager in the United States who held this hit as a secret gay anthem. And sure, Frankie Valli did it even better when he "Walk[ed] Like a Man," but only one male falsetto voice made me cry every time I heard it—Donnie Elbert's. He may have had little mainstream success, but his 1957 first rhythm-and-blues number, "What Can I Do," still sends shivers up my spine every time I listen. Goddamn, that man can wail. And when that saxophone takes off so soulfully underneath his final vocal of "What can I do, do, do, do, do, doo-doo?" he turns slang for dog shit into pure literature.

Male falsetto didn't stop here in this country; it got even more extreme in Britain. "Bread and Butter," the 1964 mod ditty, could get on any parent's nerves with its high-pitched simpleton lyrics and childish beat. I loved the end of the song best when the lead singer, Larry Henley, goes into a shrill vocal temper tantrum after finding his "baby eating with some other man." "No-no-no-no," he shrieks in a hissy fit of piercing dietary jealousy untopped to this day in foodie rage.

But the English falsetto singer that beats them all, the one man who I think may have possessed my heart and soul in 1964 (the year I finally went over completely to the side of drugs, black humor, and political lunacy), was the English novelty singer Ian Whitcomb. How I wanted to be this gawky, yet Tony Perkins–ish manboy. Ian even looked a little like me, or at least dressed the way I did at the time. His hit, "You Turn Me On," perfectly summed up everything you should always believe in: the parodying of enthusiasm, sexual confusion, and the mocking of convention. When I first heard Ian Whitcomb on record comically panting and moaning "uh, huh, huh, huh, uh" after finishing each verse, I wanted to sing along with him, giggling all the while in arousal and trembling over our shared teenage wit, which was rooted in hormonal overload.

His little-known follow-up, titled "N-E-R-V-O-U-S," is beyond a doubt the pinnacle of a great "bad" recording, combining all the elements one needs to develop perfection in musical taste: overwrought vocals, oddball storytelling, a total lack of concern over rejection, and a comic timing combined with unashamed innocence. Go right over to your computer and look up his hilarious spoof of an avant-garde, before-its-time, pre-MTV music video, and you'll feel the same joy and defiant delight I still do when I see it. Watch him stutter his lyrics, "I get so n-n-n-n-nervous" or "Come a little bit c-c . . . c-closer," on French television clips or live on *Hullabaloo* and you'll see what I mean. He's an awkward but knowing lad who turns the vocal tics of his handicap into a style. He's not embarrassed to stutter, he expects you to love him for it, and I do. Ian is still alive and lives in Playa del Rey, California, but I never want to break the spell by meeting him. I'd be too n-n-nervous!

It's certainly impossible to mention falsetto voices without bringing up some personal heroes of mine—Alvin and the Chipmunks. I have been a lifelong fan, own every one of their albums, and play their music often in all my homes (much to the annoyance of my friends) while I marvel at their effortless crossover from children's music to pop to rock to grunge to punk to techno to rap and back again to Christmas. They are gods to me, so you can imagine how thrilled I was when I *finally* got that call from my agent saying that Twentieth Century Fox wanted me for a cameo in the next Chipmunk movie, *Alvin and the Chipmunks: The Road Chip.*

This offer didn't just come out of the blue. I got the part because I had become friendly with the actor Matthew Gray Gubler, who was not only famous for being on the show *Criminal Minds* but also for doing the voice of Simon in all the Chipmunk movies. I shamelessly begged him to use his Chipmunk insider influence to get me a part in the newest Chipmunk extravaganza, and he promised he would try. I wanted to tell the producers that I'd happily be available for the casting couch, but nobody ever took me up on it. I would have had sex with Alvin in a Hollywood minute.

Is it possible to aspire to be two different people at the same time, rolled into one? If so, the two-headed transplant of my musical backbone could only be Ike and Tina Turner. I wanted to be as snakelike as Ike and as scary-sexy as Tina. So should you. Ike and Tina Turner were the best soul group ever. Not Ike alone before Tina and not Tina alone after Ike. Together. Forever.

"Ike Beats Tina to Death," the *New York Post* trumpeted when he finally OD'd years after Tina had left him. I don't blame her for splitting. He beat her, treated her the way a pimp would have, and even decorated their home so hideously that Little Richard supposedly commented after visiting, "I didn't realize you could spend a million dollars in Woolworth." I get it. Tina should have done more than leave him. She should have killed him. Any jury in the world would have let her off.

But still. Am I wrong to point out that Tina Turner never sounded better than when she sang under Ike's control? When I first heard her snarl "Your lips set my soul on *f-i-i-r-r-e*" in "It's Gonna Work Out Fine," I thought my white skin would blister, then shed. It didn't matter to me when I later found out that wasn't even Ike's voice singing back to her on this record (it was Mickey from the "Love Is Strange" duo Mickey and Sylvia). I still knew Ike was Tina's hard-core rhythm-and-blues Svengali. Just look at the cover photo of Tina on one of Ike and Tina's first albums, *Dynamite!*, and you will see a fashion icon that influenced me for the rest of my life. There she was, my new goddess, posing like a honky-tonk showgirl in a ratty mink coat, skintight sheath dress, a processed wig, and a pair of Spring-O-Lator high heels. Look closer. Above her growling lip you'll see the faint hint of a mustache.

Be selective in your musical taste as you get older. If you're going to gush, only home in on the truly oddball trends in popular music that the overly sophisticated sometimes foolishly forget. Don't be a melody maker, be a melody wiseacre. A downbeat deadbeat. A rolling unknown with a bone of his own. A melodious bitchfork ahead of the dreampop curve. If you can't influence trends in the hit parade, you are a loser, and I don't mean Beck-like. I mean mediocre like Prince. See? Controversial.

It wasn't until *way* after Ike and Tina, 1981 to be precise, that I went bananas over another soul duo. This time it began with a "situation" song (what the rhythm-and-blues world called soap-opera-ish spoken-word lyrics) that went on to be such a monster hit in the black neighborhoods that it spawned five "answer" recordings over two years. "She's Got Papers on Me" had its roots in the 1974 Shirley Brown tune "Woman to Woman," which begins with the sound of a phone ringing, being picked up, and the line "Hello, may I speak to Barbara?" The singer goes on to tell the "other woman" that the man she's in love with is hers, "from the top of his head to the bottom of his feet." She pays the note on his clothes and car, too. That's just the situation, plain and simple.

Seven years later Richard "Dimples" Fields put out an oh-so-soulful power ballad where he whines about being in love with another woman who is not his wife, but he is helpless because "She's got papers on me." I had never heard this expression before, but apparently in the African American community it was a well-known term for having any form of written contract: mortgage papers, car loans, and especially marriage licenses. I certainly adopted this expression and may have been the only honky film director who yelled "I've got papers" to a studio head from whom I was trying to collect residuals.

But what made this song such a hit was not lover-boy Dimples' endless vocals—no, it was the "Cleanup Woman" herself, Betty Wright, who came in four minutes and thirty-two seconds after the song began because she was on her way to her job and "forgot my sweater." "Well, well, well," she begins as she catches "Mr. Look So Good" singing in the bathroom about "Miss Sweet Little Thing that's always on your mind." Just like her predecessor woman-to-woman Shirley Brown, she, too, pays the note on the apartment, but this time not only does she throw him out, she announces that "you must pay me to be free" because "I got papers on you but now I'm throwin' 'em in the trash can of my memory." In my favorite breakup line ever she harrumphs, "Now take your little albums and your little raggedy component set that never worked and you can scat!" Component set? God, what beautiful detail. Well, well, well, indeed.

It was only a matter of time before the first answer record was released. Barbara Mason tried to one-up Betty Wright with

"She's Got Papers, but I've Got the Man" after Wright left Dimples behind. Fuck him. Nobody cared about the man anymore, this was now a catfight, and the claws were out and ready to scratch. "Betty, I'm addressing this directly to you," Barbara warned, and we were ready for round two.

After a fairly tepid beginning, three minutes into the song, our "other woman" finally gives us what we want—full dissing! "You see, I've never been in position to give him any material things," Barbara icily explains, "but then I've never demanded . . . no papers, no rings." Uh-oh, Barbara's gonna get personal. "I have his slippers, his bathrobe, and the component set you told him to take with him when he left." Did she *have* to mention the component set? So mean. So heartless. Is there no such thing as mercy?

Another mouthy woman, named Jean Knight, who had one hit record behind her, "Mr. Big Stuff," answered Betty, too. There seemed to be a real rush to judgment going on here. "You've Got the Papers, but I Got the Man" came out at about the same time as Barbara's rebuke, but this time the answer seemed even nastier, and to make matters worse for Betty, Jean brought along a Dimples imposter named Premium to croon along with her. Another phone call. More attitude. Meaner, yet maybe the funniest insults so far. Jean had a few things she'd like to tell Betty and minces no words, because the man they are competing for is "dealin' in class now, honey, not trash." She goes on to call Betty a "poor housekeeper" and a "terrible cook" and then accuses her of "layin' around, getting big and fat." And here comes Premium wailing soulfully about how happy he is now to be with his "sweet little thing" and how they can be together forever. This situation is getting out of hand!

Betty Wright can stand no more abuse. It is time for her to strike back. She's been quiet too long. Publicly humiliated on the radio for months by these sloppy seconds, thirds, and fourths! Besides, she's over Dimples! He doesn't even sing on this record. Plus she's got a new man and a song to celebrate him! It's called "Goodbye You, Hello Him," and this time the papers just say, "She's gone!" The furniture, too. She's left his dog, who's chewing up his clothes—"all the ones I didn't burn up or rip up." Hell hath no fury. And then the final clincher: "And oh, by the way, there are no more pimples on my face." I am overwhelmed. Completely overwhelmed. To hell with the Great American Songbook. This "I've Got Papers" answer says it better.

Learn to milk whatever success you've had. You *can* keep doing the same thing over and over as long as you have a sense of humor about not having a new idea. Just when Dimples, Betty Wright, Jean Knight, and Premium had begun to move on, along came Barbara Mason again with a new twist on the same old situation. It might have taken her three years and she was now singing disco, not soul, but she had discovered the man they were all fighting over was gay! Yep, in "Another Man," as the song was called, "another man is beating my time, another man is lovin' mine." What a hilarious development! Down-low and without papers! Just think how this new gay guy could have answered *her.*

Lo and behold, he did! A group known as Tout Sweet challenged her right away with a little ditty entitled "Another Man Is Twice as Nice." "You stole a man," they accused her, "but you wound up with two." Barbara Mason later admitted in an interview that when she first heard this song, she fell on the floor laughing. But who laughs last laughs hardest, and Tout Sweet had a dare for her about the second man: "He's got a lady too and I already know she's crazy about you."

Then it stopped. "Now, what else is going to come out?" Barbara publicly wondered, but nothing ever did. Dimples died in

2000 of a massive heart attack. He probably just couldn't stand all the trouble he'd caused. But he wound up with the papers all right. A death certificate. The final papers.

If you're a junkie, jazz is for you. Bebop *is* the sound of heroin, isn't it? Plain and simple. Every jive master I have ever loved was an addict: Chet Baker, Bud Powell, Billie Holiday, Anita O'Day, Miles Davis, Charlie Parker. The cool cats and chicks could practically ooze musical notes out of the track marks on their arms. So hep. So smooth. So *DownBeat* magazine. So Bleecker and MacDougal. Yelling out "All right" for no apparent reason as you sit with your date of a different color.

I always felt bad for my mom because she claimed to "hate jazz." When she was very ill near the end of her life and they gave her a morphine drip in the hospital, I thought, "Finally! She can appreciate Coltrane." I ran for the headphones but the nursing staff gave me judgmental looks so I backed off. I should have told my mother about the Nutty Squirrels. They did jazz and they *weren't* junkies. This sped-up vocal group who imitated the Chipmunks actually beat them to television with an animated show called *The Nutty Squirrels Present*, and they looked down on the pop sound of Alvin and his gang. The Nutty Squirrels actually had a big jazz hit with "Uh Oh, Part One and Two," but if you go back and listen to the rest of their discography, you'll be blown away by some of their other riffs. These cats were smoking! If my mom had heard jazz like this at the wrong speed, she might have loved it.

Here's another nonjunkie jazz vocalist that you can love *and* impress your family with by your obscure musical knowledge— Mildred Bailey. *My* favorite jazz singer. Despite a long-lasting career and a critical reputation that placed her second to Billie Holiday by jazz critics in 1943, then first in the following two years, Bailey is largely forgotten today. Maybe because in spite of two failed marriages, she "preferred the company of gay men." Or is it because she was remembered as "hard as nails," with "a violent temper" and "prone to nasty tantrums"? Was this what held her back? Oh, yeah, she "passed" as a light-skinned black woman her whole life even though she wasn't. When the post office put out a series of stamps commemorating jazz and blues singers in 1994, every entertainer pictured was black and Mildred was included. Yet there she was. Not black.

▣

Aren't all country songs novelty recordings in a way? A lot of people today claim country-western music ain't what it used to be, and I kind of agreed until I started listening to the Outlaw Country radio station on Sirius in my car. God, there were so many beyond-cool hillbilly musical gems before *and* after Patsy Cline, Loretta Lynn, Hank Williams, and Ferlin Husky that I had never heard before. Sure, I had hung around redneck bars all my life, but now I felt the weight of my faux-cracker musical ignorance. Suddenly I realized I was an old Caucasian listener who needed to stick his citified ears through the twanging glory hole of country music to have them rearoused. I might have known how to handle myself at a prison jamboree, but my lack of hayseed history would always make me eligible for a seat on the honky musical hayride to hell. If you can't appreciate country music, you have no soul. It might be time for a "class-lift."

How can you inject musical filler to puff out your lack of country music taste? First make an 8-track tape of all the hillbilly songs I'm going to recommend here and then play them over and over so they are drilled into your mind like the Catholic catechism. Tunes that will make you stupider in the academic world yet smarter in real life, the first step to any successful cosmetic country music makeover. These little ditties might get you laid, too.

Start with "Firebug" by J. D. McPherson. It sounds old but it came out in 2010, which just goes to show that retro is a state of mind, not a year. Who cares if the song is about pyromania? Fire prevention has always been the business my family is in (and still is), so I can't help it that a guy with a match is sometimes my Prince Charming. "Burn it up, burn it down," J.D. sings, and you can bet if there's a horndog arsonist listening anywhere nearby, he'll come sliding down your pole and ignite on contact.

If your tastes are a little less extreme but still salt-of-the-earth sleazy, "Snake Farm" (2006) by Ray Willie Hubbard is the song for you, a real mating call for the ill-bred. "'Snake farm'—it just sounds nasty," Ray snarls out, and he sounds kinda nasty, too. So what if his girlfriend in the song is named Ramona and "kinda looks like Tempest Storm"? I bet they're *both* so sexy and dirty that *one* of them will come over to your house and have a little fun if you'd just ask them. You have to aim low. Think linoleum, Gila monsters, jock itch, snake bites, venom you have to suck out of the wound to save lives. Listen hard to "Snake Farm" and you'll have a sexual musical experience all your own.

It's impossible to appreciate country music without being at one time or another in your life a drunk. "If I Could Make a Living Drinking" would be the perfect pickup song if you were looking for a date in either the welfare or unemployment office. This 2014 realistic job-hunting ditty by Kevin Fowler says it all about alcoholism as a career move. If he was paid to be drunk, he'd never call in sick, "wouldn't mind all this working over-time," and would be "too busy boozin' to ever join a union."

Sometimes a hangover is fun: staying in bed all day, taking too many aspirin, jerking off, eating junk food, and ignoring incoming phone calls. This downside of drinking has its own little genre in hillbilly music that you should become familiar with. Even if you've reached a bottom, as they say in AA, there's one place left for you: the "Hangover Tavern" (1961) by Hank Thompson. "My head is heavy, my spirit's kind of low," he sings with melancholy, "and every time I feel this way, to Hangover Tavern I go." I told you a hangover can sing if you'll just let it.

When you're feeling despondent just put on more country music. There are thousands of slit-your-wrist hillbilly songs that will make you laugh at your self-indulgence and ultimately cheer you up. The saddest, most heartbreaking, most ridiculous but touching down-home narration can be found in the 1963 Number One country hit "Lonesome 7-7203" by Hawkshaw Hawkins. What a great number! It's the telephone line the singer put in especially for his ex-girlfriend to call if she ever changes her mind about leaving him and wants to come back. She's the only person that has this number. He's disconnected their old phone because friends kept calling asking for her. "If you ever long for love that used to be," he sings beautifully, "just call Lonesome 7-7203."

I could break down in sobs just picturing him sitting around at home waiting . . . waiting for that call. For days . . . weeks . . . months! But then something worse comes to mind. There wasn't any such thing as an answering machine back in 1963. Suppose he had to go out at some point? For food? Or liquor? And he missed the call! Worse yet, suppose the phone *finally* rings and it's the wrong number? Or a hang-up? It's enough to make you jump off a cliff. But wait . . . there's more tragedy.

Three days after the release of the song, the real life singer, Hawkshaw Hawkins, was killed in an airplane crash. And the final insult? Patsy Cline was also on board and her death got all the attention. Go ahead, laugh. Your sad story ain't shit compared to his.

I hated the Beatles when they first came out because they were so goddamn cheery. I didn't listen to popular music from 1964 until 1976, when I first heard the Sex Pistols. Finally a new antihippie sound that could piss off every musical legend that came first. Before they were even known in America, I remember being taken to see the Pistols outside London and being shocked and awed at this whole new culture. Pogo dancing! Finally, the exact opposite of the cotillion ballroom dances I had been forced to attend by my parents as a young teenager. And punk goddess Jordan! Oh my God, she was a whole different ball game in radical beauty. Spiked Statue of Liberty hair! Those rubber and leather outfits! That geometric makeup on her face. Plus she could scream out vocals just as frighteningly as the Pistols. Divine took one look at Jordan and moaned, "Now I feel like plain Jane." Jordan is still alive today, living with her mother in self-imposed éminence grise, resting on her laurels as she certainly should as the First Lady of the punk lunatic fringe. No one will ever topple you from that throne, Jordan! You are our punk president emeritus in style and you still rule like a queen.

I love punk. I feel safe in that world and of course I realize it's hardly new these days. Matter of fact I have hosted for four years in a row what really is a punk rock nostalgia festival in Oakland, California, called Burger Boogaloo, brilliantly programmed by the promoter Marc Ribak. Here punk rock groups from the past (the Dwarves, the Mummies, the Damned) reemerge along with headliners such as Iggy Pop and Devo, and other more obscure groups such as the Spits and the Trashwomen who reunite and play—and *this* crowd has no trouble remembering who they are. Think about it—punk rock came out in the mid-seventies, so many of the fans are in their fifties. I've seen grandmothers pogo dancing here. It warms my black little heart to realize that for some, seeing the Buzzcocks or 5.6.7.8's is like me going to see a Jerry Lee Lewis, Fats Domino concert years ago. Punk *can* be oldies but goodies and not lose its threatening edge.

"We're middle-aged and filled with rage," I yell from the stage in Mosswood Park to the crowd of new-wave revivalists as a joke, but they don't think it's funny—they roar back their approval. Here, for two whole days, grizzled punk rockers can celebrate and relive their youthful defiance and not feel as if time has passed. "Are you bald or a skinhead?" I shout to older guys who have gotten their Bay Area punk outfits out of mothballs, and they give me a good-natured middle finger back and laugh. Stage diving? Yeah, some of the almost-senior safety-pin set would try, but at Burger Boogaloo many of the punks with guts *have* guts. A lot of them are now too heavy to catch. Does it hurt more to be dropped crowd-surfing at fifty years of age than it did at twenty?

Punk has always been down-low, hasn't it? Even today, some of the really cool young new wavers are just crazy homos escaping the square gay world to slam dance as a butch way to touch other guys' bodies. Girls never look fat or ugly if they're punk; it's the perfect disguise that turns all nontraditionally beautiful women into poverty pinups. "Remember the first time you puked in your purse?" I yell to all the proud "hags and skags," as I address them at Burger Boogaloo, and they cheer back affirmatively. Don't fuck with punk fags or chicks. They'll kick your ass. Or better yet, vomit on you.

Musical mayhem is not only a privilege of the young; it's an all-ages-admitted club in which you should strive for membership. But sometimes you need to calm down. Classical music isn't just for eggheads. It's for crazy people, too, especially when they want to be alone just escaping the frenzy of being themselves. You don't need to know one thing about classical music for it to work. Just read longhair record reviews, and if it sounds like your cup of brain tea, go ahead and buy or download it and give a listen. You only need to make two purchases (and they have a hefty price tag) to feel at ease yet excited about classical music.

First get *Glenn Gould: The Complete Columbia Album Collection* box set. It's out of print but you can find it online—all eighty-one albums remastered on CDs with individual original cover art and a 416-page book filled with rare photographs and essays. Glenn Gould is the coolest man who ever lived. The Master. The highly eccentric Canadian pianist who loved cold weather; he stood on the north side of every room he was in just to be sure the temperature would be lower. Yep, he mumbled and hummed all through his performances and refused to edit out his lunatic vocals. This reluctant public performer fetishized his taped-together broken-down piano stool, wore gloves and winter clothes onstage even when it was sweltering outside. He also thought Petula Clark had the most beautiful voice of all singers. Just listen to his elegant, sometimes frantic, always manic piano recitals, which could soothe a schizophrenic, excite a zombie, confuse a violent psychopath, and make a normal person feel at first disoriented and then inferior. Yes, Glenn Gould is the G-word and I don't just mean genius. I mean glamorous, a genie, a great man of the gramophone with gray matter to spare. A Gould.

The other purchase you need to make in music is Maria Callas. She's all you need to hear to understand opera. Anyone whose best friend was Pier Paolo Pasolini and got dumped by Aristotle Onassis so he could marry Jackie Kennedy knows how to shriek with beauty, style, pitch, and total abandon. *The Complete Studio Recordings, 1949–1969* will make you do mad scenes of your own once you listen to every one of these seventy CDs (including twenty-six complete operas). It takes a while, but once you get through them all, you will feel as if you've had a musical orgasm like no other. Maria Callas was the biphetamine of classical voices. You may have thought, "Oh, fuck opera," before you heard Callas' voice, but once you experience her life's work, you'll change your contempt before investigation. Now you've "fucked opera" and it's a whole different tune. One you'll never be able to hum.

Many listeners my age stopped liking popular music once rap came out, but not me. I don't love all of it—the gangsta "ho, pussy, fag, gun" lyrics of 50 Cent get on my nerves—he sounds like a big nell-box to me, a nouveau-riche, homophobic braggart— the Donald Trump–meets–Chick-fil-A of rap. Yet I do have a soft spot for Ol' Dirty Bastard because even though he was busted for robbery, murder, drug possession, and a shoot-out with New York police and later fatally overdosed, he was kind of funny when he took a reporter and two of his illegitimate children with him in a limousine to the welfare office to get his check and pick up food stamps. Now that's what I call a genius publicity stunt.

I love Eminem too *and* that ex-wife of his, who wore black lip liner around her mouth and upstaged my mustache fashion-wise by flaunting something equally bizarre not only on top of her lips but on the bottom of them, too. I know Eminem has absolutely no desire to meet me, which makes him even more of a hero. "Puke" is still my favorite song of his, and I actually had Jill Fannon, my onetime art assistant, remix it as if the Chipmunks were singing it and used this now helium-happy number for a time as my introduction music whenever I walked onstage to do my Christmas show.

Maybe I should start a rap nostalgia festival just like Burger Boogaloo did for punk, only bring back all my favorite one-hit wonders from the early days of hip-hop. Sort of a Whitey Watt-stax that would showcase all the rap numbers that made me feel like a curious Mr. Rogers meets an earlier would-be angry version of the poet LeRoi Jones when he first was published. "I Wish" by Skee-Lo was one such rhyme that stood out because it was happy and upbeat—a rap that put you in a good mood. "I wish I was a little bit taller," Skee-Lo lamented. "I wish I was a baller. I wish I had a girl who looked good, I would call her." Who could argue with that? He wasn't going to shoot *or* sexually harass anybody. You could almost pogo dance to it like a racial tourist on a gangsta-lite crossover holiday.

"The Vapors" was another rap number that had a big effect on me. I'd love to bring back Biz Markie (and it wouldn't be hard because he now lives in Maryland) to freestyle his hilarious hymn to the Victorian disease that high-style women caught in the Oscar Wilde days whenever they'd get so nervous or frustrated that all they could do was faint. Just picturing his hoodlums and skeezers whipping out a lacy handkerchief soaked in smelling salts to recover from "the vapors" has always been a rap fantasy I wish I could have filmed.

Basehead, a D.C. alternative jazzy rap group, fronted by Mike Ivey, would be high on my bill for my new Lollapaloser music festival. Right from the beginning of their career they confused both the hip-hop and hipster worlds with their subtle but highly original beat. As good as A Tribe Called Quest is in my book, Basehead is even better. They started out riffing on pot and depression but then switched over to Jesus and became a kind of slacker Kirk Franklin. There is no chart on *Billboard* for Pothead Gospel, but if there were, all Top Twenty would be by Basehead.

Tairrie B is my number one homegirl, the headliner of my show. The first white girl in rap who stood her ground against Dr. Dre and got punched in the face by him twice for it, even though she was Eazy-E's girlfriend at the time. Her whole life story is missing from *Straight Outta Compton* and it shouldn't be. Tairrie B was a ruthless bitch, just as one of her rap songs was called. Dressed like Mae West, she bragged, "I take apart men like I took apart Ken and Barbie dolls back when I was ten." Yeah, she was a blond bombshell from hell but not "brown or black, as a matter of fact, I'm white!" she boasted with unselfconscious racial daring. That's right—her name is Tairrie B and "*B* is for *bitch*!" I wish she'd come back and answer all of NWA's greatest hits with a comic vengeance all her own. They owe her. Big-time.

Don't get me wrong. I can also love the most commercial pop sounds of today. Like Justin Bieber. He's better than Sam Smith or Adele in my book. A *real* rock star, a child prodigy (watch him doing Aretha Franklin songs while drumming on pots and pans in his kitchen in those early YouTube videos), and a worldwide teen idol of unheard-of magnitude. I met him once. We were doing *The Graham Norton Show* in London and he was one of the other guests. When my car pulled up to the TV studio, I was shocked to see thousands of teenage girls surrounding the building screaming their lungs out—very Beatlemania. I've always believed the ultimate goal in show business is to become so famous that you can't go out. This was Justin's life already.

I didn't meet him until we were on the air. Justin was so young! Strutting out in full homeboy gangster glory, leather pants hung low showing boxer shorts—sort of like Jim Morrison meets Shirley Temple. Graham Norton has the kind of talk show where you stay on camera even when you're done and the other guests are being interviewed, and as the show progressed, I noticed that Justin was staring at me, and suddenly he blurted, "Your 'stache is the jam!" I assumed he meant my mustache so I thanked him live and offered him my Maybelline eyebrow pencil to draw on his own. After the show, the paparazzi followed him in a howling pack to a restaurant. When Justin exited after the meal, he was wearing my full pencil-thin mustache, which he had obviously drawn on with my Maybelline. The photos were plastered all over the London tabloids and later went viral online. Thank you, Justin.

Maybe we should all become rock stars. That I can't sing or play an instrument used to hold me back, but no more. Look at David Lynch. He's my favorite "new" singer. Yes! He croons electronically on the *Inland Empire* soundtrack, on his *Crazy Clown Time* CD, and yet again on his absolutely amazing eighteen-episode TV show, *Twin Peaks: The Return*. Sometimes David Lynch's vocals are twisted so scarily he sounds like the Jolly Green Giant.

Who could I sound like? If Johnny Ray cried, and Roddy Jackson snarled, what gimmick voice would I introduce? Falsetto's already been done to death so electronically I'd have to go beyond scale and pitch to a new voice level of Yma Sumac on crack to tell my story.

"I Am Fifteen and I Don't Want to Die" would be the anti-suicide tale about how J-Dog, a white boy from Lutherville, Maryland (that's me), grew up to be a hillbilly faux-soul gay-geezer rap star. By now, my homegirls Beth Ditto, Iris DeMent, and Mink Stole (who *can* sing—listen to her *Do Re Mink* CD) would have joined me for backups. Their name? The Honkettes. Already I've musically advanced up to twenty-five years from when I started at fifteen. With their help, I'm feeling much better about my musical self.

I postpone the recording session for one month and fly in Michael Jackson's onetime evil physician who's freshly released from prison where he developed a vocal cord reassignment procedure that can make any Caucasian person sing as soulfully as Al Green. It's a pricey but relatively painless operation and I owe a great deal of gratitude to the convict who donated his larynx, Adam's apple, and vocal folds before the state snuffed out his life in the gas chamber. Presto! Now I sound like Amy Winehouse meets Dusty on male hormones. Good God, I'm suddenly forty years old and I don't want to kill my musical career.

Since I'm already breaking rhythmic boundaries, I bring in white hillbilly rappers like Yelawolf, Hank III, and Machine

Gun Kelly to jam and give my sound a little injection of that "hick-hop" attitude. Imagine my surprise when Vanilla Ice crashes the session and goes beyond Shirley, Rosie, and Kathy and starts rapping while holding his nose and actually doesn't sound that bad. Suddenly I turn fifty years old and feel full of nerve. This new maturity unites our whole crew so we're not afraid to take our sound to the next unexplored vocal level.

We conspire to commit the ultimate Caucasian musical sin by covering James Brown's *Live at the Apollo* album but not his singing, just that famously insane lone fan-girl scream that comes seventeen minutes and eleven seconds in, during "Lost Someone," and makes this seasoned soul audience laugh out loud in surprise. So what if the scream is phony, as some music historians have speculated, added into the mix postproduction by sound engineers? It's still the one hormonal shriek that personifies best the power and glory of what was once called the Chitlin' Circuit. Who was that girl? If James McCourt, the great gay historian, can boast of being able to identify practically every gay man who shouts out a song request to Judy Garland on her most famous album, *Judy at Carnegie Hall*, why can't Stanley Crouch, or some other renowned black music critic, find the girl who screamed out so unabashedly for "the hardest-working man in show business"? I want to know her name. Once I do, we'd sample her howl and scratch it over and over again until all our backup singers shriek along with her from the other side of the color line and these now abstract sounds morph into a checkerboard rap beat. I'm sixty years old and ready to be reborn.

Here's where J-Dog comes in. Once I had a pair of fronts made for my teeth that had fake jewels and my initials, JW, on them. Even though I'd have to get the *W* changed to a *D*, now would be the time to get them out of cold storage. 'Cause J-Dog is a proud geezer in years but a homo-boy in attitude. Yessiree, I'm a gay player with a new kind of shade. Upscale and free from jail. Wassup? Stuck up! Fed up! And fucked up!

> No more bling and guns bitch
> I gotta new kind of rich
> I'm tired of your hating!
> I bought a Cy Twombly painting.

By now our multigenerational, all-genre outlaw rap song has caused so much novelty attention that the Grammy authorities are called. Their record police move in with warrants and accuse J-Dog and crew of inciting a comedy race riot, but we don't care if we go to musical lockdown. We'll sing the encore just like the Alvin-the-Chipmunk-meets-Johnny-Cash-Live-at-the-Maryland-Penitentiary stars that we really are. I'm a seventy-three-year-old prankster gangster and I'm livin' the life!

ACT BAD

I'm a Yippie at heart, a smart-ass late-sixties fake revolutionary who even today thinks riots are a good place to get lucky for sex. A refried radical who still knows how to throw the tear gas back at the police yet is never in the front lines of a standoff where you can get squirted with fire hoses or beaten with nightsticks. I guess even then I understood that the "revolution" wasn't really going to happen, but the anarchy surrounding the idea at the time was certainly exciting. I'm white, so I never got a "rough ride" in a paddy wagon. The few times I was arrested I was always released from lockup on my own recognizance, not on bail like a poor person. I'm a brat, even at seventy-three, and still look forward to political trouble. Civil disobedience is better than Botox any day.

God, I miss the Yippies—those "Groucho Marxists," as they were referred to by ABC News. Angry left-wing hippies who were tired of giving peace a chance and instead staged hilariously disrespectful political stunts such as throwing fake money to the crowds at the New York Stock Exchange and watching the people scramble to pick it up. Or threatening to put LSD in Chicago's water supply. "Levitating" the Pentagon with mind control during a demonstration to spook Republicans. I think

I actually pissed on the Justice Department building in D.C. with a bunch of Yippies during a demonstration. You should have seen the horrified face of Attorney General John Mitchell as he watched the "piss-in" from his office window.

The Yippie leaders wrote devilish little how-to books that corrupted further the hippie ideals of the times. *Steal This Book* by Abbie Hoffman became the first bestseller that had to be kept off the shelves and under the counter for a whole new set of obvious reasons. Abbie Hoffman was my spiritual leader—a media manipulator who used humor as a weapon against his enemy. Even Andrew Breitbart, the late right-wing activist, admitted to me when we did Bill Maher's show together that Abbie had been a big influence on him—he just used the same tactics for the other side. Abbie remained a saint in my book even later in life when he was convicted of dealing cocaine. I mean, we all need to make a living. I was sad when he committed suicide, too.

Paul Krassner was our "Citizen Kane." Not only did he come up with the name "Yippie," he wrote and edited the most radical humor magazine of my lifetime, *The Realist*. Its outrageous cover story in May 1967, "The Parts That Were Left Out of the Kennedy Book," was so timely and rude that some media outlets actually believed he had the goods on what got censored in William Manchester's book on the Kennedy assassination. Krassner's comic theory that LBJ supposedly penetrated the bullet hole in the throat of Kennedy's corpse with his penis must have been the catalyst that inspired me to shoot the entire Kennedy assassination scene with Divine playing Jackie and climbing over the trunk of the limo in that bloodied Chanel suit and pillbox hat just three months later for my film *Eat Your Makeup*.

The *Berkeley Barb* was another useful radical publication—a political weekly paper that included personal sex ads (thought to be *very* progressive at the time) and how-to advice about ripping off the establishment. Hidden in their classifieds, they published the actual AT&T codes, which changed annually, enabling you to invent phony working credit card numbers to make free long-distance calls before there was such a thing as a cell phone. I remember fondly scamming Ma Bell in phone booths all across the country for years thanks to the *Berkeley Barb*'s illegal consumer guide.

Of course, our black revolutionaries were much tougher and they probably thought us Yippies were honky pussies, but we loved them anyway, at first. Eldridge Cleaver, an admitted rapist who bragged that he practiced on white women, was too butch and violent to be funny, but his book *Soul on Ice* was required reading for all of us, which is staggering today if you read it. We should have known he'd turn out to be an asshole, but it took us a while as we watched Cleaver go from being a Black Panther hiding Timothy Leary in Cuba after the Weathermen helped him escape from prison to being a Moonie, then a Christian, a crackhead, and finally a Republican *and* a bad fashion designer whose signature look was pants with a sock-like codpiece to, I guess, display his big once-revolutionary dick.

His wife, Kathleen, was really beautiful in the sixties and inspired white and black Yippie girls everywhere with her militant fashion sense and huge Afro. She was just plain stunning. Why didn't left-wing drag queens "do" her then? Sylvester, from the Cockettes, would have captured her aura perfectly! Kathleen was even more glamorous than Angela Davis at the time. I wish *they* had become a couple. Fuck the Soledad Brothers—they were male chauvinists! Angela and Kathleen should have gone for each other and invented a new kind of sisterhood.

Kathleen *finally* divorced Eldridge and today is a lawyer who teaches at Yale. She kind of looks like the supermodels Veruschka and Pat Cleveland combined if they had both ditched the runway later in life for academia. I'm still obsessed with Kathleen Cleaver. I met Angela Davis two years ago, and she didn't disappoint, but Kathleen? Nope. She's still a stranger.

Johnny Spain was a big deal for me, too. He's the half-white, half-black Black Panther who was part of the San Quentin Six, who were put on trial in 1975 for conspiracy and murder in the escape attempt of George Jackson and other black militants. Convicted, he served twenty-one years, was released, and helped write a book called *Black Power, White Blood.* Is it wrong of me to say he was always the most handsome of the Black Panthers? When I was promoting my first Christmas spoken-word show to be performed at the Castro Theatre in San Francisco, a reporter asked me, "What celebrity do you wish would come?" I quickly answered, "Johnny Spain." I doubt many in my potential audience had any idea who he was and I completely forgot mentioning him. The night of the show I was in my dressing area and the promoter came in confused and said, "There's some guy downstairs saying you want him to come see your show." I asked, "Did he say his name!" He shrugged and answered, "Johnny Spain." "You're kidding!" I screamed. "He came?! Oh my God, let him in and bring him backstage after!" I couldn't imagine what Johnny Spain thought of the mostly gay audience *or* my brand of humor, but he did come back postshow and was shy and charming and thanked me for rooting for him and his release from prison. We became friends and for two years in a row had Easter dinner out together in restaurants in San Francisco, but then he kind of vanished. Maybe because he asked me to help him finance a project and I politely declined. Was I getting played by Johnny Spain? It doesn't matter if I was. Johnny

Spain, you're still my favorite Black Panther and I hope you're doing well today. Easter next year? I'm available.

The radical left was so homophobic that gay men were rare in the Yippie world until Jim Fouratt, one of the first queer activists, showed up at a rally to support Huey Newton at Yale University in New Haven and came out in between Black Panther speeches to rant about gay rights. Blacks may have had their Jim Crow laws to protest, but now it was time for "Mary Crow" laws to crumble, too! Both the Panther men *and* the white Yippie men blanched at Fouratt's demands. Here was a new militancy that completely threatened the left's macho ideas. With no way to assimilate, these straight-guy leaders of both races were suddenly behind the times. All in one afternoon.

Lesbians had always had a gripe with left-wing men's misogyny, but when *Rat Subterranean News* came out and combined dyke power with militant feminist hetero-rage *and* a sense of humor against male pig behavior to women, a new Yippie message was born. The fully nude cover shots of "slum goddesses" announced that some left-wing men risked getting their asses kicked if something didn't change. Underarm hair on women became the new rallying cry against the hippie male gaze. Fags and dykes together were a definite new wing of defiance.

Yet, was I the only gay man in the movement at the time who still felt excluded and hurt that there were no out queer men leaders in the Weathermen? How about the Chicago 7? Nope. All straight men. Did the prophet John Africa tell any black gay men to join his back-to-nature group MOVE before *or* after the first shoot-out with Philadelphia police? If so, I never heard about them. Was I the only gay activist in the world who felt discriminated against when I realized there were no homos inside the Manson Family? Come on, Charlie, even the most insane, ridiculous, or dangerous cult needs a little faggotry to ignite a revolution. I'm glad you're dead. *You* were the piggie. A hetero one.

ACT UP finally came to the rescue, but many of my gay friends had to die of AIDS before that happened. Sure, at first there was the Radical Faeries group, but they were a little too hippie-dippie for me, and besides, I'd look stupid wearing wings and living in the woods of Guerneville. ACT UP took AIDS militancy *and* the idea of public theater, then mixed lesbian *and* gay men's anger, and used it to wake up the world about the AIDS crisis. Larry Kramer may have been strident and obnoxious to some, but without his endless ranting about the slow testing of AIDS medications, many of my HIV-positive friends who barely made the cut between AZT and the new drugs of today would no longer be with us.

ACT UP were the warriors we always needed, chaining themselves to a New York Stock Exchange balcony to protest the high cost of AIDS treatment or shutting down the Food and Drug Administration for a day to press for a cure. Not since *One* magazine, the first gay radical publication, published the headline "I Am Glad I Am a Homosexual," in 1958 (!), had there been such unsissy brave militancy, such in-your-face defiance! When one "affinity group" of ACT UP in New York City performed a brief memorial at Judson Church for the AIDS victim Mark Fisher ("I want my own political funeral to be fierce and deviant," he had written before his death) and then walked the body in an open casket from Greenwich Village to George H. W. Bush's campaign headquarters and "indicted" Bush for murder the day before the 1992 presidential elections, even the police kept their distance in shock and maybe secret respect. Bush lost to Clinton the next day but was never charged with a crime. The crime of silence.

ACT UP soldiers were knights in tarnished armor fighting

in "cum-smeared tanks," as John Rechy so touchingly and na-ively wrote in optimism years before the AIDS holocaust. Raid-ing a mass at St. Patrick's Cathedral in New York City to harass that asshole Cardinal John O'Connor, long an enemy of the gay community, who had recently come out against safe-sex educa-tion in the schools, some gay radicals drew the line at one of the protesters, who grabbed a Communion wafer, broke it in half, and threw it to the ground.

Not me! The Catholic Church is our enemy. They have bashed me, my culture, and everything I believe in from the beginning of A.D., so I have no guilt about bashing them back right now. The anti-Pope march that was held against Benedict XVI in London in September 2010 was a festive occasion that I luckily attended. *Such* a cool and cute crowd of pissed-off gay kids and sympathizers of all races and sexual preferences. A sense of humor united all. FUCK THE POPE signs could be ex-pected, but I WOULDN'T FUCK THE POPE was even better. FUCK THE POPE BUT USE A CONDOM reflected a new spin on political correctness. Of course, child abuse by the clergy and the cover-ing up of this brotherhood of pedophiles was endlessly spot-lighted (ABSTINENCE MAKES THE CHURCH GROW FONDLERS, one placard read), and even new theories were floated with wit (JESUS HAD TWO DADDIES; OPIUM IS BETTER THAN RELIGION) "Pope? Nope!" chants went out, and when a big dyke activist leader yelled to the crowd "What do we want?" and the intel-ligent nonviolent crowd yelled back "Rational thought!" I knew English restraint had reached a new level. Rational thought? Not exactly the fighting words of revolution, but what the hell, wit can be spoken softly. THE POPE WEARS A STUPID HAT said one decidedly unaggressive protester's sign. Could under-statement be the new dangerous?

This current Pope, Francis, the one everybody seems to love, is even worse, if you ask me. Anita Bryant did more for gay rights than this co-opting, faux-queer-friendly fraud ever did. At least Anita made us angry and inspired rebellion and fury against her stupid homophobia (which eventually ruined her career). But this new guy does nothing and pretends to be gay positive. Remember that song "Smiling Faces Sometimes" by the Temptations with the lyrics "Beware of the pat on the back. It just might hold you back"? This is Francis. "Good queer," he seems to imply when he utters "Who am I to judge?" about gay marriage. Who are you?! You're the fucking Pope for Christ's sake, that's who you are!

He's even worse to women than he is to homos. The ban on ordaining female priests in the Catholic Church will "last forever," he recently announced. I guess his "Year of Mercy" is supposed to appease the weaker sex? Here he allows priests to forgive women who have had abortions—sort of like parking-ticket amnesty. He actually explained that these "expanded opportunities" would be under his order for "obtaining the indulgences." Indulgences? Is he kidding? Didn't indulgences go out with the Reformation? Again, he changes nothing. Abortion is still a "grave sin." Do all the unrepentant abortion gals join the unbaptized babies in Limbo, who are still waiting in total darkness for the privilege of seeing God, yet are now forgotten by the Church, which fairly recently announced that the very concept of Limbo had been discontinued?

Pope Francis believes in miracles even though his most recent rushed canonization of Mother Teresa came under scrutiny when doctors and state health officials debunked the claim that her prayers had cured a woman of cancer. Her cyst, not cancer, had been treated for months at a government hospital and destroyed thanks to medicine, not some Catholic hocus-pocus.

How about a real miracle for Pope Francis? He becomes the

first man to get pregnant and we give him *no* mercy on deciding what women should do with their own bodies. Not until he's given birth to a female transgender Christ child of a different color will we indulge him with a little queer mercy of our own.

I'm a big fan of the Satanic Temple. These pro-separation-between-church-and-state, antireligious advocates who believe in Satan as a "metaphorical construct" are the closest thing we have today to the Yippies. I'm not a real satanist, of course, especially after Anton LaVey and his Church of Satan made it so showbiz cheesy in the sixties. To be perfectly honest, I wouldn't have a thing to wear to a goat sacrifice. But these new comic devil worshippers who have been billed "First Amendment performance artists" who "offer tongue-in-cheek support to the fallen angel" know that the word "satanist" is a lightning rod for controversy that can be used for humorous activism. It's hard not to rise to their hilarious devilish bait.

I first heard of this group when they did one of their "pink masses" at the grave site of the homophobic Christian lunatic Fred Phelps' mother in Mississippi. A satanic graveside ritual performed after a religious enemy's death that turns the deceased once-hetero spirit gay seemed like a perfect new sacrament to me. The Satanic Temple also sued in Michigan and won the right to install a "snaketivity" display next to the Christian Nativity scene that was set up in the state capitol. You could see the confused look of the children as they gazed back and forth between Beelzebub and Baby Jesus.

When Bibles were allowed to be distributed in public schools in Florida, the Temple handed out a satanic coloring book to children in response. And in Oklahoma they unveiled plans to install right next to the Ten Commandments monument in the state capitol a seven-and-a-half-foot-tall bronze statue of Baphomet, the horned and hooved totem of contemporary satanism, sitting on a throne while two sculpted innocent children look up to him in wonderment. When the Oklahoma state Supreme Court ordered the Ten Commandments removed, the Satanic Temple scrapped the plan and moved the devil statue to its Detroit branch, where a local pastor complained that the cemetery was "a welcome-home party for evil." It now rests unpeacefully in the Satanic Temple's brand-new headquarters in . . . where else? Salem, Massachusetts.

Doug Mesner, aka Lucien Greaves, cofounder and spokesperson for the church, is charismatic in a demonic way. Yes, he wears all black and inverted-cross accessories, but what clinches his aura is a disfigured, scarred eye that never moves in its socket, which gives him a signature look that is at first unnerving and then just plain devilishly sexy. He's a troublemaker in the tradition of Abbie Hoffman but still a serious fighter for freedom *from* religion, and he's a staunch opponent of doctors who believe in "dissociative identity disorder," also known as multiple personality disorder, which resulted in the Satanic Panic that swept our country and imprisoned many innocent day-care workers following the McMartin school child-molestation hysteria (they were innocent, just in case you forgot). Lucien crashes psychiatric conventions and confronts publicly the doctors who still believe in such nonsense. You should join him. Send money. Spread the word before they commit *you*!

It's time to go beyond the valley of the Red Army Faction, over the top of the Venceremos Brigade, and beneath the valley of the Jewish Defense League to create a whole new brand of capitalist activism. One that uses a completely original positive form of comic terrorism to humiliate and embarrass our political and moral enemies. We can be rich, poor, or the ever-vanishing in-between, but we need to regroup, conspire, and attack with razor-sharp precision. College students, stop studying! High school kids have already walked out and made you look like slackers in the rebellion department. Get your lazy overeducated asses out in the streets where you belong. There's no such thing as "undecided" anymore. This time, unlike in the sixties, we're gonna win.

Don't act up, ACT BAD! No matter what your sexual preference is, pretend you haven't gotten laid in six months and use that horny drive for release in a political way. Join our little coup d'état and get out there and cause unrest no matter who's running the show. Outside agitation *is* the fountain of youth. Let it flow.

Why not kick off our new movement by bringing back Freaknik—remember that? The onetime spring-break celebration for black college students that initially horrified Atlanta when it erupted into a supposed orgy of rap music, public urination, looting, and "wilding" all in the name of fun. When Freaknik's organizers later tried to find a new home in another Southern city, white people rose up in fear, and after a few stumbling attempts at rebirth, this festival of mayhem died an unfair racist death. Next year, let's have a Gay Freaknik and burn *all* flags—the U.S. one, the Black Nationalist one, the Confederate one, even the gay one—actually, let's burn the flag of every country in the world and then we can end nationalism while ridiculing *and* celebrating one of the most outdated and corny forms of protest left. Flag burning will suddenly be au courant again.

Let's declare our *own* time zone. Hours different from any of the other ones honored around the world—especially daylight saving time. We're not "springing ahead" or "falling back" for anyone, thank you. We'd have ABT, Act Bad Time. We refuse to be pinned down by your fascist scheduling when we've never been asked to participate in thinking up the rules. A.M.? P.M.? So boring. So bourgeois. We don't do that anymore.

Going too far will be Act Bad's political platform. We'd only agree with PETA's more extreme positions, such as when its codirector Ingrid Newkirk said in 1990 with a straight face that "six million Jews died in the concentration camps, but six billion broiler chickens will die this year in slaughterhouses!" Never again. We'll demonstrate against all Christmas tree sales, too, bemoaning that ecologically, from a pro-life perspective (for once), almost 1 million evergreens are aborted internationally every holiday season by being cut down and then humiliated in a pagan way by mostly Christian fanatics who then throw out the unclaimed bodies of the dead to be desecrated by arsonists or hauled away by garbagemen to the potter's field of Christmas trees—the dump.

We'd welcome radical new splinter groups such as ecosexuals, who are erotically attracted to the land, "talk dirty to plants, kiss and lick the earth," and bury themselves in soil, surrounded by nude dancers "while the environment watches on." In other words, onetime tree huggers are now tree fuckers. These are our new brothers and sisters. Yikes! Talk about extreme!

Maybe gay people *should* stop being so nice! "Christ," a woman lawyer I know whose clientele is mostly gay men complained recently, "the gay boys don't get in any trouble these days! They don't drink, so no spousal-abuse charges or DWIs, they don't go out to gay bars anymore because they're always on Grindr so no underage-drinking busts or loitering with intent after last call. They're all married so no lewd activity in the peep shows—I haven't handled a glory-hole bust in months! How the hell am I supposed to make a living?"

Politicians need to fear us again. I remember I missed a chance I had once on an airplane. Seated in first class next to a gentleman who never made eye contact the entire coast-to-coast flight, I kept thinking, "I know this man, but who is he?!" His signature suspenders and Brooks Brothers–type suit rang a bell, too, but for the life of me, I couldn't figure it out. When we landed and everybody started exiting the plane, other passengers who recognized me started laughing and one said, "I couldn't believe *you* were sitting next to Clarence Thomas that whole time!" I thought, "You're kidding me." But, of course, it was him. That lying bastard! "I believed Anita Hill!" I wanted to yell. During the flight I should have nonchalantly ordered a Coke, and when it was served, started picking at something imaginary on the can before turning to him and saying, "Excuse me, is that a pubic hair on my Coke?" Shoulda, coulda, woulda . . .

Remember when the gay sex-advice columnist Dan Savage, who had the flu at the time, went underground in 2000 and tried to infect the antigay presidential candidate Gary Bauer by handing him the pen Dan had just licked, requesting an autograph? Savage even got a volunteer job in Bauer's office and licked the doorknob and telephone receiver in what can only be called germ warfare. If you ever get caught, turn this kind of terrorism around and trumpet the action as a pro-flu-shot public service announcement.

Gays Against Guns, or GAG as many of us affectionately call this group, is a gang that needs more of our support. Guns are fake butch. You and I do *not* have the right to own a Glock 9mm handgun. It would have been impossible for this closet queen Muslim terrorist to stab the forty-nine people he shot and killed at Pulse nightclub in Orlando. No, he needed a gun. And he shouldn't have been able to buy one. Let's join Gays Against

Guns in this "Shame, Name, and Blame" campaign to protest politicians who take contributions from the NRA. Their bumper stickers that read NRA SASHAY AWAY may be funny, but GAG means business. Why not join up with all the protesting high school students *and* GAG and plan a secret one-day demonstration where we go to the home of Oliver North, the new head of the NRA, and take a shit on his lawn? When the turd, I mean the word, is given, as Elijah Muhammad said, we must act. Any good radical knows that.

I'm against political kidnapping because of my friend Patricia Hearst, but it's hard not to fantasize one involving William Donohue, the Fred Phelps of the Catholic Church. He's been called an "identity politics ambulance chaser" and "a right-wing publicity mill" and is one of the most virulent antigay spokesmen of all. He rants that sexual abuse by priests was done by homosexuals, not pedophiles, goes ballistic against Hollywood, which, he says, "is controlled by secular Jews who hate Christianity in general and Catholics in particular," and even attacked George W. Bush when he was president for using the term "holiday season" without mentioning Christmas. In other words, Donohue is wacko. A ransom would be pointless because who would want him back? I bet even the Pope thinks he's an asshole. Let's imagine just tying him up and making him watch the Pasolini movie *Salò* over and over. Would that shut him up?

Come to think of it, Act Bad should borrow one of Richard Nixon's ideas and start its own Enemies List. Besides Donohue, we can speak ill of the dead and defame Nancy Reagan, who said in 1981, "Women's Liberation and Gay Liberation [are] part of the same things: a weakening of moral standards of this nation. It is appalling to see parades in San Francisco and elsewhere claiming 'gay pride' and all that. What in the world do they have to be proud of?" Well, Act Bad will let you know when our most crazed anorexic drag queens show up at your grave, dressed up as you as they lip-synch your most hateful comments over and over until the dead themselves judge you.

Next on our list would be Martin Luther King's still-living niece Alveda King, who said, "Homosexuality cannot be elevated to a civil rights issue. God hates homosexuality." What's with these King bitches? His youngest daughter, Bernice, participated in an antigay marriage march and commented, "I know in my sanctified soul that he did not take a bullet for same-sex unions." How about a lemon meringue pie right in your sanctified face? Act Bad is not a pacifist organization. We're theatrical and we hold grudges.

It's illegal to be gay in seventy-six countries around the world. Isn't it time for us to borrow a slogan from that new "black bloc" militant faction of protesters, Disrupt J20? "We will go to war and you will lose!" That's right. Don't we need a comic armed conflict over sexual preference? Our guns may shoot blanks but our tongues are lethal. We will kill you with humor.

Let's drop a massive stink bomb on Uganda and have our own navy "Seal and Squeal" squads round up all the American Christian evangelical preachers who went there and provoked Uganda's parliament to try to pass a bill to impose the death penalty "for the offense of homosexuality." We'd spray their thinning hair with industrial-strength hair spray and light a match. *Voooom!* Off with their hairdos! Then we'd track down the snitches who obeyed the other, more liberal Ugandan law that required heterosexuals "to report a gay person to authorities within twenty-four hours of hearing of their homosexuality or be jailed for up to three years in prison." Why this twenty-four-hour grace period? I wonder. So straights could get their hair done, flowers arranged, homes interior-decorated before the most obvious of their gay merchants were hauled away? Fag hags would be forced to go underground, where they would form their own railroad of resistance to smuggle out queers and lesbians of all degree of butchness, many of whom would later form the Lavender Avengers, who would lead a worldwide punishing squad of queer revenge.

First stop Jamaica, long a hotbed of homophobia. Parachuting in, our squad of "hit queers" would swarm out singing our new national anthem, "The Harder We Came," and raid the gay-hating community. These fuckers who attack gay men with machetes would be seized, tied up, and "teabag" tortured for weeks until our warrior balls were raw from hitting their foreheads with testicular fury. Finally giving up, these onetime homo-haters would scream out "Queer!" and we'd force them to sing a new little reggae number all our own, "A Hard-On Comes on You." A dawn of tolerance would begin in Jamaica.

Iran? They dangle gay people over cliffs and then behead them in public, don't they? We need drastic measures here! Pissed-off gay Muslims would brew a popper-like liquid that would be smuggled out and poured into the hijabs of the wives of the most antihomo religious leaders, causing their women to laugh in hysteria at their husbands' lack of sexual skill in the sack. Queer amnesty is a sudden possibility.

Other dominoes of dated indecency would begin to fall. Our vindictive and volatile gay army would, in a surprise air raid, plunder the Middle Eastern capitals of homophobia (Pakistan, Saudi Arabia, Syria) by dropping tens of thousands of pamphlets explaining in their native language the bear community, gay marriage, and Walt Whitman, followed by Bruce Benderson novels, *Mommie Dearest* DVDs, and the complete recordings of Judy Garland. Oceanic countries (Samoa, New Guinea, Tonga) would quickly change their gayly incorrect tune when they got a load of THEM, our militant transgender model squad of both persuasions who march in formation across their borders wearing armed-forces-inspired couture uniforms, swinging nunchucks in choreographed unison while chanting "Gender Surrender" for the world to hear. Those who don't flee or drop dead from heart attacks will join up with our fellow liberated citizens from foreign lands to sexually invade down-low Africa to free our homofriendly brothers and sisters. Finally we would abolish antigay bigotry through the warfare of wit. Lay waste to worldwide homophobia with fashion aggression. Invalidate universal heterosexual domination by promoting a life of erotic abandon. Judgment Day is here. We have won the battle to make gay, straight, and transgender rights the same. Together we yell in victory, "Burn, Mary, Burn."

GRISTLE

I f the revolution doesn't happen? Well, you gotta eat. I never cared much about the taste of food when I smoked five packs of King Kools a day. And before that my recreational use of speed didn't encourage much interest in cooking lessons. But once I was nicotine-free, I began to actually taste food. I liked it, and you should, too. Colleen Roome Shelton, my first assistant, explained to me, "If you can read, you can cook—you just need patience and all the ingredients the cookbook calls for." So today I *can* cook but I'm not a cook. A real cook makes up recipes. I follow them.

Going out to eat is a major part of being a grown-up. You'll need to be a "foodie," up to a point. But that zone between pretentious and sublime in a restaurant is a gray area these days no matter if you are scheduling a business dinner or using the meal as a launching pad for a sexual encounter with a new date. GET OVER YOURSELF, some fed-up hipster scrawled in graffiti over the front door of one of those pompous and preciously perfect brand-new San Francisco eateries. After dining there, I knew what that vandal meant. Who wants to consume a meal so healthy that food police would give it five stars? So gastronomically correct that trendsetters who aren't even hungry stampede the reservation desk, lining up for hours, begging to overpay for the privilege of just stepping inside?

Yet there's the other side—a radical restaurant that reinvents how you think about eating what you always did and never noticed. Prune is still my favorite eatery in New York. It's small, even cramped. Not at all fancy but confidently understated. Bohemian snooty but humble. Cooler than Coolio ever was. Where else can you order a single carrot as a side dish and be over the moon about how good it tastes? You know the kind— usually sold by itself, out of a package, and paired in a dirty supermarket vegetable bin with a few stalks of limp celery. A big ugly carrot that a horse might turn up its nose at if it was presented in a trough. But at Prune? Yummy!

Maybe it's time to open my own restaurant in New York City. I'd follow Prune's lead and pick a name that is vaguely foodie-unpopular. Like Salt in Baltimore, another good restaurant that unfortunately is no longer. How about Fat? No, too obvious. Liver . . . funny but too specific. Calories. Not bad. I know! Gristle. Perfect. Gristle would be located on the only bad street left in Manhattan. If there is one. If Gavin Brown hasn't already beat everyone else to the punch as he always does by opening an art gallery there first. We'd be the snootiest foodie-in-reverse eatery in town. "Dare to Dine Here!" would be our motto. And then the stampede would begin.

The exterior of Gristle would be purposely misleading to the uninitiated. Faux boarded-up windows and doors. Just walking by you'd think the building were abandoned until you saw the half-broken-on-purpose small neon sign with the tubes blinking in highly stylized dysfunction. The *G* in *Gristle* would be throat-like in design, and the gaseous color chemicals inside would rise up, gag, and begin to vomit out in three animated stages before swallowing and starting all over again.

We'd have valet parking, too, but the attendants would be disguised as hostile schizophrenic street people who would squeegee-attack your windshield right as you pull up. Those in the know would have figured out by now that all our valets were ex-cons, but unsuspecting first-time diners would be so rattled getting out of their cars that they'd turn over their entire key ring without worrying that now these thieves could open their glove compartment and trunk. By then, our gourmet customers would be inside struggling to be cool enough to eat our food, and the staff conspirators would have had enough time to find your vehicle registration, get your home address, and call ahead this information to a squad of burglars who would rob your house before you've even moved on to dessert.

We'll take reservations, but there's one ironclad rule at Gristle. You have to eat alone. Without anything to read at your table. Staring straight ahead. Confident. Once, I saw an older gentleman—the kind who wears ascots and gets away with it—eating solo in a tony San Francisco hotel restaurant, dressed to the nines and also wearing an oxygen device covering his nostrils, with a tube running under his jacket, down his suit pants, to the supply tank discreetly placed under his chair. "Yes," I heard him say with slight annoyance to the waiter, "of *course* I'd like to see the wine list." Pure elegance if you ask me.

Any mention of "food issues" by inquiring diners would make them ineligible for a reservation. "If you have food issues," we would icily respond, "you should stay home." In fact, they would be our specialty. "We're gluten gluttons looking for peanuts," our match covers could read. And, yes, smoking *is* allowed inside Gristle. We serve foie gras, too, but ours is made from horse corn that was forced down the throats of masochistic ducks who enjoyed being humiliated by the butchest liver-loving farmers this side of the French border. Don't care for the taste?

Too bad. My mother always told me, "If you don't like what's on your plate, just mess it up a little and nobody'll know you didn't eat it." Here at Gristle, we expect you to do the same.

Be brave. Stephen Dorff and I were in Tokyo promoting *Cecil B. Demented* and our distributor took us to an upscale Japanese restaurant where we were served some Tingler-like sea creature still alive in a bowl of boiling water who was trying to struggle out and attack us before we could eat it. "What the hell is that?" Stephen whispered in my ear as the aggressive little creature lunged toward us unsuccessfully from the bubbling liquid with its frightening little claws ready to scratch out our eyes. "I don't know," I hissed back, "but hit it with your chopstick." Stephen did so. "Hit it!" somebody else chimed in. "Hit it! Kill it! Eat it!" we began chanting together in food-bullying lust. The poor creature dying as it went down our throats was a culinary experience I can only hope to repeat here in our restaurant.

Entering Gristle would not be a welcoming experience. You'd be met by an ugly bewigged antisocial maître d' who'd explain, "Your table is nowhere near ready," and direct you into a bar area that is lit like a hospital emergency room to have a glass of wine he describes as "not unlike vinegar from a witch's asshole." The bartender, hired because of the extreme burn scars on his face, plops down two, yes, two, ready-made martinis even though you didn't ask for them. He'd explain they were made from our own brand of vodka fermented from the eyes of rotten potatoes and served warm with a lot of vermouth in the wrong kind of cocktail glass still hot from the dishwasher. The one drowned olive inside would be smelly and constantly recycled from drinks left behind after last call the night before.

"Your table is ready," the monster maître d' suddenly whispers as your full beverage is snatched away before you even have a chance to taste it, and the bill, which seems high to you, is rudely presented without anyone's offering to transfer it over to your dinner check. What choice do you have but to pay it? You notice they've added a 40 percent tip, which seems nonnegotiable.

The atmosphere in the main dining room continues the off-putting theme. The soundtrack to *La Grande Bouffe*, that shocking French-Italian movie directed by Marco Ferreri, plays on loop, and while some are misled by the supper-club tango-style music, others remember the harrowing scenes of binge eating, farting, vomiting, and jerking off topped by exploding sewer pipes that accompany the Philippe Sarde orchestral score.

The maître d' leads you past many tables (all singles, of course), each decorated with a dead-flower arrangement. We don't have salt and pepper—so predictable, so bourgeois, so pedestrian. We serve Red Dye no. 2, the only spice you'll ever need at Gristle, and a shaker of the neglected condiment will be readily available. A large Robert Indiana–inspired *EAT/DIE* painting is on one wall, but the word *SHIT* has been added in between the two more classically familiar ones.

You are seated facing the wall, which is a relief at first because you have a moment to compose yourself, but when your waiter taps you on the shoulder and you turn around, you scream out loud. He appears to have rejected corrective plastic surgery after being in some kind of chemical explosion. Both eyes are on the same side of his face and he has no nose, just two holes. He's a cubist painting after it was defaced by an enemy of modern art. You look around and see the rest of the waitstaff is in the same boat. Many must have been recruited from old Smile Train ads now that their childhood "modeling" careers have faded. Their cleft palates and hideously deformed overbites give a new meaning to *monstrous*, yet their unbridled dignity remains unchecked. To top it off, Gristle has copied the dress code of even the most extreme Whole Foods and demanded its employees feature radical body mutilation, stretched-down earlobes, horn implants, even extended lip plates. The ones lucky enough to still have foreheads have the Gristle logo branded right in the center.

The human horror of a waiter has been trained to never mention his name. You came here to eat, not make friends, and the management of Gristle respects your wishes. He does, however, give you the standard opening spiel about how all Gristle's ingredients are proudly "unnatural." All the meat comes from perverted animals who have defied nature before the slaughterhouse: steers who blew other steers, rimming quails, scat-loving turkeys, even S&M veal from calves that were erotically charged by the tiny little cages they were kept in their entire lives. Our chickens are all pillow biters and were, at first, waterboarded in solitary confinement by our angry white male chef with a history of heroin problems, whom you can meet in the kitchen at any time and marvel that he, too, wears a meat thermometer up his ass in solidarity with the animal you are about to eat. You want duck? Not only do we have it, we'll go further than that snuff Japanese restaurant I just told you about did and bring it still alive to your table so you can place it in the little culinary electric chair designed for your eating pleasure and pull the switch yourself.

Before you hear the specials, or "nothing-specials" as we call them here at Gristle—appropriating the name Warhol always wanted to use as the title for a TV show he'd host—our waiter would explain that we no longer serve water of any kind. The fashion designer Valentino once explained to me with a straight face that "bubbles make you fat," so sparkling water was the first to go. Flat water? Well, just how deep *is* that Evian well?

How come I've never seen a photo of it? I'm almost sure those plastic bottles are filled with stagnant water trickled down from a drainage ditch outside the Walt Whitman rest area on the New Jersey Turnpike and purified by the few paroled convicts who managed to get minimum wage jobs there. And tap water? So newly trendy, so disgustingly free, so aggressively hydrating. We'd explain that our no-water policy was inspired by a hilarious article by Gerald Nachman in my favorite San Francisco social-climbing magazine, *Nob Hill Gazette*, who bragged in print that he drank as little water as possible, calling it "the security blanket of Gen Xers," and lobbied to ban it altogether "on annoyance grounds alone." "The major cause of drought," he argues, "is not a lack of rain but the bottled water fetish among our thirsty youth." He's right. Water is sooo over, so plebian, so predictable. "Water can't get wet," Joy Williams once wrote, and she's not the first to notice this liquid's limitation. "I hate water," my friend Pat Moran always said, and I used to argue with her. How could you hate water? Now I realize she was right. You should never want water. Thirst is the new "needy."

Finally the wait-monster hands you the menu. The appetizers are mostly liver based, and the fine print explains that the calves and chickens who gave up this particular organ for you had severe drinking problems. There are liver sliders, liver tartare, even liver pâté char-burned until it's blackened beyond recognition and filled with tasty carcinogens.

Since we put the edge in vegetable here, we've got some treats for the vegans, too. Just the raw ends of vegetables cut off before cooking: hairy carrot tips, tough asparagus-spear bottoms, unappealing outer leaves of artichokes, scraped seeds from inside an overripe tomato, and cores of onions. Crudités were never *this* crude. You're gonna love 'em . . . or else!

The entrées are a little more traditional. We want to bring

the Southern tradition of "dirt" cooking back to the forefront of regional cuisine. These "geographic" dishes that celebrate the desire of poor people from rural Mississippi to consume soil are quite popular here at Gristle. Claylike earth would be served dug up fresh from a hill (superior to that from flatter landscapes) after a rainfall when it smells so rich and damp and tastes so gritty, rough. This caviar of sod is so downright delicious that we call it Gumbo Dirt, and it's one of our repeat customers' favorite meals. We've even gone a step further and added pica-perfect sides of nonedible items usually associated with this onetime eating disorder (paper, drywall, chalk, and paint chips). Together they have become a reinvented food group like no other. Your taste buds will now be so revitalized that you'll never complain to the waiter about a wobbly table leg; you'll just bend down and bite it off yourself. Wood chips are the new saffron if you just give them a chance.

All our meat dishes would be cooked so well-done that the final result would resemble a PF Flyers tennis shoe. Frozen vegetables that had been thawed, refrozen, and thawed again would be boiled so long they'd be dead on arrival, not a vita-min left inside. One of our customers' favorite desserts is that instant chocolate pudding with the thin layer of scum on the top that sticks to your throat as you swallow and makes you gag just like the graphics for our restaurant. There would be no sugar for your instant coffee, just saccharin. Your mother was right when she told you the government was full of it when they banned this wonderfully slimming product in 1977. Food-ies forget this ban was formally lifted in 1991. Don't worry, all our bottles of saccharin are dated early- to-mid-seventies.

Finally your waiter deigns to tell you what specials are avail-able for the evening. Tonight we are featuring recipes from the *Natural Harvest* cookbook, a collection of semen-based dishes by Paul Photenhauer. You may think we are joking or just including these dishes for shock value, but we're serious. This *is* a real cookbook, and as its chef explains, "Semen is not only nutritious, but it also has a wonderful texture and amazing cooking properties." Once you overcome any initial hesitation, he explains, you will be surprised to learn how wonderful semen is in the kitchen. Appetizers include "slightly saltier caviar" and "man-made oysters—clean shells filled with different fresh semen." If the diner has never swallowed such a liquid, these are usually the training wheels of edible ejaculation, but be forewarned, we serve the full load.

Maybe you've graduated to riskier, more high-wire culinary choices. Like extreme skiers who are dropped off on avalanche-prone mountain slopes by helicopters to ski down, you crave a taste too radical for even our most adventurous eater, one that might sicken others but to you is a new peak in palate-jarring flavor. You're lucky. Tonight we are introducing dinners that are all from *Unmentionable Cuisine*, as the food historian Calvin W. Schwabe calls some of the supposedly most repellent recipes known to man he has collected from around the world. We find them . . . well, simple, humble, almost elegant in their unsavoriness.

There's dog and cat meat. Okay, we don't support raising pets for human food, but how about the thousands of millions unwanted and unneutered cats and dogs now being humanely destroyed in city pounds and shelters just in the United States alone? What's wrong with eating them? Broiled puppy is actually a Hawaiian dish "usually prepared by flattening out the entire eviscerated animal and broiling it over hot coals." You're lucky! We have it on the menu tonight and it definitely does *not* taste like chicken. Steamed cat, a dish from Ghana that also surprises the palate, is available, too. The feline is skinned and cut into large pieces, then fried until well browned in a mixture of peanut oil and butter. We've added our own special touch—topping the scaredy-cat meal with a sprinkling of whiskers. Meow!

Undaunted, you order off the menu. "For the main course I'd like the cooked dog, but can I switch that same recipe to a litter of kittens?" The waiter grits his teeth, refusing to show his utter contempt, silently plotting revenge in the kitchen. "And instead of the tomato aspic, 'untouched by human hands and straight from the can,'" you read from the menu, "I'd like to switch to the Lazy Susan of mystery-meat dishes: Spam, scrapple, raw veal, mixed with full-fat mayo bought in industrial-size jars, unrefrigerated at Baltimore flea markets on especially hot and humid August afternoons." "You'll get yours," the waiter thinks to himself while muttering in a condescending tone, "I'll see what I can do."

Staring straight ahead, of course, you wait for your food for what seems like an eternity and begin to worry that somehow you have offended the management. It's always important to re-view mentally the rules of proper restaurant manners just in case there's a pop quiz before the entrée is served. *Never* send the food back—if you don't like it, simply never return. You don't get your money back at the movies if you don't like it, do you? Being rude to the waitstaff is strictly verboten. You know who you are—the ones who always complain every time you go out to eat. These insecure diners only reveal to the world that they grew up underprivileged in the manners department with par-ents who never taught them to treat the help with respect. Noblesse oblige must be instilled in all households without economic limitation and passed down to the next generation. Sending the wine back after that ridiculous sniff ritual with the waiter does not make you look sophisticated; it makes you look like the Beverly Hillbillies in the Playboy Mansion.

If you imagine someone other than yourself might be paying the bill (an impossibility here at Gristle), never order the most expensive thing on the menu, gold digger. In a foreign country if the poor waiter has to translate the menu into English for you, say yes to the very first thing you like—don't make him go through the whole list. Some diners always appear jealous they didn't order what you got once the meals are served. Please! So annoying—have faith in your initial taste. Food waffling is the sign of an international amateur. And finally, the Clean Plate Club is something you never want to join. Always leave a little bit of food uneaten on your plate. We're not in India. You should never look *that* hungry.

Well, look who's here—the waiter. Those kittens must have been cute at one time—all five of them. Are you hearing things or is one of them still purring? If so, this little pussy must have been happy to be cooked alive! Yes, this little bastard is definitely breathing. *Bang!* The waiter hits it with a special crab mallet he always has on hand for this type of food emergency. That settles that. Dinner is finally served.

Domestic cat tastes a little like rabbit mixed with roadkill tartare, but it's not hard to eat. Once it's browned well in trans fat and heavily seasoned with untreated, unwashed salt from the Salton Sea, then simmered over unfiltered Everglade swamp water, you don't even notice the eyeballs, which have long been a Cantonese delicacy. You have to chomp these rubbery fuckers forever to prepare them for their fantastic voyage, but these pupils eventually go down your throat like a big wad of Dubble Bubble chewing gum.

By now, your taste buds are jumping out of their drawers, they're so keyed up. You are full of shit, stunned, and slightly sickened. Dizzy with repulsive new flavors. Confused by the artery-clogging ingredients, yet thrilled to be in gastronomical outer space. Before you even get to peek at the dessert menu, you feel a pain in your chest. Naturally you don't mention it when you nod weakly at the waiter's sudden offer of coffee. "Yes . . . ," you choke, ". . . black." There's a pressing tightness in your chest—maybe that one kitten is still alive and battling to get out just like Pinocchio inside the whale. Then without warning there's an ungodly rumbling in your stomach—hope it's not those cum oysters!

The waiter brings back the coffee—the special Deadly Grounds brand they serve here that calls itself "highly caffein- ated" and boasts right on the label, "Never sleep again!" You take a sip and can barely get out the words "Thank you." Your heart starts racing and you feel like a human tuning fork on diet pills. Jitters were never this ferocious. The waiter sees your dilated pupils and runs for a bottle of that Tylenol from the recalled lot supposedly poisoned by food terrorists. "Here," he says after explaining the pill's provenance, "they work better than Tums." "But they're lethal," you sputter in food paranoia. "Oh, pooh," he answers with a chuckle, "we give them out all the time at Gristle and nobody's died . . . yet. Here's the check now, though. Just in case."

You refuse the painkiller and grab for your wallet to pay the bill. Good God, it's $1,315 and you only had one beverage! With- out asking, they have added another huge "alternative tip." It's enough to make you faint. You hand over your credit card and attempt to stand up but you feel numb all over. A severe headache throbs through your brain. Suddenly the restaurant starts revolv- ing. How could this be? In the middle of New York City. Yet it is! Just like the cheesy Holiday Inn that opened in Baltimore in the mid-sixties and then closed soon after because it gave diners such a bumpy, seasicky, unsafe-feeling ride. You try to be like a ballet dancer and focus on one point in the 360-degree turn, but since there are no windows in Gristle, that's impossible.

The waiter pressures you to sign. We want you out of here before you collapse. Your eyeballs have started to cloud over so you can't see what you're signing, but who cares? You gotta blow this spinning joint while you can. You attempt to leave but it's like walking in a rolling barrel at an amusement park fun house. You grab on to the waiter, but we'll have none of that here at Gristle. "Am I having a heart attack?" you ask in real fear. "Probably," our staff has been trained to answer honestly. Suddenly another piercing bolt of pain shoots through your head right behind your eyes. You scream. "Quiet," the waiter hisses, used to these medical emergencies as he opens the front door and you, the onetime gourmet enthusiast, see the outside world spinning. You take aim and leap out, miraculously landing on your own two wobbly feet. Gristle's door slams behind you.

Fully fed, you stand alone on the sidewalk out front for a few seconds. People stare at you, the lucky one, recognizing your new appreciation of extreme food. Suddenly a massive stroke and a brain aneurysm hit at the exact same moment. You keel over, finally having eaten a meal to die for. Foodie heaven lies before you.

DELAYED

Y ou must travel. "The day you stop touring, your career is over," Elton John once told me, and he's right. All showbiz pros know you have to stay on the road your entire life. When Jay Leno was at the top of his career on the *Tonight* show, he still went out to Middle America on his night off and did stand-up. Bill Maher does, too. You can never blink. Someone is always waiting in the wings to seize your place. Debbie Harry took a little time off right after Blondie had their first hits and Madonna came along and stole her act. *Never* blink. Nobody said it was easy to be famous.

You should always have backup plans, too. No one career lasts forever. If you can't get a movie made, write a book; if the book doesn't sell, go on a speaking tour. Better yet, do all three and make 'em all sing. You gotta stay out there. Meet your public. Press flesh. Hold babies. Do selfies. Sign autographs. When you're out, you're at work, get used to it. "Sorry to interrupt," fans sometimes say, but they're not. They paid for that outfit you're wearing, didn't they? They have the right to have a photograph of you with them. You are never "off" in show business.

You shouldn't have a fear of flying; you should have a fear of *not* flying. If I'm not scheduled to go somewhere professionally at least once every couple of weeks, I get nervous. Like Joan Rivers in that revealing documentary about her, *Piece of Work*, I don't like to see a lot of white space on my upcoming calendar. You can't hate planes. All other travel is worse. Buses? For long-term travel? Out of the question. Even fancy ones like country-western stars use. They're fart wagons. Plain and simple. A traveling "Dutch oven." Know what that means? That's when you're in bed with your loved one and you fart and pull the covers up over both of you so that neither of you can escape the odor. That is giving someone a Dutch oven. All long-distance buses are Dutch ovens. Or horror rides. Haven't you read those terrifying news stories of low-cost bus trips where the driver is drunk or speeding and has to crash into parked cars to stop? Or seen those awful photos of injured bus passengers with their spilled-out and damaged luggage, sitting dazed and bruised on the breakdown lanes of the New Jersey Turnpike after bus accidents? My own niece was on one such ride when the whole bus caught on fire and many passengers had to watch their bags go up in flames.

Even the better, cheaper bus services have issues. I often ride the BoltBus with a friend from Baltimore to New York round-trip. It's cheap, direct, and relatively painless. The big drawback is the driver's regularity. Once, in the middle of our trip, the bus driver pulled over off the turnpike and without explanation moseyed to the bathroom in the back of the bus. We waited. Passengers started squirming, looking at one another in horror. Was the driver actually taking a shit? He was! We hear the rustling of toilet paper, even grunting. Grody! Gag me with a spoon! After what seemed like an eternity, he exited and slowly, nonchalantly walked back up the aisle to his driver's seat. Without shit shame! As if it were his God-given right to take a dump on our fully paid-up travel time. I wanted to bolt, all right. Right off the BoltBus!

I used to prefer Amtrak trains for interstate travel and still do with minor reservations (engineers who speed, fall asleep, and crash; tracks that are old or untested causing major derailments), but there are a few other problems, too. On the East Coast, the Acela is great (*and* expensive), but the regional ones in the rest of the country are not as luxurious. *Lots* of stops. Slow. Major delays. Bumpy as hell, too. Once I spilled a glass of water on this traveler I didn't know seated next to me. He was so outraged that he forced me to give him $11 in exact change to pay the dry-cleaning bill for his whole suit. And it was just water, not red wine! Taking a piss? Forget about it. The unisex bathrooms are politically correct, but all men know standing up and aiming a stream on a train is a Jackson Pollock painting in the making. Ladies, bring along cleaning supplies if you're even *thinking* of sitting down for urination relief.

Riding on a train is also not easy because they keep blaring out that recorded warning "If you see something, say something" every goddamn second on the public address system, and I *do* see something: another person, a tree outside the window, a suitcase. "Something!" I holler. "Something! Something! Something!" until the alarmed conductor feels like shooting me with a tranquilizer gun to shut me up.

Cars? Well, at least you can just throw your luggage in the trunk without hassle, but there are those goddamn tollbooths where somebody in your car has to come in contact with the hands of the person who collects the money inside who may be a lightning rod for the Ebola virus—just think of all the germs on the person's fingers from touching the giant unwashed public's mitts every other second. I don't care if they *are* wearing gloves, these attendants could still be infectious. I know about E-ZPasses, I wasn't born yesterday, but even though you don't have to drive in the regular germ-filled "cash" lanes, how about the mosquitoes that fly through the air of the E-ZPass magic lanes? Couldn't they have the Zika virus? One bite and your baby is E-Z-deformed.

That leaves airplanes, and the main goal of your entire life should be to be able to somehow fly first class one day. I don't feel guilty saying that—I flew coach promoting my films all over the world until I was in my forties. But now I can never go back even though, believe me, first class ain't what it used to be. In flights under two hours, you don't even get a meal, just a basket to pick through of "free" potato chips and half-rotten bananas for an extra $1,000 or so. It's still a *lot* better than coach.

I'm amazed that air travel works as well as it does. All those flights; "weather," as they irritatingly put it—meaning *bad* weather! Human error. Still shocking to me that this huge hunk of metal, sometimes as big as a football field, actually flies in the air over an ocean. It's a "pretty good invention" as a more down-to-earth friend said to me innocently after getting off a flight, and maybe we should all stop, think, and marvel at his obvious but truthful words. A damn good invention, indeed.

But the rituals before and after the plane takes off are enough to make you commit suicide. Oh, I forgot, that's the pilots' priority. Nobody talks anymore about that German flight that was crashed into the French Alps with a full load of passengers by a suicidal pilot who first locked the copilot out of the cockpit. "There were only five or six other flights that were thought to crash from suicidal pilots," some aviation official pooh-poohed. Five or six other ones?! Don't we have enough to worry about (flocks of birds being sucked into jet engines, lightning, drunken air traffic controllers, shoe bombers) besides pilots on a bummer? You can always see the crew boarding before you get on any flight, and I always try to check out the pilot's expression. Uh-oh, he looks depressed. "Hi, Captain!" I chirp happily, hoping to cheer him up. "Just remember," I say in a singsong voice, "a smile is just a frown turned upside down," before muttering under my breath, "Please don't kill us."

I like to get to the airport early. Very, very early. At least two hours before my domestic flight, three internationally. Just in case anything goes wrong, I'm first in line to get rebooked, but that doesn't happen much because I usually book the first flight out in the morning even though I often have to get up at 4:00 A.M. to get to the airport in time. The early-morning planes are always there, the crews can't be delayed, and thunderstorms usually seem to happen in late afternoon or early evening.

I'm the opposite of O.J. running through the airport in those old Hertz ads. Me, I like to mosey. I already have printed my boarding pass, not on my phone. It doesn't always work. I've *seen* people being sent back, so I'm one step ahead of the game. Even though the luggage-cart machine can rip you off and double-bill your credit card, I get one anyway because I don't know how much to tip the curbside redcaps and am paranoid they go through your checked luggage stealing your La Mer products.

I love that the Baltimore airport is one of the few that allows you to take your cart all the way through security to your gate despite the hassle of getting it through the X-ray machines. But the regular security checks are just as tedious as everywhere else, especially now that pre-check lines are often as long as coach's. I amuse myself, as all gay men do, by watching other males remove their coats and sweaters, which always offers a glimpse of stomach or ass as they struggle to disrobe. I am appalled every time I fly by the hideous way many travelers dress. No, you can't wear shorts. Do you think others want to sit next to your hairy, scaly legs? Workout clothes? P.U.! Who wants to smell your sweaty armpits? Bare feet! How disgusting! And pajamas? You have to be kidding me! Are you a baby? Does Daddy need to hold you? Get the fuck dressed! The only thing worse is traveling with a companion animal. If you are so mentally fragile that you can't leave home without some poor creature you've condemned to a lifetime of cuddling, then you shouldn't be allowed to mix freely in society. Don't go to the airport; check yourself into a mental institution.

I need to be first on the plane, first off. At the gate, I pick the seat nearest the counter and watch the airline staff's every expression to notice even the most remote possibility of a delay or cancellation so I can be first in line to rebook. A full half hour before the boarding time, I leap up and get in the priority line even if I am blocking the departing passengers who have just arrived on the plane I'll eventually get on. I want that overhead baggage space and I want it before you!

"Thank you for your patience," the agents at the gate always say when a flight is delayed, but even though I feel sorry for these employees, I let them know in no uncertain terms that "I don't have any, so please do not thank me for something I cannot offer." They look at me blankly but not with so much hostility as they do when I roll my eyes in derision at the other fliers who "need extra time to board," who get to go on in front of me even though I'm in first class. I know that sounds heartless but so many of these passengers are faking! Especially on Southwest, which has open seating once you get on board. "What's the matter with her?!" I always want to ask the flight attendant. "Can I see a doctor's note?" I'm not being coldhearted here; most of those "disabled" passengers are liars! I see them once they get on the Jetway—it's like Lourdes! They throw down their crutches and sprint toward the airline door, laughing and singing, "Yippee, aisle seats in the front of the plane!" Bastards.

I don't mind "any active member of the military" getting to go on board before me because they're sometimes brave, always cute, and I feel sorry for them; they might die and maybe they were in those military porn movies I used to collect. Some airlines have recently and correctly changed the rules, but others still allow "families with children in strollers" to also butt in line. And, of course, a baby is always screaming. I don't blame the kid. He or she must sense they're going to be sitting in coach. But why does the mother always say to me, "He's just tired . . ." "From what?" I always ask. "I mean, does he have a job?" "Well, no," the mother answers, recoiling. "Did he just unload a truck before you got to the airport?" I challenge, and by now this parent knows I mean business and curtails her stupid excuses. Do I say ignorant stuff to her like "Just whip that little fucker with a car aerial—that'll shut him up"? No, I do not.

I always feel like Elizabeth Taylor and Richard Burton in *The V.I.P.s* whenever I fly first-class internationally. But why is everybody ugly in first class? It's true. Watch aircraft passengers deplane anywhere in the world. The first ones off the plane are first-class, and Godfrey, rich people are dogs. You'll think they're wearing Halloween monster masks, but it's their real faces! As the seating goes farther back in coach, the "cute factor" rises. Why are poor planners hotter? Why is the middle-seat passenger better looking? Younger? Hipper? Just remember, the next time you're in the last row of coach, next to the germ-filled bathroom, you're way sexier than anyone in first class.

And believe me, up front on the plane, once the flight has taken off and you've eaten your free (Ha! One-way to Australia,

$13,605) caviar and drunk all your complimentary liquor, you have to *sleep* with your fellow passengers. In most airlines the sky bed lies flat and somebody is right next to you. Sure, you get real cotton sheets, feather pillows, adjustable reading lights, but no matter how glamorous you might feel, you quickly realize you're actually sharing the space of a standard double bed with a complete stranger. It's usually a man and he is *always* snoring. And drunk. I'm constantly paranoid that he will roll over in his sleep and accidentally goose me. Roman hands and Russian fingers. Watch it, buster!

Other airlines do first class differently but seating always seems ill-designed. Delta's flat bed pods at first look appealing, but when you lie down and slip your feet inside, you can't help but be reminded of what an MRI feels like. While Virgin calls first class "upper class" (is coach "lower class"?), they at least have single beds stacked at an angle that does afford privacy, even if you sometimes feel like an anchovy in a can or your own corpse in a fitting for your coffin. More embarrassing is British Airways' first-class seats that actually put passengers in a sitting-up "69" position forcing you to stare into your adjoining passenger's face, which seems inches away unless you put up a privacy "fan" that blocks the view between seats. But that's a complicated question of manners—who puts up the "fan" first? If you do, are you uppity? Unfriendly? Subtly saying no to the person sexually? Yes, I know it's absolutely ridiculous to ever bitch about first-class seating, so feel lucky if you're in coach. You don't have to reject anyone or, worse yet, *be* rejected.

Just the sight of a family of four sitting in first class is enough to make me see red. It took decades of my hustling before I could demand to be flown noncoach, and now I'll see a mom and dad on an international flight with two kids routinely nibbling filet mignon in flat bed seats in the front of the plane. How much could that cost the family? Forty thousand dollars? Obscene! Do these Richie Rich brats realize how privileged and pampered they are? All children should be in coach until they can afford to pay for the first-class tickets themselves or scam someone other than their parents to spring for it. You're twelve years old and want to fly first-class? Go on a quiz show and win the money. Enter some contest, become a model—just don't expect Mom and Dad to *ever* pay for first class. Or me to look at you in it.

I always get an aisle seat so if there's trouble, I can grab my Comme des Garçons hanging bag (don't think I'm leaving that behind!) and knock down old ladies to get off the plane before it explodes. I've seen the passengers in coach in the exit rows that offer more legroom who nod their heads affirmatively when asked if they will be able to assist opening the exit door in case of an emergency landing. Oh, sure! You'll be able to open this big heavy door when there's been no oxygen, the plane has plunged toward earth while people are screaming and praying, and that fireball has come down the aisle toward you, setting your face on fire.

Why is it before takeoff there's always *one* traveler who speaks *way* too loudly on his or her cell phone? You know the type—the asshole who can but won't lower his voice to go over the tedious orders with the salesman at the job. Ever hear of a stage whisper, buddy? You, too, lady.

There is no need for flight attendants to be funny or hip when they go through the safety announcements. "Fasten your seat belts" should not be comedy material. If you want a stand-up career, why in the hell did you become a flight attendant? I don't think "the unlikely event of a water landing" is one bit hilarious. You aren't, either. Same with those cooler-than-thou new safety videos that airlines use to try to get your attention by joking about oxygen masks—again, *not funny*!

I always cringe when I board an early-morning flight and the passenger next to me responds, "A Bloody Mary," when asked by the attendant what he'd like to drink before taking off. "Oh, you would, would you? You big alcoholic!" I always think to myself. Who could possibly want a drink at 6:30 A.M.? A nasty, belligerent bigmouthed drunk, that's who.

Once we take off, I like to shed weight. Since I still get more than a hundred magazines by subscription in the mail every month (though, believe me, this list is dwindling), I bring a shitload of them on board, rip off the mailing labels so fellow passengers or crooked flight attendants won't steal my identity, and then race through the periodicals catching up on articles that few seem to care about these days. I used to always offer copies of *Town & Country*, *BoxOffice*, and *Vogue* to fellow passengers nearby when I had finished reading them, but these days, they politely decline. Often, they react as if I just tried to give them a turd. So, just to be ornery, I take all the gay magazines, especially ones such as the U.K.'s *Attitude*, which features semi-lurid nude photos on the cover, and leave them mixed in with all the airline shopping publications in the pocket in the back of the seat in front of me.

Who would wipe their faces with those chemically treated cum-rag-like so-called hot towels? Echhh. I used to sniff them first to see if I could get high from the mysterious fumes, but these days I refuse to even touch those filthy washcloths that anyone could lace with poison.

No matter where you're sitting on the plane, the flight attendants plot how to get back at you if you have been the slightest bit rude to them before takeoff. I don't blame them. They know that it's impossible to hear a fart while in the air, so when they serve the beverage, that's when they get their revenge. As they bend over to put down the drink for the passenger across the aisle from you, they purposely fart in your face and you can't hear it. It's silent but deadly. Don't believe me? Ask any flight attendant. It's called crop dusting. Every one of them will tell you it's true.

I never watch the movies on board because they're usually the worst Hollywood fare made even more unwatchable because of airline censorship. I want to see airplane-crash movies while flying. I love them! Just think how exciting the flight would be if the original *Final Destination, Fearless, Alive, Sully*, even *United 93* suddenly came on-screen? I always secretly wondered what films were playing on the flights that crashed on 9/11. It took me years of sleuthing, but I finally found out that on all the United flights that day two films were scheduled to be shown, *A Knight's Tale* and *Dr. Dolittle 2*. What a chilling thought. Being on those hijacked planes was a terrible tragedy, but one good thing did happen to the passengers—the planes crashed *before* the movies could be seen. Just think how horrible it would have been to smash into the World Trade Center *while* watching *Dr. Dolittle 2*.

Sometimes I bring my own DVDs on board to watch on my computer, but it can be embarrassing. Suppose you're screening some recently restored cult classic with fairly explicit R-rated sex scenes. The passenger on the other side of the aisle, one row behind you, has a full view of your screen and doesn't know what movie you're watching. They just see tits and ass and think you're watching porno! Suppose you *did* whip out a DVD hard-core classic such as *Homo Alone* and popped it in. Could anybody do anything about fellatio scenes visible to all? Once I was on a flight and a Japanese man seated next to me was looking through a porn mag that featured giant close-ups of opened vaginas. He didn't seem one bit embarrassed so neither was I.

"Nice pussy," I wanted to say just to see his reaction, but you have to be careful what you say to people these days on an airplane.

I kind of like turbulence. It's so sudden, unexplained, almost funny. I always tell people who have never been in an earthquake that turbulence is exactly what it feels like, only you're in your house, not on an airplane. I've never been on a really scary flight, and it seems as if I'm on an airplane every day of my life. Not once has the oxygen mask dropped down. No one's ever screamed. Flight attendants have never panicked. My sister Kathy has a real fear of flying, and after years of our family telling her she was being silly, she finally booked a short vacation flight. Wouldn't you know it? All hell broke loose on board. Extreme turbulence. Trays flying, people screaming, crying, masks dropping—just like that hilarious scene in Bruce Wagner's *Still Holding*, where the same thing happens to a jittery flier. Kathy has not set foot on a plane since.

Elimination is always an issue on an airplane. Even in first class the bathrooms are still outhouses in the sky with toilet seats way too small for the average size of fat-ass Americans. Men know that when seated on one, their balls can hang into the top of a turd perched above a wad of used toilet paper in that blue water in the too-shallow bowl. Wiping in the skies is crowded and clumsy, and the toilet paper is as cheap as San Quentin's. Soiled paper towels are always sticking out of the trash bin, and, God, that repellent germ-filled sink usually undrained and stopped up with that chemically poisoned water that uninformed travelers innocently drink as if it were coming from the tap of their homes.

I can be a secret asshole on board and I'm ashamed. Really ashamed. I have given dirty looks to customers who dare to violate the sacred boundaries of the velvet curtain by coming into our cabin to use our first-class bathroom. Use your own coach shitter! Keep your low-fiber feces to yourself! Even though I'd do it myself if I were them, I have reported coach fliers who sneak their carry-on baggage into the first-class overhead bins when they board, knowing those in the back of the plane are already full. And what's that damn noise I hear midflight? Some illiterate playing a video game without wearing headphones! Do you think I can stand those annoying beeping sounds when I'm trying to read Rachel Cusk's new novel? And no laughing out loud at whatever bad unfunny Hollywood comedy they're showing either. Can't you see I'm writing a sonnet?

Landing is always exciting, especially when the window shades are still not raised by the selfish window-seat passenger next to you and you don't know the plane is that near the ground and for a second think you've crashed when the wheels hit the ground. Nothing shouts amateur, idiot, or rube more than applause from passengers for a routine landing. It's the pilot's *job* to land the plane, he's not doing you any favors. Pipe down, please.

These days, the pilots always seem to announce "an early arrival," which any experienced flier knows is bullshit. About five years ago, all the airlines appeared to conspire to pad the flying time of all their flights so they could improve their on-time arrival performance. How do I know? I'll tell you how. Anyone who has ever flown one route repeatedly—say Boston to Baltimore—knows how long the flight takes. Then suddenly the airlines announced these same flights took one half hour longer. They don't. It's padding, not early arrival. Plus, now because of the fake times, the arrival gate is still occupied by another plane and you wait on the runway anyway, late as ever. All because of the airlines' bald-faced lies.

I always have my seat belt undone before we actually get to

the gate so I can leap up the second I hear the *bing* to get my overhead luggage and be the first to barge off the plane. Isn't there a more modern way to let the Jetway agent know that our flight wasn't hijacked and everything's OK on board than a knock by the flight attendant followed by a thumbs-up through the door's window? I'm always hoping for a little drama, such as a sky marshal rushing on board to bust a drunken movie star who told a perfectly nice flight attendant to go fuck herself or a jonesing smoker who really *did* disconnect the smoke detector in the bathroom midflight. I excitedly wish that the handcuffed person I saw get on the plane with an undercover marshal before the flight took off makes a getaway and races off the plane to avoid extradition. What if just once a child traveling alone, humiliated by having to wear all that special identification around his neck for the whole flight, escaped the awaiting airline employee and ran wild with no adult supervision into the terminal, knocking over junk-food displays, snatching Cinnabons out of the paws of unhealthy eaters, and swiping boarding passes from the pockets of dozing, unalert passengers in the boarding areas?

It takes forever to get your checked luggage, doesn't it? Since I'm always first to arrive at the carousel, I stand there muttering to myself, "Is there a strike or something?" I kill time by checking all the e-mails that have overloaded my phone after its being shut off for hours. I don't have a Samsung Galaxy S7, but I'm amazed *all* phones don't catch on fire and explode when you are waiting for a bag. If my suitcase isn't the first one down the chute, I immediately think it's lost. I try to hope that the fidgeting child playing on the suddenly revolving carousel isn't trapped by his jacket and dragged away for a few seconds from his horrified parents, who haven't been watching him, but the one time I saw this happen, others had to turn their heads to hide their chuckles, too. And now, after that terrorist killed five people in the baggage-claim area of the Fort Lauderdale airport, we have to worry about that? I couldn't think of a more depressing place to die than at baggage claim. No wonder I'm annoyed when the person who's meeting me chirps, "How was the flight?" "Nothing happened," I answer. These days, that's all you can hope for.

Then there's the hotel. Judge it by the trash cans in the rooms. Plastic ones are never acceptable even in the bathroom, and liner bags are beneath flophouse contempt. Metal dustbins are OK if black, but should be in every room of your suite if you're lucky enough to be in one, not just near the desk. Leather waste baskets are the sign you have arrived—every time you throw a Kleenex into one in a hotel room, you'll know your career is going well. Take a cell phone picture of the trash can wherever you stay, and later, when you look through them, you'll realize dustbin progress is like the security you'll feel watching the slow growth of a mutual fund in the stock market.

The only good thing about a cheaper hotel room is that they always have a coffee machine so you can make your own without calling room service, where a single cup, with tax, tip, and outrageous delivery fee, can easily set you back $25. Of course, these machines have no written instructions and they're often hidden nowhere near a plug. Don't get me started on plugs. There should be a lot of them everywhere in the room to charge all your laptops, phones, and sex toys. Even old-school elegant hotels sometimes don't modernize their outlets, and you have to crawl under the bed or pull out the side tables and have lamps fall over on you just to plug something in.

Reading lights are also a big problem in today's hotel rooms. Some people like to read books! Ever heard of them, hotel decorators? Envelopes with the hotel's name should be in every desk drawer, but often are not. Where else are you supposed to keep business receipts for taxes? And is it too much to ask for a pad and pencil next to the phone? Just because no one has made a long-distance call on a hotel phone in the last decade doesn't mean you don't need somewhere to write down your brilliant ideas. I always want a bathtub in my room, too, not just a shower. Any bathtub that features a soap dispenser you have to stand up to reach is prison-like without the fun of naked inmates. So tawdry. So cheap. So no-tell motel.

All this complaining is exhausting, isn't it? Still, always put a DO NOT DISTURB sign on your door and never ask for "turn-down" service. Otherwise, just when you run down to the front desk at the last minute to get help in printing out your boarding pass for the next morning's flight, right-wing Jesus freaks who have infiltrated the hotel housekeeping staff will rush into your room and plant drugs in your suitcase to punish your non-believing sinful ass. Or worse yet, pedophile sex addicts, posing as minibar refillers, will get on your computer you left open and look up kiddie porn. That e-mail you get after checkout won't be a survey; it will be a warrant for your arrest from the Feds. Wake-up call? No thanks. The bedbugs will do that for you. It's not easy being a world traveler, is it? Count your blessings, though. Staying home all the time is a lot worse. Nighty-night.

OVEREXPOSED

I f you learn to speak in public, you will never be unemployed. Lobbyist, lawyer, comedian, revolutionary, disc jockey, all these careers are possible if you don't fear addressing a crowd. I've been doing my vaudeville act for more than forty years. First I just appeared before my films were shown at colleges, coming out looking like a hippie pimp and ranting about the brilliance of nudist-camp movies, Ingmar Bergman's vomit scenes, Ann-Margret in *Kitten with a Whip*, and obscure art-exploitation films such as *Nude in a White Car* and *The World's Greatest Sinner.*

Then once *Pink Flamingos* hit, I worked with Barbara Meyer at New Line Cinema's lecture bureau and expanded my intros into a speech of sorts; I guess it was the first "art-film stand-up comedy" act. Sometimes it was billed as *Shock Value*, then as *An Evening with John Waters* and, once I realized that sounded a little too stick-in-the-mud, *This Filthy World*. I later offered up alternative titles such as *Going to Extremes*; *Negative Role Model*; *Cinematic Immunity*; *Loose Cannon*; *Ad Nauseam*; *At Wit's End*; and *John Waters Is Certifiable*; but *This Filthy World* seemed to catch on the quickest.

Since I always want to go back and play the same city where

I did well, I constantly update my material and call it *This Filthy World—Filthier and Dirtier*. I know it is permissible to do your exact same act again and call it a command performance (the code word for laziness), but I feel that would be cheating. Some comedians swear their audiences like hearing the same jokes over and over and argue, "Why else do people buy comedy albums?" But I think my audience is too smart for that. The struggle to continue to add new jokes by the time I come back to your city never ends. "Filthier! Dirtier! Holier! More Political! Nude! In 3-D, Duo-Vision, and Completely Lip-synched!"

After I wrote an essay for the *National Lampoon* titled "Why I Love Christmas," I did a holiday show with just that name at the Castro Theatre in San Francisco and later expanded this ho-ho-ho act into *A John Waters Christmas*, which I've been touring with every December for the last fourteen years. Now averaging eighteen cities in twenty-two days, it's a big part of how I make my living. I have a big Christmas list—this way I know I can afford all the presents I have to buy. It's my part-time Christmas job and you should get one, too.

I also have a version of my show I do at horror conventions, called *This Filthy World—More Horrible and Dirtier*. For years I've been trying to steal Vincent Price's career, and while I haven't been successful, at least I've hijacked that early TV monster-movie host Zacherle's. "You don't make horror films," some gorehounds complain, but I just answer, "Ask my mother, she thinks they're all horrible!" Real movie stars (or my idea of them) appear at these horrorthons: Dyanne Thorne (*Ilsa, She Wolf of the S.S.*); all the survivors of the cast of *Texas Chainsaw Massacre*, including Edwin Neal, who played the hitchhiker with the birthmark on his face, my type if there ever was one. And oh my God, recently I got to meet the Amazing Kreskin himself, my idol. A man who tours more than any other living performer and knows his plane will be delayed before anybody else. He could read my mind all night for all I care because I have no secrets—my only thoughts were how much I loved the idea of his entire career. Kreskin, you are king!

I know it sounds redundant, but if I'm speaking at an LGBT film festival, I have a gay version, too: *This Filthy World—Gayer and Filthier.* Often do-good gay groups whose work I support such as GLAAD and Outfest offer to "honor" me, but I know that just means they want a free speech, so while I'm flattered, I tell them "my regular honorarium fee would have to be part of the honor." It usually works. I'm happy to be a good queer of the year but I'm gay-for-pay, all the way.

I can think of an angle to use on any speaking job. I've been known to exploit Valentine's Day and my birthday, too, by touring on these occasions. I can imagine a Mother's Day and New Year's Eve version, too. I'm shameless. Is *Groundhog Day—Filthier and Sunnier* far off? I play music festivals a lot. Yes, *This Filthy World* goes to Coachella, Bonnaroo, and Fun Fun Fun in Austin, and I love being the oldest person to come out in those big tents with all the young kids screaming and do my rock-and-roll comedy routine. There's now the John Waters Summer Camp every September in Kent, Connecticut, which lasts a whole weekend and has to be experienced to be believed. Guest counselors like Mink Stole and Traci Lords join me and the truly gonzo fans in what we like to call "Jonestown with a Happy Ending."

I've played everywhere. At a *Wizard of Oz* celebration in Chicago, I described my dream sequel of Dorothy returning to Kansas, and when she can't stop ranting about her trip to Oz, Auntie Em loses patience after months of telling Dorothy, "It was just a dream," and Uncle Henry puts his foot down and forces his defiant niece to see a psychiatrist, who gives her shock therapy, but even that doesn't cure Dorothy of her yearning to return to the magical land. She tries LSD, but these hallucinations are not the same as the poppies of Oz. Mushrooms, too, but there's no great and powerful anything much less a wizard. Finally she sniffs poppers and it works! She's back in Oz. The Scarecrow is old but still brilliant, the Tin Man is a yoga instructor, and the Cowardly Lion is now a drag queen named Roara. They give her the Wicked Witch's magic broomstick and Dorothy flies back to Kansas, starts cross-dressing as Margaret Hamilton, and opens a gay bar called the Yellow Brick Load.

I also spoke at "William Burroughs' 100th Birthday Party" in Lawrence, Kansas, and have been the keynote speaker at the national Public Library Association convention (librarians are always smart, a little nuts, and know how to party), art events (where once I was falsely accused in the press of encouraging my fans to vandalize Donald Judd's sculptures in Marfa, Texas), and a gathering of every mayor in the United States that was hosted in Baltimore by our mayor at the time, Stephanie Rawlings-Blake. Since she had no idea what I was going to say, I have to give her credit for her nerve. Who books an act called *This Filthy World* for a group of politicians in the town she governs? I was a little nervous, but the mayor seemed to laugh even when I suggested we have a "win a date with Marion Barry" contest and then followed up by telling them their own children were sexting just as Anthony Weiner had been accused of a few days before. "I thought Richard Pryor was crazy," one elderly African American mayor quipped to me as I finished my show and left the stage. Now *that's* what I call a good review.

Sometimes I feel like a low-rent Oscar Wilde touring the coal-mining towns of America as he did in the 1880s. I've performed in nightclubs all over the U.S.A. and been in the classiest dressing rooms to the worst, but the one I remember most was at the Ice Palace on Fire Island, the last place Carol Channing did her act before retiring. It was hot as hell inside, no AC, and on the floor was a left-behind size 15 drag queen high-heeled shoe—just one of them. Whimsical, if you ask me.

I'm proud to say I've sold out the Royal Festival Hall in London and the Sydney Opera House in Australia, too. *This Filthy World* has traveled to Sweden, Belgium, Denmark, Finland, New Zealand, Spain, Austria, Argentina, Italy, and France, and to even more foreign lands such as Las Vegas, where I shared a bill with the headbanger metal band Slipknot at *Fangoria*'s "Trinity of Terror" event on Halloween night. The most radical booking of all? My dad's Rotary Club in Baltimore. When the meeting began with the members leaping to their feet and bursting into the Rotary "Hello Song" ("Hello! Hello! Hello! What a wonderful word *hello*!"), I was actually scared. Was this some voodoo white people chant? Were they going to cook and eat me alive? "Crossover" was never this complete.

I remember when I was young seeing the great street tabloid photographer-turned-artist Weegee give a talk. Warhol, too, appearing onstage with his superstar Viva. He'd come out at a college, flashing his camera at the audience as Viva just motor-mouthed whatever came into her mind, and the audience loved it. They felt Andy's fame oozing out and blessing their own wish for celebrity. Andy, Viva, and Weegee inspired me.

I used to use opening acts and I've had some great ones: Wanda Jackson, Elvis Perkins, Jonathan Richman, Matthew Gray Gubler (hosting, dressed as me), and Peaches, the female performance artist (not Peaches Christ, the talented producer, movie director, and drag queen friend of mine). I wish I could have Elena Ferrante impersonators or even Levi Johnston himself, who could finally come out and make good on his promise to show his dick while I sing "The Star-Spangled Banner" in pig latin.

But these days it's just me onstage with my big mouth. I never explain my jokes. Sure, not everyone gets a Marguerite Duras or Michel Houellebecq gag or a Bruno Dumont reference, but so what? Look it up when you get home. I talk fast, too. I've had simultaneous translators just give up midshow in foreign countries. And signing for the deaf? Except for the one in San Francisco where she got an ovation of her own for acting out the sex parts so hilariously, usually the signers are so mortified by what they have to mime they panic and run off the stage in embarrassment.

If you don't get the last joke I cracked, it doesn't matter, I'm on to the next one. Seventy minutes of scripted, memorized material. *If* I even remember it all. Every night (and I always forget something different each show) it's exactly the same once I "freeze" in all the new stuff. I don't use any notes. If I had them in my pocket for safety, I'd probably peek. I don't take my glasses out with me onstage either so I couldn't read them even if they were there. The amount of dough the venues charge to see me ain't cheap so I figure the customer expects me to know my lines just as if I were in a Broadway play. Of course, when it's a one-man show, like mine, there's no other actor to whisper you a cue. You're working a high-wire act without a net.

That's why I have to be in my dressing room for forty-five minutes before I go on. I learned early *never* to have even one glass of wine beforehand. Your timing is completely thrown off if you do. I'm a Method speaker. I have to get in the zone. Click in my mental outline of abbreviated dialogue-slash-words that cues my memory of the entire script. Even if I'm in the middle of the tour and have been doing the show nightly for weeks, I *still* have to have my private time before I step onstage. And every night I think, "Suppose I can't remember it? What then?"

I feel sorry for rock-and-roll bands. They have to split the fee between all the members and the road crew. That's a lot of people. Me? I just tour by myself. Sure, the agent or promoter gets a percentage, but I get all the rest: 50 percent on signing contract, 50 percent day of the show. Every single detail of my tour is completely worked out by my expert team (Ian Brennan, Susan Allenback, Trish Schweers, Jen Berg, Toffer Christensen, and Barbara Meyer) before I even leave home, so usually the dates run pretty smoothly. Except for the three times I got ripped off: once by the Georgetown Film Festival in 2002, later by the Shock Pop Comic Con in Fort Lauderdale, Florida, and most recently by Go Cedar Rapids in Iowa. I'll get you one day, my pretties.

I'm no Grace Jones—I have the simplest rider in the world. The fee. First-class airfare and hotels. Per diem ("walking around money" is something you should always ask for). Cars to and from home and the venue. A cordless microphone. A small stool onstage off to the right where I keep my timer (why I still use one I don't know—the running time of my act is exactly the same after I test it on the first night) and the props I throw into the audience (Maybelline Velvet Black eyeliner pencils and travel-size packages of anal-bleach gel).

My dressing room demands for the theater are also non-divaesque. No all-green M&M's for me. Just Evian water, hangers, Kleenex, some healthy snacks, and for after the show a bottle of wine and some beer for my backstage guests. I like to be taken to the stage area a few minutes before I go on so I can feel the buzz of the crowd, and I don't like to talk to anybody there because I'm all prepared and revved up. I need a strong voice-of-God announcer offstage ready to warn the audience that there is "no videotaping, audio taping, or photography of any kind permitted during the performance," because if my act is on YouTube, who will ever pay to come see me? I like a *short* intro, please; I'll be the one to get the first laugh, not some sponsor. "Ladies and gentlemen, John Waters" works just fine.

I've never canceled a date. It's true what they say in showbiz— yes, the show must go on. I've done my act with a bad cold, a toothache, an ear infection, even with the raging flu. Telling jokes with snot pouring from your nose is tricky to pull off onstage, but you learn to time the handkerchief *and* the wiping to the laughter in between.

If your health issues get serious, you have to figure a way to go see the doctors *in between* showtimes. Once in the middle of my Christmas tour I discovered I had a kidney stone. It's so humiliating to be recognized in some doctor's waiting room in a strange city, yet if you hadn't been at all famous, you wouldn't have gotten your initial "emergency" appointment in the first place. "Hey, are you John Waters?" a fellow sick person yells, and I sink down in my seat, filling out insurance forms. Alerted but confused, another waiting patient bellows out for the world to hear right in front of you, "Who's John Waters?" I try then to keep a low profile by mumbling politely, "Oh, I made the first *Hairspray* movie." Then another wiseacre yells out, "Yeah, but what's the *matter* with you?" "Leprosy," I want to answer, but rather than up the ante, I just say, "A touch of the flu," and silently pray for the words I'm dying to hear: "The doctor will see you now."

The kidney stone finally struck the day *after* I completed the eighteen-city Christmas tour. I was home at least. The worst pain I have ever experienced. Screaming out loud. Scaring people around me. Rushed to the emergency room. Suppose

I had been onstage? A kidney stone attack hits almost instantly. What if I had been in an airport? Or worse yet—*on* a plane?!

Nobody would have known about my ordeal if it hadn't happened on December 23, the date that year of my annual Christmas party in my Baltimore house. I was in the hospital, the caterers had already delivered the food, and it was too late to call the two hundred invited guests to cancel. "Have the festivities without me," I told my assistants, and they did. Everybody showed up, heard the news, and realized the mood would be a little different without the host, but still many stayed until the wee hours. Maybe not being at your own party is the most chic thing you can do. I recommend it highly.

One of the guests blabbed to the press, though. The next day, after I had been released from the hospital with a stent and was at home, a local reporter who lived in my neighborhood was snooping around my house and caught a friend outside who was emptying the sad bucket of the previous night's party's cigarette butts. "So is he OK? What's the story?" the reporter wanted to know. My friend mumbled the noncommittal but undramatic response "He's fine." After hearing the reporter's reply that he was going to run the "missing my own party because I was in the hospital" story whether I commented or not, I hurriedly sent him an e-mail hoping to kill the piece, saying that it was no big deal and I was already home and feeling better.

His article came out online, the *Baltimore Sun* picked it up, and then I guess it was a slow news day because Page Six of the *New York Post* ran it and this Christmas stop-the-presses article went viral—and then a tabloid in London featured it and finally it spread internationally. My agent in L.A. actually heard I had died! So ludicrous. So overblown. Most of the two hundred guests began calling to see if I was OK, as did business associates and other press, and while they meant well and I appreciated their concern, my office was closed for the holidays, so no one but me could answer the phone, and it became a giant pain in the ass to go along with the pain in my penis. But I was fine. I had only been in the hospital for one night!

The next day George Michael died. Then Carrie Fisher. And, yes, death does come in threes—Debbie Reynolds croaked, too. Somehow my hospitalization got dragged back in and linked to these deaths. My whole nonstory got a second wave of hype. "Aren't you glad *he* didn't die?" one nice gay publication asked its readers. Aggggghhhhhh!

Your personal life never gets you out of a performance. Even if someone close to you *does* die, your contract doesn't excuse you from showing up. Even if it's family. When my younger brother, Steve, tragically passed away after complications from a brain aneurysm, I left the burial following the funeral ceremony a little early to catch a plane for the first night of my Christmas tour. From the grave to the airport directly to the stage without even checking into the hotel. Nobody knew. I did the show. Another time, I left for a German tour knowing my mother was about to die. She was in hospice, we had said our goodbyes, and the doctors had told me and my sisters that Mom would never regain consciousness. The show must go on and I think my mother would have understood.

Midway through the German tour, I got word my mom had died and I didn't tell a soul. How do you do a comedy show after informing the audience your mother just died? You don't. I went out and did the act before a sold-out audience and nobody was the wiser. The night I got the news I even attended a party Wolfgang Tillmans threw for me at his amazing flat in Berlin. He had gone to a lot of trouble and it was too late for him to cancel, so who was I to ruin his good intentions? I didn't mention anything to him until it was time for me to leave, a little too early since the party was still in full swing. "Don't say anything," I whispered to him at the door, "but my mom died today. Thank you so much for this lovely party." He looked stupefied. But I did the right thing. I finished my tour and made it home in time to do the eulogy at Mom's funeral. Everybody rested in peace. Including the tour manager.

The venue *can* cancel *you*, however. Too few ticket sales (this only happened once in my whole life) and weather issues. But long ago I figured out if you somehow show up, they have to pay you. Once I was with one of my best promoters, Ian Brennan, and we had just done my Christmas show in Toronto, and the next day we were supposed to do the same thing in Montreal. But the worst blizzard ever to hit Canada struck and all the flights were canceled. We took the train. In a full whiteout. Often the train had to stop while the railroad workers unfroze the switches in the tracks. By the time we somehow made it to Montreal, it was illegal to even be out. Full emergency curfew. "We're here!" we told the club. The show must go on!

The venue couldn't even find us a way to be picked up at the train station, but two crazy female fans took over and showed up with a car. We slipped, slid, and skidded our way to finding a hotel (our original one had closed). By showtime it was a complete disaster outside. Snowdrifts. High winds. A winter horrorland. But our trusty fearless punk rock drivers somehow got us to the club, and I was shocked to see people actually showed up! Not as many as would have on a regular night, but still a good crowd. I did the show, maybe a hastily rewritten blizzard version, and the club, God bless their soul, had no choice but to pay us. It took days for us to get out of town afterward, but so what? I had fulfilled my contract, and again, the you-know-what went on.

There are some gigs I won't do. Parades. No thanks; me on a float is something you'll never see. I've turned down *Dancing with the Stars* twice, the first time for a lot of money, the second time way less. Oddly enough, my mother was appalled when I got the offer. "You do *Dancing with the Stars* and I'll never speak to you again," she joked. Why, I don't really know. She watched it when Ricki Lake was on *and* my mom loved to dance. *Hollywood Squares* also was interested in having me on, but I felt I was a little too close to Paul Lynde as it was. I'd never know the answer on *Celebrity Jeopardy!* because I don't do crossword puzzles, but my mom would have wished they *had* asked me. She was always impressed when my name was an answer on *Jeopardy!* To her, that proved my fame way more than a *New York Times* profile.

Sometimes today, when I'm doing shows, when I come out I get a standing ovation because I'm old. A standing ovation *after* they hear what you have to say is the only one that counts. Once I'm ranting onstage, it's almost as if another person is doing the show. After a few nights in a row, I can step out of myself and think about where to get my dry cleaning done, airport pickup times, even arguments I need to have with a boyfriend—and not miss a line or fuck up my timing. I sense when I've skipped something, and my mind races to remember what, as I'm continuing the monologue. Once you remember what you left out, you do the bit without trouble—the hard part is remembering where you left off and how to get back *in* the narrative order as seamlessly as possible. It's kind of like entering a jump-rope contest midjump without missing a rotation and still joining in on the chant.

I almost never get hecklers. With the spotlight on you, you can't see the audience when you come out except for maybe the first two rows. Often I don't know how big the theater is or the size of the crowd until I hear the first applause. The few problems I've had with audience members have been because they are *too* enthusiastic, often drunk in the first few rows because they got there too early. They hoot and holler when you're trying to set up the first few jokes and laugh obnoxiously when there's not even a punch line yet. They mean well, but the rest of the audience seems pleased when they pass out, usually about fifteen minutes into the show.

Once you're done with the monologue, the easy part comes: twenty minutes onstage for questions and answers. I think, by now, I've heard all the questions, but once in a while I can still be surprised: "Mr. Waters, I'm a straight guy and I've never kissed a man. Can I come up onstage and give you a kiss on the lips?" "Well, of course," I answered—he was cute and bold, so why not? Another woman threw me by telling the crowd that her father told her he "almost went home with you from a bar in Baltimore." Almost? What happened to that "Everybody looks good at last call" cliché? "Tell him hi," I said, thinking fast on my feet. Some questions demand comic improvised answers. "Did you ever blow Tex Watson?" one ticket buyer asked. "No," I replied. "Next question." "Have you ever eaten pussy?" another inquiring mind wanted to know. "Yes, but I don't know how successful I was at it," I responded truthfully. "If you had to have sex with one of the presidential candidates, who would it be?" a politico wondered right before the presidential election of 2016. "Oh, boy," I thought, "I better be careful!" Martin O'Malley, the onetime governor of Maryland, was by far the best looking of all the ones running, and I knew him, too, but I feared some smart-ass journalist who might be in the audience would use it in a pull quote—"John Waters wanted to have sex with Martin O'Malley"—so I was politically incorrect and answered, "I'd come *in* and go for Hillary." Leaving the stage,

I'm always confused and have no memory of where I am or the location of the dressing room I was just in ninety minutes ago. The backstage staff has been warned of this problem and gently leads me back to reality.

I immediately brush my teeth because "monologue breath" can be a nasty problem in this line of work. Then my backstage guests are admitted, but I don't have long to chitchat because usually I have to do a meet and greet after the show (you always get sick later from close contact with "huggers"). Originally started by country-western stars, this routine is becoming quite commonplace today for all traveling entertainers, even though Chris Isaak, who also tours, told me he had a manager once who said, "If you're *really* famous, you never let them meet you." "Does Madonna do meet and greets?" this realist asked. "Well, no," admitted Chris. "But Dolly Parton does!" I countered. I'd much rather be Dolly Parton than Madonna, wouldn't you?

I sell books after the show, too. Once, when I scolded a girl for bending the paperback cover back far enough to break the spine when she asked for an autograph on the title page, she snapped back, "I bought the book, so I can do anything I want with it!" In other words, take your library-science bullshit and shove it, Mr. Know-It-All.

I've signed asses, dicks, tits, stomachs, backs, even tongues. For a while there I had a run of transgender men asking me to autograph their mastectomy scars. When the fans tell me they want to get my signature tattooed on their body, I used to try to talk them out of it, but now I just offer the advice that I'll pose for the photo op of signing their body, but in reality I should sign a plain piece of white paper so I can do it neatly and then the tattoo artist can put it in the computer and make it any size when he inks it on. The smart ones do so.

At a CD release party for my *Date with John Waters* at Amoeba Records in San Francisco, I saw a male fan way back in the long line waiting patiently, totally nude. When it was finally his turn, he said he was straight but asked, "Could I sit on your lap" for a picture he wanted to "use as a Christmas card for my mother?" I happily obliged.

In another city I could see this angry girl waiting in line so I knew something would be up. When she finally got her turn, she snarled, "Will you sign *any*thing?" "Sure," I said. She reached under her skirt and pulled out of her vagina a bloody tampon and splatted it down on the autograph table. I signed it. She bought the book, didn't she?

I never encourage this kind of behavior, but recently this "period stalker" got topped in meet-and-greet shock value as I signed and posed happily at last year's John Waters Summer Camp. A girl in line got to me and asked if for the photo op she could actually eat dog shit in front of me and the rest of those waiting. I was momentarily stunned, but what the hell—she had it all ready in a deli tray. Knock yourself out. She did so, but I turned my head and didn't look.

For some reason, lately, men have been asking women to marry them in front of me. The couple waits in line, and when it's their turn, the guy gets down on one knee, pulls out a ring box, and asks the unsuspecting girl for her hand in marriage. The crowd cheers. The girl always says yes. Sometimes I want to warn her that her new fiancé looks gay to me, but I keep my mouth shut.

Another couple waited patiently so they could be last in line and, once they got up to me, whipped out a marriage license and, since they had read I was an ordained minister in the Universal Life Church, asked me to marry them right then and there. I did so. Just recently I played that same city without remembering this and they surprised me by showing up still married. I don't know why I was surprised. Of the seventeen couples I've married, only one has gotten divorced so far. The Pope of Trash has a better record than any of the popes in Rome. My blessings work. Theirs often do not.

My fans are so great; they're smart, well-read, and know how to dress. I could be in Paris, Arkansas, or Boise, Idaho, and they all look the same—cool and sexy. They get their roots done for me, too! The Internet, Netflix, and social media have been quite democratic in the hipster eradication of local color. Everybody everywhere in the world is bohemian chic these days—at least the ones that come to see me. Nowadays you don't have to leave where you were born. Actually, you *shouldn't* leave. Stay where you are and make it better! There's no new youth movement happening in New York or L.A. that you are missing. It's too expensive there for any revolutionary ideas to even breathe.

The fans give me great presents, too, alarming portraits of me that they have painted, highly collectible paperback books with titles such as *From Here to Maternity*, *Those Hollywood Homos*, and, my favorite one of them all, *Lights Out, Little Hustler*. A really edgy lesbian once gave me the "packer" she was wearing in her jeans—that's a limp plastic penis that some girls "stuff" to give a subtle suggestion of a "package." It was still warm. I took it back to the hotel room but realized I couldn't take this through airport security! What gay man travels with a limp-dick dildo?

A few tips for fans. On tour, I can't carry anything with me. I already fight with airline officials on baggage-weight restrictions every time I check in. Do you really think I can carry that heavy sculpture you are trying to give me? I mean, I love some of the artwork you do, but don't bring any of it to the show, mail all items to Atomic Books in Baltimore—I *will* get them.

And don't answer, "Me," when I ask, "Who would you like the book personalized to?" "Me"? How am I supposed to know your name? Do I look like Kreskin? If you are awaiting my flight at an airport with a whole stack of stolen-from-the-Internet, no-photographer-credit-given pictures of me you expect me to sign so you can sell them on eBay the next day, forget it. I used to believe you when you said you wouldn't, but as soon as you say you don't want them personalized, I know you are lying. Get a job!

I get great fan mail and I actually do read it. Quickly. Most of it *very* quickly unless your letter grabs me in the first few sentences. No scary, tiny handwriting. Keep it short. No form letters for your autograph collection or pleas to back your project. You can send your scripts or DVDs or books, but my lawyer won't let me watch or read any of them because you might sue me falsely for stealing your material.

I'll sign and send back my own books and head shots if you enclose them in properly addressed and stamped return envelopes. If you don't pack them well and include that in the weight for postage, your stuff will come back damaged or not at all. I don't sign multiple copies of film stills, pirated items (that means you, Etsy!), or blank file cards, and even though I enjoy some of them, I don't answer letters from prisoners (well . . . so far I haven't).

But sometimes fan letters are so great that I feel bigger than an awful Oprah, prouder than a ghoulish Gandhi. Here's my favorite one—from a female:

> Dear Mr. Waters,
>
> You saved my life and I thank you. A couple years ago I saw your Christmas show in _____. You did a bit on rim jobs which prompted me to more consistently attend to my

asshole at shower-time. So, I found a small lump. Over a few months the lump became bigger and bigger.

Turns out it was anal cancer. I was treated last fall, just had my 3rd set of clear scans and do not have scans scheduled for another year.

I want to thank you for sharing that bit which saved my life.

If I can ever do anything for you, please let me know.

Fondly,

———————————

Let me set you straight. Whatever you might have heard, there is absolutely no downside to being famous. None at all.

FLASHBACK

Maybe it's time to take LSD again. Why not go back to our bad-boy and bad-girl roots and take another psychedelic inner journey? An LSD trip is not something most seventy-year-olds would consider, but maybe they should. Old age sometimes needs the cobwebs shaken out, and what better spring cleaning of the psyche than a fresh dose of pure acid? I hitchhiked across the country so I could write about that adventure in my last book—isn't this similar? A stunt to prove to myself (and others) that I'm still open to new ideas, not stuck in my privileged life? Why not celebrate irresponsible risk at my age? Now, when I'm even older and can't remember stuff, I'll have the perfect excuse. It's no senior moment—I took acid at seventy years old!

I've had a pretty good history with drugs. I think I've tried almost every one and mostly had good experiences with each. I never was a drug addict but I certainly *was* a drug enthusiast. I had always thought that "I'd *never* take drugs," but as soon as they were offered, I jumped at the chance. Gold hash came first for me, in 1964, probably smuggled into the port city of Baltimore by merchant marines, who always seemed cute and criminally friendly. Marijuana was next in line. I smoked it every day for the next seven years. As soon as I heard about LSD, I knew this was a drug for me and couldn't wait to get my hands on some. Then speed reared its ugly head (what a great drug for seeing three or four movies a day), black beauties being my favorite diet pill. As soon as heroin was offered to me, I had to try it (by needle of course) but luckily I hated the high. Sitting around, nodding, and puking was just not my idea of a good time.

Let's see, I sniffed glue (so low-rent, but it does work in a chemically harsh and ugly way), huffed Carbona on a rag and felt like a crazy dishcloth, inhaled nitrous oxide (just to talk in a funny voice), smoked bananas (it doesn't work), and ate (after boiling off the poisons) the contents of package after package of morning-glory seeds (Heavenly Blue, Pearly Gates, and Flying Saucers were the only brands that delivered). Afterward you would puke and puke for hours, but then suddenly you'd go into a strong and cheap psychedelic state—second-class acid for the proletariat. I even ate belladonna leaves—yeah, I know they're poison, but what the hell. I was fearless in my search for the outer limits of sanity and I sure found them with this drug. Never again.

I loved poppers (especially the "real" kind of amyl nitrite that you used to be able to buy nonprescription in some drugstores—the kind you snapped and then inhaled) and later the liquids you sniffed from bottles for both fun (even on roller coasters) and sex (yes, it *does* make it more intense). Much later in life I created a large sculpture of a bottle of poppers spilled out on the gallery floor. The owner of the Rush company liked my using his brand name in an art exhibition so much that he sent me a lifetime supply, which I'm embarrassed to admit I'm now out of. I felt bad when I later read that this same popper executive had committed suicide. I hope not from a Rush OD!

Even in "the winter of my years," I used to throw an annual "popper party" in the middle of the Provincetown Film Festival, where I host screenings and interview our annual Filmmaker on the Edge directorial winner. I finally had to stop this downscale gala after *The Boston Globe* wrote about the party, outing me as the popper Perle Mesta, and then in a scene right out of the movie *Mother!* the whole town crashed the event. But, ah, the memories! I have seen Academy Award–winning directors, actors, cinematographers, even big-time film critics, all doing poppers (often for the first time) inside my beach apartment. One year, a younger, cute, but somewhat naive heterosexual man *drank* them, not knowing you're only supposed to sniff out of the bottle, not guzzle from it. After seeing this poor guest gagging and vainly trying to blot his tongue, another Rush enthusiast shared a worse popper story with me. A friend of his, a heterosexual woman, told him she had heard gay men used poppers to relax for anal sex and she'd like to try some for the same reason. He bought her a bottle and gave it to her thinking she knew how to use them. But she didn't. She poured them up her ass! This is why we need popper education in public schools today. So your children . . . our children know how to use poppers correctly *and* responsibly.

Like everybody I know of a certain age, I loved Quaaludes in the seventies but was confused when some of Bill Cosby's victims later claimed he gave them the same pills. I gave people Quaaludes all the time and others gave them to me. None of us woke up the next morning, felt our asshole, and hollered in confusion, "Ow!" And we drank with them, too! I thought he gave them roofies (something I never tried) or maybe that drug Michael Jackson liked that made him so sleepy he felt happy-dead until he really was dead.

I liked cocaine but not as much as everybody else did in the eighties. I only bought it a few times but often snorted it when it was offered to me at parties. The problem for me was, I loved the high but it only seemed to last ten minutes, and then you had to do more and then you crashed for a month. I smoked cocaine once so I guess I've done crack, too, but if I liked it I was too high to remember.

Once, at a dinner party in San Francisco, I joined the other guests in "stuffing" opium up my ass in the bathroom between courses, but this high was one of the last I tried. And I guess because of my mother's strict upbringing on table manners, I recoiled at the very idea of "stuffing" itself. Magic mushrooms I ate twice, but both times they made me slightly paranoid so I quit them. Let's see, I never took ecstasy because who wants to love everybody (what a terrible high that sounds like), but I did take MDA in the seventies and I think they're pretty close. I only tried angel dust once and I hated it, but I was already prejudiced against it because it not only led to David Lochary's death but also to my wonderful friend David Spencer's. I'm still mad at him for dying. I'd come home to his San Francisco apartment where I crashed for months in the early seventies and see him crawling around on the floor crying, high from angel dust. "*This* is high?" I'd think. No thanks!

I guess I stopped taking drugs around the time of "Molly" or "Tina" or "G" because it seemed bad biker at first and then sloppy gay. I saw that video of Miley Cyrus on salvia, so I'll pass on that drug, too. "Meow meow" seemed interesting (I love the name) until I read about that kid who ripped off one of his testicles while high on it ("Then what?" I wondered. I hate when they tease me with narrative). Besides, meow meow's real chemical name is mephedrone, and how embarrassing to be addicted to that. You'd go down to the "bottom" to cop and beg other junkies, "Got any mephedrone?" And they'd think you were just stupid. "It's *methadone*," they'd correct you condescendingly. "No," you'd have to explain, "it's mephedrone . . . Help me . . . help me . . . *mephe*drone . . . meow meow . . ."

Bath salts I've never even considered. I saw the news reports about the guy who bit off the other guy's face in Florida ("It's so unlike him," his girlfriend supposedly said. I hope so!), and then another cannibal case happened in Baltimore. It seemed it was always a younger man on bath salts biting off the face of an older gentleman. Was this sexual? A new way to dominate? Was Jeffrey Dahmer on bath salts? Was he the ultimate "top"? I didn't want to find out.

I did love the idea of "gravel," or "flakka" as it was also called on the street. "Want to come over and do some gravel?" has a sexy ring to it, but when I learned this drug (which only costs $5) keeps you high for three days with feelings of extreme power *and* paranoia (oh, great) and was especially popular with the homeless, I decided maybe I'd take a rain check. One girl had been arrested running down the street nude, covered in blood, and babbling about Satan. "That's *Carrie*," I wanted to tell her, clarifying her cinematic references, but I'm not sure she would have cared. Another teenager on flakka impaled his buttocks on a metal fence. I mean that's just flakka wakka. Plus a third gravel enthusiast was caught fucking a tree. Well, this I understand. Aren't trees nature's very own porn? Just look at those filthy little bark things all covered with vaginal and anal openings. I feel like fucking a tree myself. Even when I'm sober.

But LSD again? I remember how long it lasts! I have back problems already; what will they feel like now after a senior-citizen acid trip? I have a lot to lose these days, too. My filth empire. My friends. My mental health. My relationship. LSD may have given me confidence then, but do I need greater self-worth now? That might make me completely insufferable. I exhaust myself as it is.

Suppose I go crazy like Diane Linkletter? Would that be poetic justice after I made fun of her death from a supposed bad LSD trip that resulted in her suicidal leap from her Los Angeles apartment window in 1969? Would my having a nervous breakdown on LSD in my dotage be a karma kickback for my early underground short film *The Diane Linkletter Story* ("The Girl . . . The Tragedy . . . The Gap"), starring Divine as Diane, which I directed and premiered at a Baltimore college auditorium around the same day as her funeral? Would God punish me for starting a short-lived trend of drag queen reenactments of politically charged events? I didn't make the Cockettes-starring vehicle *Tricia's Wedding*, which premiered at the exact day and hour of Nixon's daughter's real wedding, but I'm not sure this film would have happened without *Diane*'s lead.

Even though *The Diane Linkletter Story* has been out of distribution for decades, the coincidences have continued. We didn't hate Diane Linkletter, we hated her father, the Republican talk show host who was a buddy of Nixon's and Billy Graham's and tried to blame Timothy Leary for his daughter's death, even though the autopsy revealed she was *not* on LSD when she jumped (at 10:00 A.M. after reading the *Story of O*!). She wasn't on anything—no booze or drugs were found in her system—so Linkletter changed his story and claimed she had a "flashback." For years he targeted Leary. "If I ever get my hands on him, I'll kill him," he ranted, and decades later, when Leary was ill, Art (around the same time he was cracking AIDS jokes) boasted he was "glad Leary is crippled." We always wished Diane had run off with us.

Mr. Linkletter had worse taste than I did concerning his daughter's death. One month after her suicide, he dusted off some old spoken-word recordings he had done with Diane about her having a bad trip and turned them into a kind of "answer" novelty record, where he, in his own voice, begged her to "come home," and released it as a two-sided single, "We Love You, Call Collect" backed with "Dear Mom and Dad." To listen to it is to marvel at a new level of insensitivity, topped only when Joan Rivers and her daughter, Melissa, played themselves in a TV movie about the suicide of Edgar, Joan's husband and Melissa's father. "I've met a lot of weirdos," Diane argues back to her dad, "but I've found out how to tell the beautiful people from the phonies." "Come back," Art begs from the other side of the grave, "before you're trapped in a life that daily grows more aimless and unreal." "We love you," he sobs, "call collect." Good God.

What are the odds that a close friend of mine bought his condo in L.A. and found out the very next day after he moved in that his apartment was the same one from which Diane Linkletter had jumped out the sixth-floor window? He was actually completely freaked out by this and didn't think it was one bit funny. I didn't think it was funny, either. I thought it was predestined, maybe even spiritual. I begged him to have a séance with me there to see if Diane would contact us. He refused but did let me see the apartment. All the windows had been changed and replaced architecturally, so I don't know why he was so uptight. I thought maybe I should ask him if he'd like to trip with me when I decided to do it for the book, but realized he had no interest in riling up the ghost of Diane Linkletter, who, like it or not, was still his roommate and might have been interested.

But *who* could I take LSD with? Naturally I thought of the Dreamland survivors, the very same people I tripped with in the sixties. I asked Pat Moran, but she shrieked in my face, "No! Are you crazy?" Mary Vivian Pearce at least contemplated it, but then turned me down, laughing and saying, "At *our* age?" But, hallelujah, Mink Stole said yes. She reasoned we both had never had bad trips when we took it together then, and since this was the fiftieth anniversary of our meeting in Provincetown, why not do it there again? But we needed a third person. I mean Mink and I have been through a lot together, even had our moments of being estranged, but that was all so long ago I barely remember why. But suppose one of us freaked out? We needed a buffer, a third buddy who was neutral. Frankie Rice, a close friend of mine who is much younger but always seemed comfortable around older people, would be ideal. He is an artist, married to a man (I performed the ceremony), handsome, funny, and more importantly, a townie. Perfect.

But where do you cop acid in 2016? I had two friends who were still plugged into the Northern California drug scene both legal and illegal, and I knew I could trust them and their contacts to come up with the real thing. I mean, how will I know how much to take? I don't want it to be a microdose disco hit that techies now take to "explore" at work, nor do I want the LSD to be so strong that I lose my marbles. Finally, through channels that were almost royal in the tripping world they got me the proper dosage. On little wafers. Each was supposedly 100 milligrams, and we were told to take about 125 to 150 for best results. I only wanted to do this once! It couldn't be so weak that it meant I was chickening out or so strong that I'd think I could fly off my third-floor Provincetown porch. I even took a photo of my "man" handing over the drugs to me. Yes, she was a woman. So what? She had done her due diligence. The last thing either of my connections wanted was to be blamed for me or Mink going postal. I didn't even tell them about Frankie. They were pretty sure what they had gotten for us was pure. Who wanted to be John Waters' Cathy Smith? Remember her? The one who sold John Belushi the coke he OD'd on? No sirree, we were in good drug hands here. Susan, my assistant, drove the psychedelic little babies right up to Cape Cod in my car without knowing it along with my usual office stuff at the beginning of summer, and I later placed them in the freezer. They're sitting in there right now, waiting to be gobbled.

I'm kind of nervous. I *did* tell my shrink and he seemed to take it in stride and gave me Ativan pills in case I got the horrors, but he also told me what I already knew: that friends "talking you down" is the best solution if things go south. "Oh, you'll be fine," a great friend who's in AA advised me, much to my surprise. Mink said she'd try smoking pot if she freaked out because marijuana relaxes her. Frankie admitted he had had a bad trip when he was young because he didn't think his dosage was working and then took more and it all hit at once and freaked him out. He said he was bringing art supplies in case the muse struck.

I remembered listening to certain LPs when I tripped when I was young, so I brought these same ones up on CDs with me from Baltimore: Dionne Warwick ("Once in a Lifetime" is the cut I remember most because Divine used to lip-synch the entire number as the acid began to build), Fellini's *Juliet of the Spirits* soundtrack, and, oddly enough, the saccharine score to *Born Free*. Could they possibly still work?

I remembered that looking in the mirror on acid was weird then; now it might be horrifying. I don't think I ever saw my partially drawn-on mustache while tripping—suppose I lose it when I see how ridiculous it looks sitting on my face as it has for over forty years? Worse yet, what if I "see" through my skull? Am I well-adjusted enough today that I won't see the ravages of time or my receding hairline reflected in the old, already-distorted bathroom mirror here?

Suppose I have to take a shit? On acid! Just the thought of all that straining and wiping while tripping is enough to give me a panic attack. Did I ever do such a disgusting thing on acid when I was young? Even now, I can't bring myself to ask Mink such a repulsive question. I'm not eating one thing for two days before blastoff.

I guess I will have a little hootch on hand just in case we feel like having a pre-LSD cocktail, but being drunk *and* on LSD seems kind of ill-advised no matter how "bad" I'm trying to be. Snacks? I don't remember ever eating on acid. And sex? Ewwwww! An orgasm on LSD? Mink, Frankie, and I had agreed not to have any of our love interests present. We needed to bond as friends on neutral emotional territory.

July 15, our agreed date, was fast approaching. I was already settled in the apartment I rent every summer on the beach in Provincetown. "I guess we're really gonna do this . . . ," Mink had written months back announcing that she'd drive up the day before and stay at the house of Channing Wilroy, another Dreamland survivor. I had sneakily "auditioned" Channing for our LSD reunion by nonchalantly asking him if he had good memories of tripping, and his answer, "Absolutely not," was immediate disqualification. I love Chan, but God knows he can be grumpy, and it was a stretch for me to imagine him "peaking" with joy. Chan's just not a smiley-face kind of guy.

I had made my trip mates take a vow of silence. Nobody could know about our little experiment until the pub date of this book. I had included the idea of my tripping in the treatment of *Mr. Know-It-All*, and both my editor and agent had said, "Be careful." Huh? If I was being careful, I wouldn't do it, would I? Would Farrar, Straus and Giroux now be liable for damages if, high on LSD, I cross-dressed as Robert Motherwell, who used to live in Provincetown, and ran up Commercial Street attacking tourists? I hadn't mentioned that Mink was joining me, but I figured FSG would only be happier with this chapter on my lunatic geezer reunion with my movie past included. Mink had already asked if she could use the night as material *after* the book had been published, and of course I answered yes. Unspoken is the question of what *are* the rules if one of us *does* have a bad trip and goes mental. I guess we all should think back to that famous line in *Tea and Sympathy* when the older woman kisses a much-younger closeted gay boy and says, "Years from now, when you talk of this, and you will, be kind!" We will.

We're not using a "guide." Remember them? Most people don't when waxing nostalgic about LSD. A guide was supposed to be a person *not* on LSD, who might have been part of the drug culture, but who volunteered to be around a group of trippers making sure nothing went wrong. Kind of like the chaperone at a party. We had already made fun of that concept in *Multiple Maniacs* when Lady Divine's gang of psychos dropped a net on suburban gawkers inside her Cavalcade of Perversions and then shot them up with acid. "I'll be your guide," Divine evilly snarled as unwilling LSD victims screamed in horror. Who could be our guide? My eighty-six-year-old landlady downstairs? My art dealers here, Jim Balla and Albert Merola? Our trip is scheduled for a Friday night in the middle of summer—they have to work, I can't ask them. Who could stand spending twelve hours stone sober at a Dreamland multigenerational LSD party *and* keep their traps shut? Nobody. We'd have to take our chances.

But suppose something goes wrong? As LSD-day approaches (two more days!), I admit I'm as nervous as I was before I began my cross-country hitching trip that became the book *Carsick*. This I hope will be a shorter ride than the nine days that trek took, but I have no choice, other than to once again imagine the "best" and "worst" that could happen. I can't be clueless like Lana Turner, who told me that before she filmed the ludicrous but wonderful LSD melodrama *The Big Cube*, in 1969, no one, including the director, had bothered to tell her what LSD was. When she shot her freak-out LSD scene (which has to be seen to be believed), she still didn't know what LSD was. For better or worse, I do.

Maybe I'll go crazy and never be able to write again? Or commit murder like the Z-Man character in the best LSD musical of all time, *Beyond the Valley of the Dolls*? Will I have flashbacks to the finale of that trashterpiece and try to behead Frankie and Mink? God, I hope not. Or reenact that great Jody Reynolds suicide song "Endless Sleep" and wade into the ocean like handsome Rick Morrow (Ricky in *Multiple Maniacs*) did when he was freaking out with Mary Vivian Pearce and me on acid in Provincetown way back when? He lived then, but would I now?

Is an LSD-related death what I want as the lead in my obituary? Actually this might be kind of cool. Talk about eternal street cred! Yet I still have a lot I want to say in life. Or do I? Will LSD make me think, "Are you nuts? Why are you working so hard when, all things considered, you don't have that much time left? Take off! Spend the rest of your life traveling, reading. Never work again!" Or will I have anxiety attacks that I'm still not working hard enough? Sixteen movies, nine books, speaking tours, art shows, that's not enough, you lazy bastard! Nobody will remember you after you've gone. Get your lazy ass to work.

Suppose I gouge out my eyeballs while tripping like the guy we all knew in Baltimore who did just that and has been blind ever since? Could I be the Stevie Wonder of Filth? I hope I don't experience flashbacks of my poor mother's face in the mid-sixties the morning I arrived home tripping out of my mind as she was just leaving the house with my brother and sisters, all dressed up for Sunday mass. Our eyes locked and never did the slogan "Psychedelicize suburbia" seem sadder. Sorry again, Mom.

Turn on, tune in, drop out, as we used to say, could be a painful process back then, but today I'm much more worried about the effects of LSD on my psyche. It's been hard to plan the many meetings or conference calls I have to schedule *after* my trip date. Suppose I don't know who I am anymore? What if I turn into one of those "zombie" drug fiends in Brooklyn who, after taking bad doses of K2, a kind of synthetic weed, foamed at the mouth and staggered around screaming and attacking neighbors just like in a horror movie? An art show I'm curating in Provincetown opens just *one* week after our planned LSD trip. It's called *Catastrophe* and I hope it doesn't end up being about *me* instead of the paintings, drawings, and photographs of car accidents and freak occurrences I've included.

But I'm a glass-half-full kind of guy. I think taking LSD at seventy will be a wonderful adventure. I read online about "the plastic fluidity of the dream state," "the geometric patterns you see with your eyes closed," "the subtle rainbow hues," "the wonder and delight of renewed psychedelic experience," and I feel excited. Maybe this trip will be a gateway to further senior-citizen drug experimentation? If it goes well, why not take every drug I ever took in ten years or so and see what happens? Could sniffing glue at eighty be my new frontier? Is experimenting with PCP at an elderly age a life-or-death crisis or a new way to say "old people want to have fun"? Suppose I get magic powers on this trip? Experience sudden automatic writing and finish this book in a day?

It's the day before we do it. What supplies should I get? Ice cream sounds good. An ocean of Evian. Coffee, although I doubt staying awake will be a problem. Mink e-mailed me yesterday,

"What are you wearing?" That question startled me because, for once, I hadn't even thought of what to put on! Let's see. Definitely not my Comme des Garçons jacket with the skull patterns. Mink had mentioned something about "being comfortable" and I agree. For me, that means 501 Levi's white jeans, what I always wear in summer. Aha! Here it is in my closet. The perfect "trippy" shirt from Issey Miyake—the one with the blurry black-and-white geometric swirls that will go perfectly with the mismatched-on-purpose CDG paisley-patterned shoes I love. I better go to the beach today for one last dose of suntan maintenance so I'll at least look healthy if I go crazy.

Will we go out while under the influence? I remember driving to Race Point Beach on acid long ago and hallucinating the sand dunes shifting and melting in the distance, so that cured me for good of driving a car on LSD. When we used to trip in Baltimore, the acid was so strong that just sitting in a chair was an experience. You *were* the chair. Will I *be* a chair again? I sort of hope not. The chairs in my summer place are a little rickety, not all that comfortable. Maybe I'll turn into one of my landlady's, Pat de Groot's, paintings. That would be nice. One thing for sure. I'm going to keep real busy today and tonight so I don't dwell. I'm actually going to do this. Acid at seventy.

Okay, it's the morning of July 15: blastoff day. There's no way I can chicken out. Like a murder plot conspiracy, it's too late to stop. Will the next twelve hours be my last morning of sanity? "Christ," I mutter out loud, "what does a grown man have to do these days to get a book deal?"

Do you clean your house for an LSD party? I did tidy up for my popper blowouts, but there were a lot more guests than two and most were already liquored up when they arrived, so I doubt any of those Rush heads were running their finger across my writing desk checking for dust. I will clean my toilet for Frankie and Mink. This I know.

I'll buy flowers, too. Yep, that is a festive, positive, trippy way to decorate for the occasion. I just took the doses out of the freezer so they can defrost in time. Does LSD even need to be defrosted? Who knows, but I did it just to be safe. I put away all work-related materials and get out just that little pocket tape recorder I used on my hitchhiking trip in case I need to remember details. But will I be able to work it while I'm high? Or will I "be" the tape recorder? I also dig out an old digital camera to take a few photos of us—I guess *before*, not after. From my memory, an LSD trip is not exactly a recipe for beauty. Drained is a tough look at my age.

Suppose I blurt out deep dark secrets? Or have a heart attack? I've been an A-fib sufferer with no symptoms for decades but never asked my heart doctor if an LSD trip was advisable. What if there's yet another terrorist attack while I'm tripping? I hope none of my media-freak friends call to tell me. Now that I think about it, I'll be scared if the phone even rings.

Shit, I just noticed *ants* in the kitchen. Every summer I have this problem, but this year I thought I had beaten it. But no! Now I have to get more of those disgusting little white plastic poisoning trays and place them around the sink. They don't work instantly! We'll be tripping and still see ants. Just like that surrealist Buñuel film, *Un Chien Andalou*—not exactly the cinematic reference I had on the menu for a suggestible mind. Fucking ants!

Oh, stop worrying, John; it's going to be fine. "Just do it," as Jerry Rubin used to say. Just say yes, as Nancy Reagan most definitely did not say. It's LSD time, be happy!

Frankie arrived at 7:25 P.M., early as always. I laughed out loud
when I saw his outfit—a tank top and cargo pants freshly tie-
dyed for the event. I had slipped into my LSD-friendly pat-
terned shirt, and he laughed, too. Seven thirty-five P.M. Mink
was late. I couldn't imagine her chickening out and I was
right—she just hadn't been to my Provincetown apartment for
years, and finding the entrance to my place around the back of
this Grey Gardens–type house on the beach is never easy. She
was dressed for comfort, and we were thrilled to be together on
this secret little adventure celebrating our fifty-year friendship.
Mink admitted that Chan, whom she was staying with, may
have been a little miffed not to have been invited to whatever
we were planning—after all I had met him *over* fifty years
ago, even before Mink. "I was going to tell him we were going
to have sex, just so his feelings wouldn't be hurt," she admitted
with a chuckle. Yikes! "That's a good excuse!" I responded in
friendship conspiracy.

Frankie and Mink had barely met in the past but gave each
other an LSD-ready hug. I put all our doses on a plate and took
my usual onetime Polaroid, now Fuji, instant photo of them
both together, the way I always do for every person who's ever
set foot in any of my homes, and labeled it *7/15/16. Our LSD
Trip.* We sat around the table and I asked that we hold hands
for a second. "We are here for each other," I said, "so let's watch
out for the other person. No pretending to be freaking out. It's
gonna be beautiful. We're in a safe place with friends. It's going
to be a great experience." "And," Mink added, "if anybody sees
God, please keep it to yourself." Each picked a colored candy
wafer with the hopefully equal dosage in the center; I took

green, Mink took pink, and Frankie chose purple. We turned off our cell phones.

I had the music all cued up and pushed the play button. "A chair is still a chair," sang out Dionne Warwick in that beautiful voice, setting the surreal tone of a house being a new kind of home on LSD. Yes, she was right when she sang about a chair not being a house, but a room can bloom on acid, Dionne, and a house *can* be a chair if you dare. A home. A chair. A house. We could be all three.

But not yet. We had been advised it would take sixty to ninety minutes to "come on." The first thing you feel—and I had completely forgotten this—was the certain thickness in your throat when you swallowed, a mucousy chemical phlegm that lets you know liftoff time is near. We went outside to my third-floor porch, which overlooks the bay and the very tip of the end of Cape Cod—about as far away as you can get geographically from Hollywood ("3,716 miles" as the vintage "Coast to Coast, Provincetown, Massachusetts, to Los Angeles, California" postcards read). We chatted, suddenly not nervous, and it seemed like less than ninety minutes, but the first thing that happens is the concept of time vanishes. You start seeing some "trails" on movement, a few color flashes, and then *WHAM!*

All at once, we were peaking full tilt. "I'm tripping balls!" Frankie hollered with a big grin on his face. And he was dead-on. So were Mink and I. Suddenly the seascape before us came alive, rolling, pulsating, hallucinations coming toward you like footage of the ground undulating in an earthquake. Every sparkle of the moon on the water turned into pinwheels and prisms of pop-art beauty. Boats speeding at us suddenly disappeared. The sky lit up: shooting stars, fireworks, colors flashing (mostly red), a planetarium of lunacy beyond compare. *WHAM! WHAM! WHAM!* it hit but none of us was freaked for one second. This stuff was strong, we all realized, maybe stronger than what we had had as teens. Definitely pure. Right out of Timothy Leary's asshole. No wonder he had his cremated ashes blasted into space. We had exploded too! And amazingly, the waves of hallucinations were hitting all three of us at the exact same time. The strobing colors and throbbing shapes may have been different inside our heads, yet we seemed to "see" the same forms of intense LSD visions together.

Yet we felt calm. In awe. The cinematic hallucinations were straight out of vintage LSD movies such as *The Trip*, *Easy Rider*, and *Hallucination Generation*, only they weren't cheesy or funny; they were explosive and classic like in *Taking Woodstock*, which includes the best LSD cinematic scene so far in movie history, in my opinion. In the sixties we said, "Wow!" But this time around it was "Whoa!" We responded with wonder to the exaggerated and chemically altered universe that had us huddling in stunned amazement. This was fucking fun! There's a clip on YouTube from the fifties where a doctor interviews a research subject hours after she has ingested LSD. "If you can't see it," she struggles to explain, reaching out into the air in front of her, "you'll never know it. I feel sorry for you!" We felt the same.

When we moved back inside my garret-like apartment, our trip got even more intense. The knotty-pine walls and ceilings came alive for me, sliding, pulsing. The little holes in the wood became like a chorus—shining beams of light down on us and singing songs to Frankie and Mink like the Chipmunks (even Alvin came along on LSD!). Every little framed picture on my walls was melting, becoming animated, performing for me. A postcard invitation for an art show, *Paul Swan: The Most Beautiful Man in the World*, lit up and blinked, begging to be noticed above the others. A recent stunning but blousy self-portrait of Nan Goldin, dressed in a bra, pulling down her slacks over her middle-aged stomach, which I'd clipped from a magazine, winked at me, started pulsating, split into fragments, and began twirling. A photograph of a very young Cy Twombly revolved in its frame, dissolved in and out, and changed from black-and-white into color. The bouquet of lilies on the table grew in size almost comically. All perspective was gone. I felt like *The Incredible Shrinking Man* happily reunited with Audrey II, the plant in *Little Shop of Horrors*. The fragrance was almost overpowering. Years of smoking cigarettes had erased my sense of smell, and it barely came back when I gave it up decades ago. But on LSD, I *was* Francine Fishpaw in *Polyester,* completely overloaded with a superdeveloped sense of smell.

The music I'd played on my first trip still worked well today. Dionne Warwick, I love you! Divine's lip-synching ghost was happily celebrated and conjured up on the "Once in a Lifetime" cut from Dionne's *Here I Am* album. Fellini: your soundtracks are still the perfect accompaniment to LSD—especially the *Juliet of the Spirits* CD. And, lo and behold, that corny, ridiculous score from *Born Free* soars again and can trigger endless bouts of hysterical laughter when you're tripping. The three of us howled so hard singing along that we, too, "roared like a lion," just like the lyrics. I got "launched," as Frankie called it when I often started ranting happily about something I feel strongly about when high, and went into a whole acid-induced rap on how Frankie reminded me of Little Ricky Ricardo playing the conga drum on *I Love Lucy.* Not sure exactly what triggered that nonsensical babble, but it was enough to send me into further bursts of hysterical cackling. If anyone had come over for a visit, they would have thought they'd stumbled into a mental institution. Thank God we didn't have a guide. They might have brought us down. *Or* called an ambulance.

We never once mentioned the possibility of going out. I'm not sure that would even have been possible. The thought of facing the Bear Week celebration in this state of mind was beyond even our perverted imaginations. Just sitting here with Mink and sharing this fabulously fractured night was such a wonderful high. I'm sad for people who don't have old friends. Audiences have said how they love growing old with Mink on-screen in our movies, and I'm even luckier to do so in real life. Fifty years of rebellion was bringing Mink and me together once again. Plus the fact we could be "bad" influences on young people (Frankie) was kind of nostalgic. We weren't juvenile delinquents anymore, we were finally mature multiple maniacs.

Frankie and I had had some wild "Friday nights" out carousing in the bars in Provincetown, but this was definitely the best one ever. Frankie looked so beautiful to me tripping, not in a leering or sexual way, just aesthetically; his gestures, his posture, his young body moving about so elegantly on acid. I realized Frankie is just about perfect.

I did forget how to do certain things. I couldn't clear the table of empty glasses. Frankie couldn't figure out how to get ice out of the freezer. Mink and Frankie both smoked a little pot during the trip, which surprised me because pot does anything but relax me in normal circumstances. Nobody seemed to see the irony of their using that pipe I've had for years, the life-size gold-plated revolver one where you stick the wrong end of the gun in your mouth and light the grass on top and inhale.

I had put off looking in the mirror up until now, but I finally did so and, hey, I looked fine. I had a suntan. Urinating was weird though. Taking out your penis felt like a ridiculous chore you wished you could take a permanent vacation from. We certainly didn't see God, as Mink had earlier feared, but we did see a renewed, exaggerated universe that proved anything could be out there just waiting to be discovered. Never once did I think of picking up the tape recorder or the legal pads and pens I had laid out to document our trip. I didn't have to wonder if I'd remember wonder.

"Peaking" lasted about six or seven hours. We sat back outside, and while we were still hallucinating (the moon somehow hovered directly above the Pilgrim Monument, vibrating up and down like a Silly Putty prophylactic before sliding down over the top with ease), we started to come down a little. I realized I hadn't worried about one thing since the trip started, but I did wonder if the blaring music was now being heard by the neighbors. I also didn't understand why not one person was on the beach at 3:00 A.M. taking photos of the beauty we saw. Were they blind? Oh, well, it didn't matter. We were just so happy to be alive and together. Nobody was thinking about being in control. We were *so* calm. The birds landing on the incoming tide out front seemed to be performing just for us, especially the lone blue heron that morphed into a cartoonlike old man as we watched him trolling for minnows. The nearby sandbar seemed to be in the exact same shape as a whale's head. Yep, it actually *was* groovy!

Way in the distance, day started to break, and as we descended back to earth (those speeding-boat hallucinations were the last to go—Mink kept seeing them, too), we relaxed even further. Frankie admitted he had been so nervous about taking this trip that he had been waking up all week every morning in a panic worrying about it. Mink said she purposely hadn't dwelled on it during the eleven and a half hours it took for her to drive here from Baltimore in summer vacation traffic. If I'd known beforehand how strong our doses were going to be, I *would* have been worried, but now I felt the way I did when I got the last ride on my cross-country hitchhiking trip a few years back—relieved and content. I had made it. But there was absolutely no reason to ever do it again.

The sun came up. A beautiful morning in Provincetown. The landscape was almost back to normal; the seascape had switched off from the LSD job of entertaining us. Mink felt fine to walk back to Chan's, and Frankie was clearheaded enough to drive back to Truro. I walked them both out to the street, and thank God, we saw no one—our bug-eyed happiness might have been off-putting to anyone on a "walk of shame" home after a night of wild casual sex. We hugged. We felt safer than ever.

I walked back upstairs and sat down, more serene than I'd felt in years. There was no reentry or hangover like I remember from my youth. My back didn't even hurt much. I was tired but not depleted. I texted my boyfriend that I was fine, and he seemed glad to hear it but not overly concerned. I knew my assistants, Susan and Trish, had mixed feelings about this whole LSD idea. They had researched much of the material in the first part of this chapter and had been tight-lipped about the second part—me actually taking it. I let them know I was home free. "Really glad it was so pure," Trish texted back. "Glad you didn't fly off a roof" and "I just hope you don't experience any aftershock" and "I'm glad you're OK," the more traditional Susan responded right away. Pat Moran and her husband, Chuck, were relieved, too, but Pat couldn't help scolding back, "Hope it's not a habit." I didn't even have to take those "in-case" pills my shrink had given me, and when I told him I was fine, he said he'd like to take LSD again himself! I let my dealers know that they had done a great job and weren't going to be blamed for any mental meltdowns. "You are going to reinvent the market for LSD," one half of the team joked. Well, I don't know about that.

My mom always used to be horrified when she'd read interviews with me in the seventies where I'd say, "LSD gave me the confidence to be who I am today." "Don't tell young people that!" she'd beg. I'm not. If you didn't take LSD back then, you're probably not brave or insane enough to take it today. Why would you? You're busy with your new designer drugs, virtual reality headsets, and DJ-ing your way into becoming a billionaire. But senior citizens? Yes! You're stuck. Do what Mr. Know-It-All tells you to do and take LSD now. Be placid on acid. Turn on, don't yawn! Tune in and win! Drop out and shout out, "I'm proud to take LSD at seventy!" Would my mom from beyond the grave now update her plea? Will I hear her spookily scolding voice whispering in the wind like in a James Purdy novel? Am I having a flashback or did I just hear her plead, "Don't tell *old* people that!" with a concerned urgency? It's too late, Mom, I just did.

ONE-TRACK MIND

THE TOILET
• MEMBERSHIP   APPLICATION •

MEMBERS
·Application·

Name _____
Address _____ Apartment Number _____
City _____ State _____ Zip Code _____

MAILING ADDRESS

City _____ State _____ Zip _____

Age _____ Height _____ Weight _____
Color of Hair _____ Color of Eyes _____

I do/don't want to be notified by mail of up and coming Club events.

Signed
Signature _____

Approved by _____

O K, if you ever write a book, you must have a dirty chapter. Here's mine. I feel sorry for young people today because they missed the wild sex years before AIDS ruined everything. The promiscuity that was so widespread and accepted in the sixties and seventies will never come back in the lifetime of anyone who is reading this book no matter how long it stays in print. Yeah, I know about the high-end *Eyes Wide Shut*–type hetero sex parties that take place in fancy mansions these days, and the young queers are fucking like rabbits again on PrEP medication, but it's still hard to imagine that it was once normal (at least in my world) to have sex with a different person (sometimes more) every night of the week. Plus you could do it in public.

That's right, in public. I've had sex watching *The Blue Angel* at the Bleecker Street Cinema in New York City and made out with a male inside the Crookedest Man's House in the Enchanted Village children's theme park outside Baltimore. In a truck that pulled over right inside Manhattan after exiting the Holland Tunnel. In a graveyard, on the beach. On lawns, inside peep shows. In cars. Men's rooms. Parks. Even in a real dump. All gay men from my generation did the same things, or worse.

The most radical thing you can say these days is "I still love sex!" But you should. A robust sex life does not have to be stopped because of political correctness. You can still be horny, act on it, and not be a pig. The easiest way to position yourself in today's touchy, not-feely times is to pick a specialty sex act early on. And just like women in Baltimore who still wear the same hairdo they did in high school, no matter what their age, stick with it. You'll never get anywhere defining yourself sexually in the crowded field of the missionary position. So old hat, so traditional, so your parents. Better to concentrate on another sex act and excel at it.

I'd get specific if I were you. "The first thing I tell a male partner," a female friend confided to me, is that "they must go down on me. That is nonnegotiable." She had the right idea. Don't pussyfoot around, lay down the law. "So what if you can't get it up," another woman I know told an impotent male partner, "you've got a mouth, don't you?" Oral sex is the way to go. Choose a side and become an expert. It's just as challenging to be good at getting oral sex as it is to give it. Shaken not stirred. Eaten in, not out. Soon potential sexual partners will hear of your specialty, and if they are on the other end of the oral stick, your good word of mouth (so to speak) will pay off.

Oral sex should be included in every marriage vow. But not simultaneously. The sixty-nine position has always seemed awkward to me plus vertically discriminating if both parties are not the same height. You can't concentrate. Please your partner or get pleased. You can dedicate yourself to one oral side like a Democrat or a Republican or go back and forth like an Independent. Even switch sides for a surprise attack.

Oral sex can then wander into unexplored areas. Shrimp-

ing (toe sucking) is safe, you can't get pregnant, and licking
those little piggies as they go wee, wee, wee all the way home
adds a certain surreal quality to any mouth adventure. Rimming
has always been unmentionable in some circles. But I know a
few enthusiasts who swear this is sex at its most intimate. Was
Dennis Cooper wrong to write that the asshole can be thought
of as "an alternative face"? "That's why the good Lord placed
the anus where it is on your body, so you can't look at it," a
Christian family doctor explained to me as a teen in the middle
of a routine proctology exam. "Then why did he invent mir-
rors?" I wanted to ask, but I hadn't yet learned to question au-
thority with quite as much sass as I did later in life.

Militant rimmers are the Jehovah's Witnesses of anilingus.
Always knocking on the door of the asshole but accepting if
turned away. Real anal sex with a penis involved is more plun-
dering and fascist, and unless you're a young person with an
eager and energetic asshole, it's always kind of disgusting. Scat
is whack no matter which end of the rear entry you find yourself on. Dingleberries are never erotic, and anyone who shaves
his rectum is an asshole, in my book. Butt fucking is messy, un-
comfortable at first, awkward, and prone to accidents. Logjams.
Mudslides. Gravy. Who wants to put his dick in a squishy turd?
Yes, you can take the endless precautions to clean yourself out,
but aren't enemas more appropriate before a colonoscopy than
a coupling? Plus aren't you supposed to wear one of those ugly,
wrinkly rubbers that traps cum in that unsightly dam of plastic
to protect yourself against AIDS? Yechhh. How do you throw
that out without stopping up your toilet? Horrifying your garbageman. A compost pile is disgusting enough without this! I
say assholes are for shitting, then cleaning, followed by licking,
but never fucking. Accept that and you'll be a happier, sexier
individual.

Autosexuals, the new pro-masturbation militant group, believe you only need yourself to be sexually satisfied. And since you know how to work your own equipment better than anyone else, why have any partners at all? One is *not* a lonely number to these whackers. They've added a new voice to the sexual chorus by reasoning that sex with anyone else makes you unfaithful to yourself.

Texting is the new way to have phone sex, but I still don't understand the subtleties of this masturbation aid. Is misspelling the new way to be butch? Bad grammar equals rough trade? And Skype? How could *anybody* send back and forth dirty pictures of each other on this app? Never has there been an uglier camera angle or worse lighting than on Skype.

I may have a one-track mind but I have limits. Water sports are better to imagine than actually do. S&M looks silly at the beach, and besides, young people today refuse to feel guilty over sex. Wearing some ridiculous biker Halloween costume (unless you're in the Tom of Finland cult) and getting spanked or tied up in public is not on their menu of how to have a good time. Adult babies are beneath contempt, and I'm not marching for these fuckers anywhere. "Feeders" and "gainers" try to make eating disorders sexy, but give me a Boney Maroney any day. Even bears are getting so huge these days. Is fat suddenly the new butch? I pretend to get it but I'm not sure I always do.

Gay bars are vanishing. Some queer historians mourn their passing but not me. It seems like actual progress. Young gay kids don't want to be ghettoized. They want to hang out with other cool kids of any sexual persuasion of either sex. While I've always said I don't have nostalgia and think what comes tomorrow is way more interesting than what came before, I do think a few of those sex pits from the past deserve to be remembered.

Some were so appalling that I get misty-eyed just thinking of them.

Hellfire was my all-time favorite. Built underground around an abandoned old subway platform beneath Ninth Avenue, this dungeon-like sex club was the first to cater to gay and straight perverts alike, mixing together, watching, whacking, blowing, fucking, or just plain voyeuring like happy sex tourists. It was all the rage for a while. A fat woman in a nurse's outfit and surrounded by enema supplies collected the admission price (and I seem to remember that women were free). The author Jerzy Kosinski seemed to be there every night (until he committed suicide). I even once saw Angela Lansbury checking out the scene. You could be talking to an uptown museum curator about the novels of Alain Robbe-Grillet and a dick would pop through a glory hole next to you and knock your drink out of your hand. You'd both chuckle, move down the bar to a safer location, and maybe switch the subject to Samuel Beckett. Sharon Niesp and her girlfriend, Cookie, had a fight in Hellfire once and it got physical and one hit the other over the head with a chair. A crowd of masturbators quickly gathered around them, watching the action and jerking off in a frenzy of sexual glee. There was Pop, as we called him, an elderly man who could pass as anybody's long-lost uncle at a family reunion. Every night he strung himself up in a sling, totally nude, with a dildo up his ass, while he smiled and waved to the bar crowd as if he were perched atop a float in the Easter parade.

Using the bathroom at Hellfire was complicated, but you learned how to cope. There were two bathrooms, one with a long line and normal toilets inside, the other with no line and a nude man sitting in a bathtub waiting to get pissed on. You didn't have to touch him. After you got over the initial shock you realized the line next door was awfully long. Just whip it out and hose him down and you were outta there in a flash. Close your eyes and think of . . . well, a new experience. It didn't seem abusive. After the guy got pissed on, he thanked you! I always felt these first water-sport experiences at Hellfire broadened me intellectually. Still, I tried to imagine these piss freaks going home as the crack of dawn broke over Manhattan. Talk about a walk of shame. Didn't their doorman get a telltale whiff? I guess co-op boards weren't as strict in those days as they are today.

The Toilet took faulty toilet training to a whole new level. It was located in the Meatpacking District in what was known as the Kelly Building, right up the street from Hellfire, and you had to be really in the know to find out how to even get in. The rickety freight-elevator ride up to the loft directly from the street was enough to scare away any faint-of-heart water-sports enthusiasts, but once you got in, well, you were drenched in fun. *Number one* took on a whole new meaning. Were there any real toilets? I don't remember any—just human ones and they seemed quite willing to flush. No wonder the management gave out free drink tickets! Hard to process today, but this was a private club and you could actually apply for membership. I know it is not a figment of my imagination because I have the application framed and hanging in the bathroom of my New York apartment. One trembles to imagine what you'd have to fill out to be rejected. Urinary tract infection? Blood in your urine? This was not exactly a to-the-manor-born type of club. No, you went there to piss on somebody or get pissed on, not to play tennis.

In the late seventies it seemed each city had its own Glory Hole club. Today you can buy online a "Portable Glory Hole" that "mounts to any wall" and is "quick and easy to set up and use at home or away," but back then these little entry holes had their own community centers. And why not? Erotic lounges made economic sense and were cheap to open with little overhead except for a carpenter with a hole saw-blade drill and a lot of Lysol. The one in New York was on the West Side Highway—Eleventh Avenue between Twenty-First and Twenty-Second Streets, near the leather bars the Eagle and the Spike. You paid a high admission price, then entered to hear loud, awful disco music and the banging of wooden doors. A maze of booths lay ahead of you. Each had a glory hole on three sides with a screen-door handle for each hand above to hold on to if you were getting blown. It was a leap of faith to stick your dick through the hole because you couldn't know what was on the other side. There were always wild tales of castration but I think that they were just fantasies of fear. Usually all that awaited you was a warm mouth. There was even a Grove Press novel called *The Softness on the Other Side of the Hole*. Sometimes as soon as you entered a booth, three dicks would come through all three glory holes and you had to choose the lucky winner. Wouldn't you worry it might be somebody you knew and hated on the other side? You couldn't see his face; all you could see was his dick. Suppose you had just blown Rex Reed?!

Were there manners at the Glory Hole? Yes, in a way. Sometimes you'd kneel down to look through the hole and another eyeball would be staring back at you. You might jump back, but you never screamed. Banging the door shut when you moved to another booth was considered bad form, just as it would be at your parents' house. Sometimes poppers were offered through the hole and it was considered good form to accept. If you wanted someone to join you inside the booth, you didn't lock the door. If you were operating strictly alone, you bolted the handle. Being the last customer left when they closed the door at 4:00 A.M. was nothing to be ashamed of. Usually the one employee would blow you just to get rid of you so he could lock up and go home. Today, the onetime New York Glory Hole is a super-trendy restaurant, Lot 61. I bet they don't offer anything as good at closing, probably just a goddamn mint.

I always wondered—what did the Glory Hole's tax forms say? Who were the actual owners? Mafia types? If so, did their wives know the Glory Hole was a family business? One so successful it seemed to become a chain? There was a Glory Hole south of Market in San Francisco that I used to stagger to high after an uneventful night at the Stud, the first hippie gay bar for men. I don't remember much about the club except for sex. The DJ told the *Berkeley Barb* at the time that it didn't much matter what kind of music he played. "No one ever says I want to hear something to suck cock to. If they did, I'd probably play it."

The concept of the Glory Hole bar sank to new Bay Area lows when the Hungry Hole opened at 1190 Fulton Street. Here was a bar with a backroom with glory holes for assholes. Big holes. Butch asses. Tough tongues. Indiscriminate rimming. My friend Van Smith used to go there and he told me all about it, but I never had the nerve. I figured you'd need a gamma globulin shot first and I never planned that far ahead.

Leave it to Los Angeles to make the glory-hole-bar template showbizzy, exhibitionist, and, yes, more discriminating. Rechristened as Basic Plumbing, this sex club at 725 North Fairfax (a later one on Hyperion was shut down by the authorities but I never went there) had doormen that demanded customers pull up their shirts before entering and show their stomachs. If yours was flat or muscular, you were in like Flynn, but if not, hit the road Jack and don't come back. No fats, fems, or bare feet. Just hot hornball dudes.

Inside, the booths were bathed in an eerie red light, and newcomers were startled to see that some of the glory holes' compartments were made out of clear Plexiglas, not wood. You could still stick your dick through the hole to get blown, but both participants could also pose and whack for each other's enjoyment before the main course was served. So L.A. So Hollywood. So porn star in the making. I always felt slightly inadequate in Basic Plumbing. Not good enough. Don Knotts with a hard-on.

Some of the other sex clubs around the country were really ridiculous. The oddest and most ludicrous was Night Shift, a blow-job theme park located above the Hollywood Twin porno theater at 777 Eighth Avenue in Midtown Manhattan and owned by Nick Marino, producer of *Hollywood Chainsaw Hookers*. Getting upstairs to the second floor was harrowing. The one trash-strewn, scary elevator had no attendant and came up directly from the street and was often manned by junkie muggers looking to rob the gay and often inebriated clientele. If you were lucky enough to survive the trip up, you were momentarily stunned when you stepped out into the "cruising area," an actual set of an outdoor public park, complete with pathways, grass, benches, even fake birds in the trees, tweeting away mechanically. Kind of like a studio soundstage at Paramount, only with blow jobs.

The Night Shift's two clienteles were completely at odds with each other. Horny gay guys mixed with unsuspecting homeless men who had checked in for the night (it was open twenty-four hours a day) hoping to find a cheap good night's sleep on a park bench ("Newly Heated" the ads read). But the equally clueless queers didn't realize the sleeping bums might be offended when their dicks were grabbed or circle jerks formed around them. "Hey, get off me!" you'd hear some confused, pissed-off hobo yell, while a haughty homo would argue back indignantly, "This isn't some shelter! It's a gay fuck room!" Class issues were never more apparent than they were at the Night Shift. I was always scared there. Today, it's the headquarters of Gray Line sightseeing bus tours. If they only knew.

It wasn't just gay people that had unhinged sex pits. Heteros had their own "eros centers," like the Copenhagen Room in San Francisco's Mitchell Brothers O'Farrell Theatre. Headliners could make up to $3,000 a day by showing up, stripping, and letting the men in the audience examine their private areas like amateur gynecologists. "Touchie-Feelie" performances, they were called, and while hetero men are more prone to blue balls from being more sheepish about public masturbation than their gay counterparts, one can only assume they were doing just that or at least "banking" these images mentally for a red-hot whack-a-thon in their heads later that evening when the show was over and they were safely tucked into their beds at home.

Even Edy Williams, Russ Meyer's ex-wife and star of *Beyond the Valley of the Dolls* and *The Seven Minutes*, played the O'Farrell Theatre, putting on eight—yes, eight—shows a day beginning at 1:00 P.M. and ending at midnight. And you thought vaudeville was a grueling schedule. Imagine undulating in a "calisthenic style," as the San Francisco reviewer Peter Stack so hilariously put it, while men in the audience lit up your vagina with beams of flashlights provided by the management as you talked dirty and continued your floorwork (as split-beaver posing is known in the trade) for eleven hours a day! Is this the lowest rung of show business or the highest? I'm still trying to figure that out.

Could there be a new kind of revolutionary promiscuity? I want to open my own sex club in Baltimore in the Pigtown community, a mixed neighborhood of many rednecks, art-school dropouts, homeboys, and brave homesteaders with their families.

To publicize our hot spot, I'd sponsor an exchange program for out-of-town guys with confused dicks and gals with vagabond vaginas. I'd encourage all the gay women from Provincetown to crash the Meat Rack in Fire Island, and then all those muscle Marys would, in turn, panty-raid Baby Dyke weekend in Provincetown. In both places, gay men and gay women would have sex with each other for the first time, and a new sexual minority would form. Gay heterosexuality. Then these radical warriors would relocate to my hometown and begin to refine this vanguard movement of advanced perversity that would confuse even the most advanced LGBTQ leaders. My hot spot's name? Flip Flop. Soooooo 2019!

Our men's and ladies' rooms would be open to all interpretations of gender, but since there would only be commodes, not urinals, in the men's room, gentlemen would have no choice but to sit down to pee, feeling for the first time what it's like to take a passive piss. Women, on the other hand, would experience the thrill of aggressive urination by standing up to relieve their bladders into those now highly collectible female urinals that were manufactured in the early sixties but never found favor.

Music? I'd defy expectations and just play on loop the three-LP, six-sided 1966 spoken-word version of the Marquis de Sade's *Justine, or the Misfortunes of Virtue* "recorded previously" and read "anonymously by a distinguished repertory company." It's on the Sadisc label, and just the overkill of the constant replaying of this amazingly graphic pre-audiobook presentation should be enough to inspire the badly needed freshly filthy vocabulary of dirty sex talk that will give meaning to our bi-hetero homosexuality. Eat that pussy, cocksucker! Swallow that dick, carpet muncher!

That's right. The new gays will come out to invade heterosexuality. M.F.K. Fisher may have asked her culinary readers to "consider the oyster" in the kitchen, but I'm asking gay men to consider it in their bedrooms. I know, it's new, it's wet, but it's time for us fags to face the nation. Lesbian pussy may be foreign to some of our more timid gay brothers, but it's time to broaden our horizons and give muff diving a chance. Fellow se-men demons, loosen up. "Sneezing in the cabbage" could be a whole new clitoris closet you could escape into if you'd just open the door. And, lesbians, "having lunch downtown" can have a whole new meaning for you if you'd only stop the "clam snack-ing" and just "talk into the mike." All I'm asking is that you "polish the knob" of a gay guy who's just tried "goin' down South in Dixie." We're all in this together, aren't we? We're here, we appear to be queer, and sometimes we're straight when we sal-ivate. Get used to it. We're not. But so what? It's time to heat things up.

MY BRUTALIST DREAM HOUSE

B e willing to change everything. Even where you live. My house in Baltimore is a 1925 Mediterranean-style stucco four-story dwelling designed by the architect Laurence Hall Fowler for himself. It faces wooded grounds that remind me of a small private mental institution. But architecture isn't fair. Whenever I'm alone here and lying in bed listening to my heartbeat before I go to sleep, I realize this building will outlive me. It won't care if I die. The walls will still be standing after I'm six feet under. I'm loyal to my home but it is not loyal to me. My house spits on my grave and looks forward to housing whoever comes next. It pisses me off.

There's really only one thing you can do about it. Tear down your existing home. Fuck your past. Torch all those Chippendale heirlooms, that Jean Roger furniture, your midcentury antiques, that arts-and-crafts crap. It all goes out of style one day anyway. Take a flamethrower to your beautifully landscaped garden, too. You need to move beyond any kind of taste to a new level of architectural defiance. There's only one way to start over. Brutalism. The new ugly.

I want to level my existing home and build my own brutalist dream house and call it Monstrosity Manor. Raw "crap" concrete.

Repetitive detail. An oversize-for-the-property geometric night-mare that references a block cement prison with no windows. Stalinist chic, Stasi nostalgia. Designed to be unfriendly. Hostile. Cold and uninviting. The neighborhood association would be apoplectic, but what do I care? I want a house that everyone can hate.

Yet these days brutalism is making a comeback. I'm distressed that this style of architecture has become cool. I *want* the unsophisticated idiots to continue tearing down these classic but reviled buildings from the sixties and seventies so I can be the only one left with a brutalist home. Can't somebody stop all these I Love Brutalism websites from celebrating this once-loathed style of architecture?

It seems all brutalist architects were heterosexual. So I'd hire the meanest, grumpiest one, who would barely speak to me, and let him go way over budget to design a fortress that would invoke fear and elegance, discomfort and sophistication. I don't want Monstrosity Manor to be "heroic," as some brutalist groupies call this style. I want my home to be hermetic, with boxy, windowless wings protruding at clumsy angles from the main compound built out of the rubble of the now-destroyed Morris Mechanic Theatre in Baltimore, designed by the grand pooh-bah of brutalism, John M. Johansen. Once this "world's ugliest building," as it was often called, was torn down on the orders of Baltimore's planning commission, brutalist fans everywhere went into deep mourning, and many have never recovered. I'd cover this new building material with green lichen, an ugly organism that especially likes to grow on bare rock and reproduces sexually all on its own.

Needless balconies some would call eyesores of ugliness would purposely dot the rest of the manor, and I alone would know their secret entry passageways. My Evita-like appearances would enrage the angry mobs of traditionalists from my neighborhood, who would gather below to jeer at my architectural perversities before I zapped them like the mosquitoes they really are with flames shooting out from the side of the building, so red-hot they are actually blue in color.

We're no Fallingwater here. Frank Lloyd Wright was all right but think of Monstrosity Manor as tougher, more manly. Nobody's coming over to borrow a cup of sugar. The grounds would be unforgiving even to students of architecture. Surrounding the property would be copies of those vaguely communistic concrete statues of inspired underprivileged children long displayed in front of the McCulloh Homes housing project in Baltimore, only their facial expressions would be altered to alarmingly hostile glares. My front gates would be made out of the rescued barbed wire of the now shut-down Jessup Correctional Institution in Maryland and then electrified by paroled prisoners to a much higher voltage than is used for invisible fencing for dogs. A NO TRESPASSING sign would be totally redundant.

The lawn itself would be scorched of any natural vegetation by a vintage fire hose left over from the Vietnam War. Dotting the grounds would be a few of the artist Roxy Paine's stainless steel tree sculptures to reinforce the "industrial nature" look I now believe in so stringently. Tumbleweeds made from lightweight razor wire would blow into you without warning.

There'd be a pool, but only a fool would want to swim in the salty, *E. coli*–friendly, chlorine-resistant water I'd have scientists concoct. Urine, sweat, old makeup, and traces of watery diarrhea are always part of the bacteria in even the most well-maintained pools. But I'd add to this unholy mix half-alive bitter sea nettles ready to sting even if you just put a toe in to test the water temperature. Ornery little barnacles would be waiting, too, hoping to scrape and cut your feet as you climbed up the pool's ladder in panicked escape.

The driveway, made from alpine white gravel dyed an especially putrid shade of puke green, would lead to hidden storm-cellar-type doors in the earth that would open up electronically to reveal a steep ramp down to the garage, where I'd keep my own personal vehicle. The actual 1971 black Lincoln Continental customized by George Barris to star in the 1977 driverless-killer-car movie titled . . . yes, *The Car.* Don't even think about getting in. It will eat you alive. I told you not to come here, didn't I?

Inside? Well, brutalist architecture has always been known for its interior drafts, so I'd purposely use this supposed flaw to surprise, chill, and finally move you to embrace the mistakes of my despised design before it kills you first. The Europeans have always been paranoid about cold drafts (Visconti's *L'Innocente* even features the murder of a baby by *courant d'air!*), so I'd embrace this phobia by cracking the few windows just a tiny bit in each room. Since the rubber sealing between the edges of the casement and the frame would have been purposely omitted, the windows would vibrate as the air rushes through the cracks, causing a loud moaning hum that has a maddening musical pitch, which moves up and down the little three-note scale as the wind gusts and subsides. It's called a thrum and it would drive you crazy. Hee hee hee.

I wouldn't have heat. Cold gives you nature's face-lift. Why do you think David Letterman kept his TV show soundstage so freezing that you could see your own breath when you were on his show? To keep himself tight, that's why! Skinny windows would contain special glass that would act as a magnifier, with such intense sunlight piercing the chilly rooms that little decorative fires would break out inside and inflame any of your personal items if you were stupid enough to leave them out unprotected.

The living room—and boy, would it be a stretch to use the word "living" here—would feature the artist Doris Salcedo's hideously heavy, cement-laden thrift-store furniture that has been molded together for maximum ugliness and lack of function. Forget that these randomly placed monstrosities that I've crowded into one corner are sculptures with political undercurrents. Just marvel at furniture that not only rejects you but also negates all forms of comfort.

My impenetrable security system would include a panic room you'd enter off the library by pulling a faux spine of a book you grab like a handle and the whole shelf spins around. Once you saw the horrifying selection of fascist books displayed here in my little satellite reading room, you'd feel anything but safe. *Hitler at Home, Dead Funny: Humor in Hitler's Germany, Magda Goebbels: First Lady of the Third Reich,* and *Born Guilty: Children of Nazi Families.* We've got all the other monsters, too: Idi Amin, Pol Pot, Ronald Reagan, even *On Democracy* by Saddam Hussein. (I remember watching his public hanging on my computer crouched on the floor with Baroness Marion Lambert, who was dressed in full couture right before she threw open the doors of her Gstaad chalet to let in her New Year's Eve party guests.)

I know brutalists are supposed to be minimalists. I try to live with nothing. Alone. At one with ugliness. I'll have a high-end screening room: State-of-the-art digital equipment. No chairs. You have to stand to watch the only movie I would ever allow to be shown in this section of the manor, *Blue*, a seventy-nine-minute static shot of the color blue accompanied by the director Derek Jarman's smart, angry, sad musings on his fast-approaching demise from AIDS. I'd turn off the soundtrack and just show the picture now that he's dead. It's even more tragic. Yep. Utal-bray.

The grounds may be barren outside but inside would be a whole different story. Yes, I'd have plants, and all the ones lining the downstairs halls would be black. Black Scallop bugleweed would be allowed to grow between a few cracks in the concrete floor and join the black hollyhock flowers that only live a short life but put many of their merely purple, black-impersonating competition to shame color-wise. The devil's tongue has been called both "sinister" and "brazen," and inside, its enormous black stem can tower five feet in satanic height. The nearby hooded Griffith's cobra lily is like an uncircumcised flower, and after a week or two, a single large dark leaf pokes its head out like an eager penis. And all through the first floor, hidden discreetly in awkward cinder-block vases are black pussy willows, ironically the male version, which is easily forced inside. *Forced* is always a good word if you're a brutalist flower.

Up the concrete staircase past Damien Hirst's first dead-fly painting, *Untitled Black Monochrome*, the one that smelled so bad that the collector Miuccia Prada had to get it out of her house after she bought it, you might need to settle yourself on the stairs. Not because of the stench. There's no handrail to balance yourself, and if you're not careful, you could trip over the sculptor Carl Andre's twelve small copper tiles that were purposely designed to be hidden on the side or back of the steps for your minimalist artistic danger and enjoyment.

Once you've made it up, you'll see my master bedroom at the end of the hall, guarded out front by one of Pino Pascali's Arte Povera "cannons" that point at you with impotent male aggression. A few plants are up here, too, only they are all poisonous. My coyotillo shrub would hopefully tempt unwanted neighborhood historical busybodies to nibble the black berries it produces

once a year. They will kill you. Slowly. Paralysis sets in sometimes several days, or even weeks, later, beginning at your feet
and working its way up to the lower legs and after that bringing
the respiratory system to a halt, shutting you up forever.

My bunker penthouse with faux windows would offer a view
of a phony brick wall that is a mere illusion of set design. The
only art displayed in my most personal of rooms would be Lee
Lozano's untitled two-panel giant painting of a seemingly hostile, damaged C-clamp; so angry, so painful, so threatening, it's
spiritual. Only one potted plant would ever make it up here after
a ruthless final edit of Monstrosity Manor's dangerous green-
ery. I wouldn't have known about it if I hadn't gotten my hands
on the botanical-atrocity guidebook to poison vegetation *Wicked
Plants* by Amy Stewart. It's called the deadly nightshade, once
thought by a botanist to be a plant not only capable of love but
also of possibly holding grudges before it kills you. Here is a
flower that can hate. Maybe it will warn me of unfaithful lov-
ers *before* they even get in my bed—of nails. What did you expect? Torture must be complete in home decor if you expect to
be taken seriously by the brutalist community.

Now it's time to lie down on my bed of punctures and concentrate on the beauty of ugliness. Before I drift off to dreamland tonight, I think I'll look through one more time my favorite
coffee-table book, *This Brutal World* by Peter Chadwick. It's so
exploitative in its naked adoration of brutalism you could almost
call it art porn. Go ahead, try pleasuring yourself to it. Look at
the hideously repetitive circle of balconies of the Druzhba San-
atorium building in Yalta designed by Igor Vasilievsky and you
might get a tingling feeling down there. Arouse yourself further by gazing at the photo of Didier Fiúza Faustino's insanely
top-heavy and clumsy Misfit Tower in South Korea. Fondle
yourself in an impure way as you ogle the colossal holy hideous-

ness of the architect Gerhard Mayer's Wotruba Church in Vienna, which exaggerates a pain worse than anything Christ could have suffered on the cross.

The text of the book could turn on a castrato. "Ugliness is, in a way, superior to beauty because it lasts," reasons the singer Serge Gainsbourg, and this book's author knows his one-armed readers like dirty talk just as much as they do brutally sexy pictures, so he gives erotic pull quotes prominent display on the pages.

Damn, that giant concrete mushroom sprouting rigidly from the top of the Geisel Library in San Diego (architect: William Pereira) is hot! As you turn the page frantically, feel up the photograph that shows the erotic monotony of the Temple Street Parking Garage, designed by Paul Rudolph, as you begin to build to your brutalist climax.

Is it possible to penetrate a building? Only you can decide. How about that Casar de Cáceres bus station in Spain? The architect, Justo García Rubio, surely knew during the pre-#MeToo movement times that the circular openings here for the world to see were practically asking for it. Jesus, look at that staggering unwieldiness of scale in the Alberto Linner Díaz and Cesare Galeazzi Jenaro Valverde Marín building in Costa Rica. Couldn't you just explode?

The final turn of the page to the unbelievably space-age ridiculousness of J. Mayer H.'s border checkpoint in Sarpi, Georgia, will surely do the trick. Let's hit the brutalist big O together! Then a new Zen afterglow will wash over us all just as it does me here in Monstrosity Manor. A house so big. So ungainly. So hated by the rest of the world that I reach sexual peace through architectural fury.

NO VACATION

Mr. Know-It-All understands you need a vacation, but not a real one. Take a "no vacation." That's when you work *and* relax and are never idle, bored, or unproductive for a planned period of time. A no vacation will give you the much-needed break from your usual routine yet allow you a new daily grind that can become just as delightful as punching the time card at home.

Pick a place. Make sure it's a good one. I first came to Provincetown, Massachusetts, a bohemian fishing village, in 1964, and I've spent every summer there since. You can't mix and match summer resorts. You don't live on Fire Island and visit Provincetown in the summer and Key West in the winter. That dilutes your loyalty and makes you an amateur vacationer. No-vacation enthusiasts and Percy Faith know there can only be one "Summer Place," and you don't need Sandra Dee or Troy Donahue to make it your own. You just have to pledge eternal loyalty as I have.

Yes, I am fond of sand dunes and salty air as Patti Page used to sing in "Old Cape Cod," and I am proud to be a militant seasonal resident here. You'll know it's really summer if you see me riding my beat-up bicycle down Commercial Street because

I come here every year on Memorial Day and leave on Labor Day. Everybody likes to complain about how Provincetown (saying "Ptown" seems lazy and too familiar) has changed, but to me it's exactly the same as it was fifty-five years ago. I feel that if I dropped a piece of gum on the corner of Bradford and Court Streets in the late sixties, it would still be there today. I must admit I do ask myself every year after I arrive, "Am I crazy? What adult goes to the beach for the summer?" Isn't that for college athletes who flip burgers and prom queens who get pregnant? Yet here I am, year after year, unpacking my summer whites and getting ready for another season of frolicking in the sea and doing laundry in an actual Laundromat.

Provincetown, the Last Resort, it's been called because of its remote location at the very end of Cape Cod's tip, but its sexual reputation is what's really made its name over the years. When I first arrived, Provincetown was known as an "artist colony," which was code then for "gay." Many kids who were still in the closet only told their parents they had summer jobs on Cape Cod, never Provincetown. It's still the only place I have ever lived that my parents never visited. I still can't picture my dad walking down Commercial Street (the main drag that Tennessee Williams wrote a play about with the fitting title *Parade*). Just last night I saw a man walking home after the bars closed wearing nothing but a jockstrap, football helmet, and athletic shoulder pads.

Even the street signs read like double entendres: PROVINCE-TOWN EITHER WAY was a famous one that announced, or warned of, depending on how you looked at it, the initial split in the road when you drive into town of the more popular-with-pedestrians one-way Commercial Street and the auto-friendly Bradford Street. The sign was stolen so many times that the town must have given up because they eventually stopped replacing it.

Even the two-way Bradford Street has a lowbrow T-shirt of its own that reads BRADFORD STREET GOES BOTH WAYS. It's just that kind of place. Remote. Beautiful. With sex lurking at all times.

It's not easy getting there. The only good thing about taking the bus (which can stop in every little town all the way to Provincetown) is that it drops you off right in the center of town near the wharf by the public restrooms, and you get to make a great film-noir entrance as you step off, carrying your one piece of luggage just like Constance Towers did in that amazing Sam Fuller movie *The Naked Kiss*. Alone. Brave. Fleeing something but ready to begin again in this town called Province.

You can take the ferry, but a lot of times the whole boat is filled with pukers. It can be rough out there in that two-hour ocean ride from Boston. Once I picked up a friend who had taken it and the whole side of the boat was covered in vomit. Passengers were staggering off, some olive green and still heaving. My friend told me 90 percent of the passengers on board were violently seasick, some lying flat on the deck of the ferry vomiting into their own faces. Not exactly how I want to start my no vacation.

You can drive, but that means you take your life in your hands on killer Route 6, in my opinion the most dangerous road in America; a highway of sorts where you can go sixty miles an hour that also has dirt roads and driveways that directly exit onto it with little warning. People drink on the Cape. They're excited. They are oohing and aahing the sights and *bang*, they rear-end a car that has suddenly braked to turn into a roadside jelly stand. Don't say I didn't warn you.

Cape Air is the way to go. It's a tiny commuter nine-passenger Cessna 402. A lot of people transferring from jumbo jets at Boston's Logan Airport panic when they arrive at the gate and see the plane outside the terminal window, but not me. I love this airline. What other carrier has a sign warning passengers that bringing poppers on board is illegal? The Boston–Provincetown flight only takes twenty minutes versus two and a half hours if you drive, and that's *without* traffic. Michelle Haynes, who handles press relations, will even hold the plane for your boyfriend's connecting flight if you are a good enough customer. You can't beat that service!

There's only one pilot, though, so if she or he (and sometimes they appear to be about sixteen years old) has a heart attack during the flight, you're screwed. I always watch how the pilot lands in case I ever have to take over, but after decades of flying on Cape Air I'd still be no Penny in *Sky King* if there was trouble. There's one harrowing story I love about the most frightening flight Cape Air must ever have had (there's never been a fatality, which makes me nervous; if *one* had died, the law of averages would be better that another would not). The Provincetown weekly local paper, the *Banner*, covered it well, as did the *Cape Cod Times*. It was winter. The Cape Air flight from Martha's Vineyard to Hyannis began with a high-frequency beeping sound and no heat. Halfway through, the pilot became disoriented and said he was flying to Hyannis as scheduled even though the passengers could see Provincetown in the distance. The plane started going up and down and right to left. A female passenger on board, Melanie Oswald, a Cape Air security employee with only fifty hours of training, told the other three male passengers that they needed to get the pilot out of his seat midflight.

As the plane got nearer to Provincetown, there was "total panic" on board, according to the published report, and the pilot resisted giving up control so two male passengers grabbed him from behind and pulled him up as Oswald took his seat and finally got control of the headset and began to land the plane with the landing gear still up. It banked steeply and descended rapidly and all of a sudden out of the darkness the lights on the Provincetown runway lit up. The airport was closed, but another pilot, hearing about the 911 distress call one of the male passengers had placed in the few seconds there had been cell phone coverage, had remotely turned the lights on. The aircraft belly flopped with a screeching sound. Nobody was injured, yet once they realized they had landed safely, no one knew how to turn on the lights inside the plane. Somehow these survivors got out of the aircraft, then ran across a field before stumbling into freezing water. When the cops finally arrived, the pilot was still in the plane and Ms. Oswald was "in distress." No wonder! "She apparently had turned off the fuel so there would be no fire," an officer marveled, and she "skidded the plane along and slid into the grass." Damage was minimal. By now the three other passengers had walked back to the terminal and were picked up by a local cab (that's it?) and taken to Hyannis in "very high energy." Nobody ever figured out how our heroine Melanie Oswald got back to her home in Yarmouth, and at first she declined to speak with reporters. Did someone ask her when she got home that night, "How was your flight, honey?" I can imagine her saying, "Don't ask, just don't ask."

Six years later the pilot pleaded guilty to making false statements to the FAA and lying about his diabetes, which had caused his medical attack during this *Airport 1975* Karen-Black-as-stewardess-who-takes-over-the-Cape-Air-flight-near-disaster. Melanie Oswald finally broke her silence by writing to the court, "Thoughts of everyone I held dear passed through my head in an instant and harsh reality hit me that I may never see them again. It's a feeling that I have never been able to quite let go." I guess not! Does she retell the story over and over at cocktail parties today, or does she refuse to mention it? The pilot was fired and sentenced to jail for sixteen months. I located a phone number for a Ms. Oswald in Naples, Florida, and Cape Air services that area, so maybe it was her; but when I called it, the number was no longer in service. Upon further research I saw she is now head of corporate security at Cape Air! She should be! But I'm scared to contact her. Why would she want to relive the most "horrific" experience of her life with a sensation-monger like me? Besides, these days she might think I'm al-Qaeda.

I do the exact same thing every single weekday in Provincetown, timed down to the second. I wake up at 6:00 A.M. (it gets light here at 4:00 A.M. in June so I pretend I'm in an Ingmar Bergman movie in Sweden) and take a bath like an old lady (and apartments with a tub are hard to find in a summer resort!) and then go down and get all my papers, which are delivered by the best *and* most glamorous paper "boy," Tony Jackett, the handsome onetime main suspect in the infamous Christa Worthington murder case, who was eventually and correctly cleared of all suspicion. I drink my hundredth cup of Harney & Sons Earl Grey Supreme tea, think up twisted things (that's how I make my living), then eat a light lunch of turkey burger with no bun or my "cat-food special"—a single small can of tuna fish packed in water. I then drive to my favorite beach in the whole world— Longnook, where you need a special sticker for your car. I'm so obsessed with getting the number 001 pass each season that I'm there at the beach office waiting in line before they open the first day the beach stickers go on sale. Being number one at my number one favorite beach makes me feel that I have won.

After passing the Larry-Clark-meets-Kennedy-Compound-like teens who are employed to check your car's sticker between bouts of making out, you park your vehicle in the lot (which I used to hitchhike to in my pre-beach-sticker days) and approach the cliff-like entrance and see the amazingly cinematic views of this beautiful place. It's like credits to a soap opera— endless vistas both right and left of empty beaches and an ocean with sometimes crashing waves. I get excited every single day just seeing this incredible beach. There are definitely sharks. Last year one attacked a bather in the same spot I swim in every day, but it didn't scare me away. It made the beach seem much more glamorous to me.

Bodysurfing in the ocean at Longnook is perhaps the happiest feeling in my life. It makes every bit of past troubles disappear. Looking up from the surf to the steep mountains of sand and the clear blue sky above, I feel healthy—a sensation that does not come easily to me anywhere else in the world. I experience complete bliss for seconds at a time, and a feeling of well-being washes over me every time a wave knocks me down. This is why I come to Provincetown every summer. Plain and simple.

Sometimes I run errands after leaving the beach, such as going to the only real grocery store in Provincetown, the Stop & Shop, even though like all old-timers I still call it the A&P because that's what it was called when I first arrived. Here's a supermarket that respects the demographics of the town and its traditions. During Bear Week, the annual celebration of hairy, overweight homosexuals and those who love them, there are giant display bins of candies, cookies, crackers, and all sorts of fattening foods for the fellas, all up and down the aisles. Provincetown has all sorts of "weeks" dedicated to different sexual minorities, and the Chamber of Commerce lists lots of them. There's Single Women Weekend, on Memorial Day, and it's

like a lesbian version of *Girls Gone Wild.* College girls drinking, fighting, going topless—Burning Man goes to the Isle of
Lesbos. July 4 is Circuit Queens, and the disco beat is heard
everywhere in the still of the night. Special K and meth rule,
and the Stop & Shop can look like *The Day After* in the bottled-
water department because, apparently, the more water you drink
on these drugs, the higher you get. Girl Splash week is later in
July and it's sporty dykes—the Dinah Shore Golf Tournament
types.

Bear Week seemed a little less crowded this year. I'm worried because these guys seem to be getting fatter and fatter.
I saw one walking down the street shirtless that was so huge
and so hairy that I thought it was a hedge, but it was a person!
I hope these big boys aren't having heart attacks. Family Week
is supposed to be for heteros, too, but gay parents seem to have
dominated. A lot of the shop owners secretly hate it because
the parents want to take cell phone pictures of their kids with
all the items for sale and not buy anything. "This is not a prop
house for children," a friend of mine who owns a shop sniffed.
There's Women Craft Week, which used to be for prison-guard,
old-school Johnny Cash look-alike gals, but that seems to have
faded. And both Daddy Week (I hope nobody thinks I'm here
for that!) and Gay Pilot's Week (huh?) have seemingly faded in
popularity. I want Fag Hag Week. Both kinds could come—the
mentally healthy ones who hang around all gay men as friends
but have a hetero male fuck buddy, and the twisted sick ones
who fall in love with gay men, thinking they can change them,
and then get suicidal when they can't.

Actually, the ones who really deserve a special week in Provincetown are straight people. Aren't they the minority? There
are only a few straight bars, almost no children were born here
all year, and the high school closed. Hetero Pride Week. Let's

have it off-season in February to be even *more* outrageous. Think of the support groups: Parents of Provincetown Hetero Children ("My straight son is so brave—he works at Tea Dance!" or "Our hetero daughters actually live among these lesbians, yet have never experimented with cunnilingus despite being feminists"). We could honor heterosexual folk dancing (the Electric Slide), have male male-impersonators doing imitations of Norman Mailer, and women's softball games ironically played by heterosexual femmes.

Sometimes, usually on Friday nights, I still go to the bars. In theory, the Underground, located in the worst tourist-filled block in town, is my favorite since it's a straight-minority bar in a gay mecca and filled with locals and hipsters, some of whom are definitely on the down-low. My kind of place. Unfortunately, drunken bachelorette parties have also discovered this watering hole and, whenever they barge in en masse, act as real cockblockers in the pickup department no matter what your sexual tastes may be.

Scream Along with Billy is a great event on Friday nights at the Grotta Bar, and a mixed, cool crowd is always on hand to see and hear Billy Hough sing tributes to his very un-gay-favorite performers while he plays the piano accompanied by his sidekick, Susan Goldberg, on the guitar. What other gay man do you know who can sing entire Eminem or Velvet Underground albums in between patter about his own bad nights of shooting up drugs or having lewd sex with crazy people? Billy's an amazing talent who has to be seen live and in person in Provincetown to be believed. He puts the queer straight in covers like no other.

I don't go to the gay bars in town much these days because I'm against mandatory fixed sexual identity, but the history of some of these places has always fascinated me. When I first got here in the mid-sixties, every summer on Memorial Day the gay and straight clientele of the two biggest bars in town, the A-House (still there) and the Back Room (now the Crown), would draw their sexual lines in the sand. One bar would end up the gay one for the summer, the other one straight. Both were good. It happened spontaneously. At the end of the first night of the season, each sexual team would choose, and that's the way it stayed until Labor Day. But you couldn't be sure it would stay that way next year. It was back and forth, gay one year, straight the next. But never the two shall meet.

Then Piggie's opened in the early seventies and everything changed. Gays danced with straights. Bisexuals cruised fishermen. Townies and fashionistas took drugs together for the first time. It was the best bar Provincetown ever had. Since it was located outside town on Shank Painter Road, the entire crowd had to walk back into town together once the bar closed, and the shortest route was through the graveyard, where many, in these pre-AIDS days, had sex. Very *Zabriskie Point* orgy scene meets *Night of the Living Dead*. Nobody seemed to mind. Including the deceased.

Provincetown is a lot like Mortville, that fictional town in my film *Desperate Living*. If you reside here year-round there are no real laws—you live outside polite society freely as long as you don't ever leave. So of course there are characters. Everybody remembers the late Ellie, the onetime straight male Christian evangelist who had three ex-wives and five children who came to town and began living as a woman. At first she worked in drag at the local supermarket and was often seen at night making out with biological women in the local straight bar, but then she found her true calling, standing out front of Town Hall (even in the dead of winter) in full female attire singing along to Frank Sinatra albums (the same one, day after day) that blared from her boom box she pulled along in a wagon. LIVING MY DREAM, her handmade sign read.

But I remember Moulty even more fondly. He was a teen-age townie who became famous all over the world in 1965 (the second summer I was here) with his band the Barbarians, who had one big hit, "Are You a Boy or Are You a Girl." The first time I saw Moulty hanging outside the bar he played in, the Rumpus Room (I love that name), I was starstruck. His hair was so long! "How could he have grown it to the middle of his back when the Beatles had *just* come out?!" I'd ask anyone who'd listen. I knew his song wasn't about gay or straight or unheard-of-at-the-time transgender rights, it was just about getting hassled for your hirsute splendor. I remember pulling into gas stations when I had long hair and the attendant would approach from behind and say, "Fill it up, miss?" Then I'd turn around and snarl, "A dollar's worth, funny!" Hairdo politics were a big deal then and Moulty was my leader. Better yet, he had a hook for a hand. Oh, God, how I idolized him. I had always wanted to have a hook for a hand. Even as a child, I bent coat hangers and wore them up my sleeve to pretend I was Captain Hook, and now, right before my eyes, here he was: a hippie Captain Hook, a reason to live. When the follow-up record "Moulty" was released, I was even more excited to hear in the melodramatic lyrics that his hook was a result of a homemade pipe bomb's exploding in his hands in 1959! A fashion explosion that to this day excites me. Moulty is still alive. I read he lives in Arlington, Massachusetts, right outside Boston, and I think he owns an upholstery-cleaning company. I'm gonna call him up. Right now.

Don't be afraid to contact your idols. You never know. As I've said one thousand times, a no is free. What are they gonna do? Hang up on you? Beat you up? Call the police? Most famous people pretend they hate being well-known, but they're liars. It may help if the idols you are trying to reach are slightly fallen. Doesn't that make your love for them even *more* special? Isn't the fan-idol relationship now on a more dignified and even term? Their vulnerability is suddenly human in a way that is untarnished by the vulgarity of mass success.

Yay! The number I found for Moulty by spying online on Intelius still works—I can tell by his voice on his answering machine. As I start to hurriedly leave a message explaining who I am, he picks up. Moulty himself! Other people's bucket lists may include talking to Paul McCartney or Bob Dylan on the phone, but not me—it's Moulty! I've been wanting to hear his voice for half a century.

When I introduce myself and start gushing ("I like you already," he jokes), Moulty explains that he can't talk now, but could I call back tomorrow? We pick a time. I don't think he knows who I am, but why should he? I never had a hit record *or* a hook, so just by these facts alone, I am a lesser man. I accept this with humility. Moulty is the man.

When I call back at our appointed time the next day, he picks right up ("Glad you're punctual"), and he's just what I had hoped he'd be: unpretentious, funny, and, well . . . ever hip. And yes, everybody does still call him Moulty even though his real name is Victor Moulton. "In the first grade in Provincetown," he remembers, "they had to tell me, 'Your name is Victor, you ignorant Portugee, don't say Moulty!'" But that nickname could never be crushed.

"As you know," he continued, "Provincetown is a fabulous place. I love Ptown so much tears come to my eyes when I think of it. I was a wild son of a gun and a guitar player when I was just fourteen. Then I made a bomb and blew myself up." "What were you going to do with that bomb?" I asked, thinking today he'd have Homeland Security up his ass in thirty seconds. "Oh, blow up the railroad tracks—just act crazy. Not going to kill anyone." Knowing these train tracks were no longer active even then, I knew he wasn't a terrorist, and I told him so. "I wasn't a bad guy either," he says, just so he's sure I understand. Ah, the days when a boy and his bomb could still be innocent.

"But how," I wondered for the millionth time since first seeing Moulty, "did you grow your hair so long then? The Beatles had just come out and their hair was positively short compared to yours." "I was wild, I grew up on the beaches of Provincetown," he explains. "I wasn't like the other people. I really wasn't. My idol was Johnny Weissmuller, Tarzan. That long beautiful hair. So I had long hair before anybody. When the music business came along, I just let my hair grow longer and longer, and then when we hit, I had the longest hair in rock and roll." "Weren't your parents pissed?" I quiz him, remembering my own mom and dad's horror. "Oh, yes!" he cries, then imitates his father: "'Your grandma doesn't want to tell you she's ashamed of you. Cut that hair!' Big fights! But then as soon as we hit—'Look at my son!'"

When I tell Moulty "I spent a year of my childhood with a coat hanger up my sleeve pretending I was Captain Hook," he stammers for the first time. "Wow . . . hahaha," he says as I continue blurting my obsession with his prosthetic hand, not realizing at first that pretending to have a hook and really having one are two very different things. "When I first saw you, I couldn't believe it," I continue, maybe digging myself deeper into a hole. "Here is the guy I want to be, and you made that hook a complete fashion statement." "A lot of people say to me," he replies with a little bit of concern, "'One of the reasons you made it in the business and had hits and everything is because you had that hook,' and I say, 'Stop it right here. Let me tell you something. In those days no one saw you until *after* your records came out, and they knew what you looked like after they bought your stuff, so it had nothing to do with that!'"

"Did you know Provincetown was a gay town then?" I ask, bringing up for the first time something that could be touchy for the townie kids growing up here. "Fags!" the other high school teams would taunt the Provincetown High School teams whenever they'd play other schools in sporting events down Cape. "Provincetown began as a fishing village," Moulty remembers, "with a small community of gay folks—we were kids—the queers were over here. We didn't care. Everybody got along. When our song came out in 1965, a lot of the gays in Ptown thought I made it for them. I didn't make it for them, but I didn't say anything. Let 'em buy it." That's the first time I've heard "gay for pay" applied to record sales, but I sure as hell get what he means. Straight people love *Hairspray* and I just keep on letting them buy the different soundtracks, too. We're both gay-for-music-pay.

His much lesser known song "Moulty" is my favorite. It's kind of like a male Shangri-Las record, emotionally distraught, talky, and hilariously over-the-top. Moulty didn't even want to record it, but the follow-up hit to "Are You a Boy or Are You a Girl," "Hey, Little Bird," the one they did on *The T.A.M.I. Show*, costarring the Rolling Stones and James Brown, didn't chart, and neither did their next single, "What the New Breed Say," so their manager, Doug Morris, who later went on to be CEO of Sony Music Entertainment, pleaded with Moulty to release this crazy almost-novelty record that explained how after losing his hand, "something deep" inside Moulty told him "over and over to keep on going" and that all he needed now was "not pity, but a girl" to make him a "complete man." Oh, brother. Moulty at first refused to sing it, but after much pleading from his manager, he reluctantly agreed, and since the other Barbarians were not even *on* the record, Moulty still wouldn't approve the release. The label put it out anyway without telling him, and it became the hit they needed. Even though Moulty admits today that song sometimes gets even more attention than their first hit, neither the Barbarians nor Moulty ever played this record live even once. Not then. Not in their later different reunion tours. Not ever.

Moulty may have been back on the charts in 1966, but suddenly he was busted for possessing pot in Provincetown and had to serve four months in prison. "You got time for just pot?!" I marveled. "Yep," he responds without any apparent bitterness. "They said I was a bad influence and I was. A year later it would have helped our careers," he reasons, since by then many big rock-and-roll stars were having their own legendary drug problems, but in 1966 it was the final curtain. "That ended your career?" I ask sadly. "Yes, it did," he says. The Barbarians were over.

Suddenly I remember the final question I've been wanting to ask Moulty forever: "Did you know Tony Costa?" He was Provincetown's most famous *Life*-magazine-covered hippie murderer—kind of a pre–Charles Manson who was suspected of killing seven young women but convicted in 1965 of murdering only two and cutting up their bodies in his marijuana-growing patch in the woods and gnawing on their remains. "Very well," Moulty answers without missing a beat. "There were many other girls killed," he continues, and "nobody knows about [that]." "Did you suspect?" I wonder. "We knew girls that he had killed, but we don't know where he hid the bodies. A lot of us knew what was going on. I was traveling so I didn't see as much as my friends in Provincetown did. They'd tell me . . . [a last name] . . . 'Oh my God! I went out with her! She's gone! Tony got her!'" "This was common knowledge?" I ask incredulously. "Oh, yeah," he deadpans, still the most unruffled and unaffected man on earth. Moulty, I love you. Please do one more Barbarians reunion tour and for the first time sing your song "Moulty" live. Just for me, your number one fan.

When I think of the Town Crier, I go beyond even my Moulty obsession. In my mind, I am the Town Crier of Provincetown. There've been many of them over the years and I've followed the career of each. My favorite was Fred Baldwin, the grouchy one that scared children even when he gave out lollipops and was really mean to all hippies. One day, I saw him picking up his Pilgrim outfit at the dry cleaner's, and it struck me in such a beautifully pitiful way that I started to spy on him. What an existence he had, every day walking up and down Commercial Street in Provincetown, ringing that damn bell, yelling "Hear, ye! Hear, ye!" and posing with tourists. He seemed to have no friends. Then he'd go home, change into some drab clothes, and watch TV. Such a double life, *so* Clark Kent.

For many years the Chamber of Commerce paid the Town Crier and a gift shop was even named after him. He'd announce official events such as the Blessing of the Fleet, ride in parades, and appear at church bingo events. But as the town got gayer, the role of the Town Crier seemed to fade. The town stopped paying him and it became a volunteer job. One crier seemed antigay in his public behavior, and there were whispers of child abuse against another. Then Ken Lonergan got the job and the Town Crier was back in a big way. He was "openly gay" as they say these days and would often belt out show tunes while keeping up the tradition of bell ringing. Not everybody approved. "I think it's awful the Town Crier is now gay," complained a friend of mine's liberal mother, who was supportive of her only son's gayness. "He used to be serious," she griped, unfairly in my opinion, "but now he's just gay. It's not right." Go figure.

I decided I wanted to experience what it would be like to actually *be* the Town Crier. So I plotted to have myself photographed dressed as the Town Crier for purely artistic reasons and hang the results in an upcoming art show I was having at the Albert Merola Gallery. But like a cheapskate drag queen I had to ask the real Town Crier if I could borrow his outfit. Ken was quite understanding. I went over to his modest but neat apartment (I'm always trembling with excitement whenever I'm near a Town Crier's actual living space) and tried on one of his tunic tops and drawstring knee breeches. I slipped on the white Pilgrim collar and felt for the first time like a complete public figure. Was I a film director caught in the body of a Town Crier who suddenly felt the urge to "pass"? Ken patiently explained where I could send away to get the white leggings I would need plus lent me the buckles to clip on any pair of black oxfords I might have with me. When I tried on his floppy hat, it fit! My transformation into total Yankee lunacy was almost complete. "Could I hold your bell?" I asked in cross-dressing glee. "Yes, you can," Mr. Lonergan answered benevolently, handing me the prop I'd so long yearned to ring.

When the big day of the photograph finally came, I got into full Town Crier drag alone in the privacy of my apartment. James Balla, Al Merola's partner in the gallery (and in real life), was scheduled to pick me up in his van so I could ride into town in the back, unseen by the public, and we'd pull up to the exact spot where the photographer I had hired, Jennifer Moller, was all set to take the picture. But I had to get *to* that van first. I took a deep breath, held my head high, and walked out of my door for the first time in full Town Crier drag. Could I pull it off? I felt like a complete fool as I walked down the two sets of outdoor steps to the beach and didn't look over at the families that sunbathed there every day and by this time knew me by sight. I didn't hear any shouts of derision, so maybe I had them fooled. I paraded around to the front overgrown yard, and, uh-oh, Pat, my landlady, was right there, weeding her garden. I walked right past her and just said, "Don't ask." She looked up at me dressed as the Town Crier and said nothing. Her mouth fell open. I just kept going, out the front gate, and thank the Lord the van was waiting. Jim Balla took one look and tried not to laugh in my face and opened the back door. I hopped in and we were off.

He called ahead and the photographer said she was ready. It was a go. I felt as if we were about to execute a bank robbery. We pulled up, and as rehearsed, Jim jumped out, opened the van's back door, and I emerged onto the streets of Provincetown as the new Town Crier. "Is that John Waters?" I heard a dumbfounded tourist sputter. "No, it's a look-alike," Jim said. I made no eye contact with anyone, went to my mark, rang the bell, and Jennifer took the picture. I could hear some laughter from the usual packed crowd of summer tourists but I was not crier-bashed or judged in any way. I jumped back in the van. We peeled out and later the photograph was sold in a small edition and Bryan Singer, the director of all those *X-Men* movies, bought one, I'm not sure why. He's never been to Provincetown as far as I know. Maybe he's just a Town Crier hag, too.

OK, time to put on the brakes. Ever notice all the books about this town never mention anything negative? Well, No Vacationer, sometimes somebody has to speak up or forever hold his summer lease. It might as well be me. Here are my summer gripes: Those damn trolley tour buses (no local would ever be caught dead on one) that are too wide for our little streets and block foot traffic every time they stop to announce obvious facts. What the driver *should* be pointing out over the PA system is that tourists should never be seen wheeling their luggage up Commercial Street. That is the sign of a true amateur. Commercial Street is our center stage. Bradford Street is where the scenery and props are changed, and here is the *only* place you should ever be seen with your transient baggage. I also hate couples (even gay ones) who hold hands walking up the middle of the street, daring bike riders to speed through them the way I do, breaking them apart and narrowly avoiding injury. Yes, you can be in love in public here if you are the same sex and I know maybe you can't do that where you live, but *still*, I am trying to get to MAP, the best clothing store, at the other end of town, so use the fucking sidewalk.

Here's what's really going to get me in trouble. Sometimes it's *overly* gay here. There are many great drag queens appearing here (Dina Martina is my favorite), but I'm still scarred from the awful ones from the past that seemed like the Amos and Andy of gay culture in Provincetown when I first got here. Would any gay man really want to be Arthur Blake, the insult comic who had been in Bette Davis movies but spent his later years in Provincetown drinking and giving all gay people bad reputations by performing in hideous Tallulah Bankhead drag? Worse was the potbellied drag queen Sylvia Sidney, who played here for years and horrified passing tourists every afternoon when he'd "bark" his act out front of the club as drag queens are still contractually obliged to do today. "You ugly cocksuckers," he'd yell at families through his missing teeth, dressed in a Clarabell red wig and ill-fitting tacky gowns.

Not every gay man in the world wants to be a woman. Recently I was minding my own gay business on the street, talking to a friend, and a big lug of a queen came over to me and said,

"Hi, girl." I was momentarily stunned. Had I "dropped an earring," as they used to say in the old days when you were publicly mincing? Had I been flitting? Why had he referred to me as a girl? Just because he knew I was gay? Do I look like a girl?! I'm not the butchest thing in the world but I'm pretty obviously a man. I looked to my left, I looked to my right. "You couldn't have been talking to me, could you, sir?" I asked dismissively. Too familiar or too gay? You be the judge.

I hate dogs. Well, not dogs themselves. They can't help being held prisoner by their deaf owners, who never seem to hear their captives' barks. "He's just talking," one actually said to me when I complained. "Yeah, well, arf! Arf!" I said. "That means shut up!" Provincetown has been named the Most Dog-Friendly Town in America and I'm afraid to tell you it's true. I live on the beach, and every day while I'm trying to write, I hear, "Fluffy, stop it!" "Fluffy, stop barking." Do these jailers think their dogs are taking notes? I wonder. "Heel!" I want to shout about a hundred times a day—that's the only word a dog understands. Sometimes the yapping goes on for so long on the beach below that I throw caution to the wind and yell, "Shut up!" Stunned silence. They can't see where I'm yelling from, but some vaguely point up to the vicinity of my apartment with confused outrage.

I've since solved the problem of annoying barking by sending just $4.95 plus shipping to the *National Enquirer* for one of their advertised "bark stoppers." It supposedly sends out a high-pitched pulse sound that is inaudible to humans yet I guess annoys the shit out of barking dogs. I change the batteries every summer and set it to high. "Does it work?" pet lovers always ask in alarm when they visit the apartment and I show it off. "Well, do you hear any dogs barking?" I respond snappily. When they admit no, I realize this product doesn't even need to offer a money-back guarantee.

Then there's the Pilgrim Monument. All these years in Provincetown, I can't decide if I love it or hate it. I had always heard the old wives' tale that if you actually lived here and climbed to the top of the 252-foot tower that dominates the town's skyline, you would soon move away for good. Like a curse or a hex. But I finally did so in the early 2010s and I'm still here every summer, so that is bullshit. I always wanted to buy that painting I saw in the local paper just *before* 9/11 happened that showed a small plane crashing through the Pilgrim Monument, but when I tracked down the artist credited, he refused to admit he painted it or that there even *was* such a painting. It wasn't as if I thought he was a clairvoyant terrorist or anything.

"Now tell me about this ridiculous tower," a smart art-collector friend of mine said to me as she linked her arm in mine and we strolled up Commercial Street on her first visit to Provincetown. Ha! I was shocked at the blasphemous-to-locals statement, but she wasn't being snarky. I guess unlike most tourists here she *had* seen the original Torre del Mangia, in Siena, Italy, from which ours is completely copied. Neither monument has anything to do with the Pilgrims *or* Provincetown. It *is* kind of ridiculous. A Boston architect complained, "If all they want [in Provincetown] is an architectural curiosity, why not select the Leaning Tower of Pisa and be done with it?" *The Boston Globe* reported, "Even the people of Provincetown are not at all enthusiastic about the design but are glad enough to get almost any sort of monument." Weak praise indeed.

But I guess I'll agree with all the locals today and love the Pilgrim Monument, too. Channing Wilroy, who appeared in many of my films, is employed there and takes the money when you park your car. He'll be happy to pose for selfies if you ask him politely. The gift shop is pretty great, and right outside is a popular spot for gay weddings and receptions (Hillary Clinton *and* Cher appeared there together *with* Cher drag queens, too, to raise campaign money for the 2016 presidential election). It may be "ridiculous," as my friend innocently commented, but it's ours. Climb to the top and you will finally be able to accept and embrace the stupidest, most despised-by-locals mispronunciation of their great town's name. You're on a no vacation in "Providencetown" and no better place could you be.

BETSY

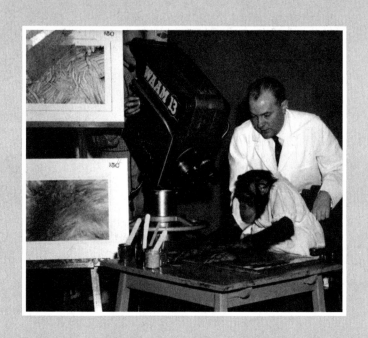

When David Byrne was recently asked by a reporter "What art are you collecting these days?" he answered, "Who can afford to buy art anymore?" He was right. The days of going in that one cutting-edge gallery you thought only *you* knew about and buying an artwork for under $5,000 by an artist who's having a second show there after getting his or her first good review are long over. Today's "great" collections are made up of blue-chip art bought for astronomical prices from auction houses.

Every movement that changed the art world and ended up being worth money was first hated—abstract expressionism, minimalism, video—but now it's all accepted. A few artists still go out on a limb, such as Gelitin, the collective from Vienna who had a sculpture show at Greene Naftali Gallery in New York, where the work was displayed on pedestals with levers gallery-goers could step on to launch the sculptures off their perches to smash onto the floor. You couldn't restore the works once the show was over because, by then, they had been broken so many times nothing was left but rubble. But *still*, that rubble was art, and in its own faintly powerful way was still respectable.

So what's left? Only one collectible art movement from the past hasn't been reinvented, hoarded, or parodied. Want to speculate in the art market? I'm telling you what to buy—monkey art. Yes, paintings by chimpanzees. The second half of the 1950s was the Golden Age of Monkey Art, and artist apes were used as a tool to make fun of abstract expressionism and then to establish a market value, first for charity, followed by profit for their high-minded dealers. It has been said these "monkey painters do not take the slightest interest in their product," and isn't this the ultimate fuck-you artists of today are constantly trying to affect? Isn't the ultimate lack of concern for the collector just plain too cool for school no matter how hard you try to be transgressive?

Thierry Lenain's *Monkey Painting*, with an introduction by Desmond Morris (the Clement Greenberg of ape art), published in 1997, is the holy grail of this semi-forgotten-dying-to-be-rescued art movement. Here you can read the complete history of creative chimpanzees of the canvas and you will also meet the stars. For me, there is only one, Betsy, and like the female artists Bridget Riley and Sturtevant, she is just waiting to be rediscovered and deified. Betsy was the first famous monkey painter and she lived in Baltimore. Thanks to the showboat director at the Baltimore Zoo at the time, Arthur Watson, the Betty Parsons of gorilla art, Betsy became an international phenomenon.

But before Betsy came Babs, my first monkey idol. I knew her from being a guest with my Cub Scout troop on the local TV show *This Is Your Zoo*, where she often appeared dressed in gowns or fur coats, along with Dr. Watson, the host of the show. Babs was mostly loved by the audience for being such a brat on live TV—biting the guests, refusing commands, knocking over the set, and occasionally letting loose a frightening jungle screech. I was so impressed as a kid that I later named Divine's character in *Pink Flamingos* Babs in her honor. "Babs?" snarls Divine's disdainful enemy Raymond Marble, played by David Lochary. "What a stupid fucking name!" "Sounds like a chimpanzee on a tire swing," Mink Stole's character, Connie Marble, bitchily adds. Ha. It was.

But Babs got too unruly as she got older and, worse yet, became pregnant, so Arthur Watson groomed her successor for fame too, plus she had talent to boot. After a contest on the show to select a name, "Betsy" made her debut and was an immediate hit. She painted on live TV. Her local publicity got so big that she had to go national. Realizing he had a true star, Dr. Watson took Betsy on the road. Wearing a white bonnet and carrying a pink suitcase, she arrived in New York City for a round of appearances, including *The Garry Moore Show* on CBS and *Tonight* on NBC. Her work was already selling, too, raising much-needed money for the zoo animals' fund back at home.

The media frenzy eventually went international, and Congo, a male chimp from the London Zoo who was also a painter, issued a "challenge" to Betsy to come to the United Kingdom to see who was the better artist. Congo painted with oil in an abstract way and used an actual paintbrush or two, while Betsy much preferred finger paint. Congo may have felt like an uppity Lucian Freud looking down on Brice Marden, who also didn't paint with conventional artist tools, but wasn't Betsy way ahead of her time in refusing to show "craft," mocking the very idea of a "good" and "bad" painting like a primate Neil Jenney? Congo was referred to by his people as "the master," which furthered the tradition of male chauvinism in the art world. To me, Congo was dull, old-school, stuffy, and a bit of a copycat without the slightest thought of appropriation. Let no one forget—Betsy came first.

Finally the art establishment across the pond began to take notice. The Institute of Contemporary Arts in London hosted a show of these two competing artists in 1957, titled *Paintings by Chimpanzees*, and called the canvases "the only genuine works of abstract art in the whole history of art and painting." Congo must have gotten cold feet, because as the opening approached, he came down with a sudden case of pneumonia and didn't attend. The rest of the cognoscenti did, though. "But, darling, just how contemporary can you get?" one trendy art maven gushed to the press. Betsy's work was more "mature" and reminded one critic of a "highly magnified detail from a Van Gogh." "It's inspired, just inspired," moaned another Betsy fan to a reporter that magnificent night. Even though Congo was being billed as the "Cézanne of the Ape World," some scribes thought his work "brash" and worried if perhaps he "gave the impression of a sense of insecurity." No matter. The macho-male collector artists went for Congo. Picasso acquired one, Miró swapped two of his paintings for one of Congo's, but Salvador Dalí nixed both, commenting, "The hand of the chimpanzee is quasi-human, the hand of Jackson Pollock is totally animal." The Russian press panned both Congo and Betsy, too. "To exhibit the daubs of these two chimpanzees—is this not the most shining example of the decay of bourgeois art?" Finally, what an art movement always needs to succeed—condemnation. Monkey art was now history.

Was Betsy a victim of misogyny in the art world? The Baltimore Museum of Art's male director at the time sneered that finger painting was worthless. The Maryland Institute College of Art Alumni Association borrowed Betsy's paintings for a meeting to welcome the new head man on the job, but when the press found out, the trustees dove for cover, claiming the artwork was there for "amusement" and certainly did not "compromise an exhibition sponsored by the school." When Betsy's work was entered in a Berkeley, California, art show, a male artist howled to the press, "No chimpanzee is going to make a monkey out of me," and she was given the boot.

It seemed Betsy's manager, Arthur Watson, who had become practically the Colonel Tom Parker of the monkey business by now, couldn't trust the lasting fame of a female artist, either. He brought in one of Betsy's old cage-mate boyfriends, a four-year-old chimp from West Africa named Dr. Thom, and made him Betsy's public boyfriend. But according to the press at the time, Dr. Thom was disturbed and jealous of Betsy's success. "Having his mate suddenly catapulted to fame and fortune caused tremors in the fragile ego of Dr. Thom," one reporter presumed. So Dr. Watson tried to make him a star in his own right, buying him a piano and hoping to donate some of the recordings of his banging on the keys to the public library to be cataloged and placed alongside the composers Beethoven, Bartók, and Brahms. The library politely declined. Dr. Thom was no Van Cliburn of the jungle, no simian Glenn Gould, and the public knew it. Betsy was the real thing. Dr. Thom was a charlatan.

Betsy presumably put up with this sham marriage until she took on a companion named Spunky, who was bought by the zoo with funds raised by the sale of Betsy's artwork. Betsy may have had to pay for love but at least she found it. It must have been too much for Dr. Thom, though, because just a few years later, in 1960, he dropped dead, maybe from a broken heart and a failed career. Then in an artwork horror story to rival Jackson Pollock's fatal car crash, Betsy's paramour, Spunky, accidentally fell on her from the top of their cage and broke her leg just a few days after the death of Dr. Thom. Betsy was rushed to a human hospital and given emergency treatment including open-heart surgery, but, alas, she passed away, too. An autopsy revealed that Betsy had also been suffering from cancer of the stomach and liver. Like many geniuses, Betsy was doomed. Her heirs were unknown. Spunky the monkey faded to obscurity quickly. Betsy's obituary appeared in *Time* magazine, and one Baltimore paper in a front-page story remembered her as the "Picasso of the Primates." Betsy was dead. But her legend was just beginning.

For a monkey who lived only nine years, 1951–60, Betsy certainly left her mark in art history. But it took a while. In 1962 Desmond Morris published his serious study of monkey art titled *The Biology of Art*, subtitled *A Study of the Picture-Making Behaviour of the Great Apes and Its Relationship to Human Art*. In my opinion, the author overpraised Congo just because he could draw circles. Big deal. Betsy wasn't traditional, maybe her smears *were* circles, only abstracted. Yet her detractors still called her a "zoological joke." Why? Because she didn't paint with a brush? Yves Klein didn't always either and nobody gave him grief, did they? No, because he was a man.

At least Desmond Morris included two of Betsy's finger paintings in his groundbreaking book, even though they were reproduced in black and white and Congo's were in full color. But it's all about image, correct? More important to Betsy's reputation was that Morris also ran, right up in the front, that great WAAM, Channel 13, press photo of the TV camera filming Betsy painting. There she was in full Baltimore glory, costumed in that smock dress, creating monkey art for the world to see. As powerful an artist photo as the one Mapplethorpe did of Patti Smith. And talk about a look! Betsy was the Frida Kahlo of finger painting.

Like Warhol, she could bang out paintings, sometimes working on four easels at the same time. Was the Baltimore Zoo Betsy's "Silver Factory"? Of course, some tried to say she was insane. When her creations were shown to a child psychologist, they were interpreted as that of "a fiercely belligerent ten-year-old girl of the schizoid type." But Betsy was no baby Camille Claudel. No homicidal Tracey Emin. She may have died before her time like Basquiat, but she was her own person. She was Betsy!

Yet her place as the First Lady of primate painters still needed cementing. Pop art came out about the same time as Betsy's first serious appraisal in the Desmond Morris book, but the press moved on to a whole new movement to ridicule. Monkey art was abstract-expression oriented; old news. Pop artists were themselves now the monkeys.

In 2004, the Dime Museum, a local Baltimore antique shop and gallery started by Dick Horne, hosted the first retrospective of Betsy's paintings, complete with a catalog of sorts—well, OK, a brochure that gave an overview of Betsy's history and press reviews. For many young Baltimoreans, this was the first time they had heard of Betsy, and notices such as "a painter of genius" from Reuters News Service in 1954 were considered without a grain of salt.

Two years later, a longtime Betsy supporter and collector, Rebecca Hoffberger, found a way to include Betsy's works in the *Home and Beast* exhibition at her Visionary Art Museum in Baltimore, the only American institution dedicated to "outsider art." Again, Betsy was being taken seriously in a well-respected academic setting.

Betsy was the ultimate outsider artist, wasn't she? You could call her anything you like—"charlatan," "amateur," even "an animal"—but she wouldn't care. Write any lie you can dream up—it's legally impossible to libel a monkey. And, yes, Betsy was mentally challenged. Studies have been done, according to *National Geographic*, on captive animals compared to ones raised in their natural habitat. True, Betsy was pampered by her handlers, but the Baltimore Zoo couldn't hold a candle to the lush jungles of Liberia, where she was born. Did Betsy feel the "depression-like" symptoms of other animals kidnapped from their native countries by well-meaning zoologists? In nature, if one animal has "behavioral disorders," it may "impair their chance of survival" and they are preyed upon. But who would eat Betsy? Not the art world.

A year earlier, three abstract tempera paintings by Congo were sold at auction in London for nearly $30,000, and again the press had a field day, but at least "the golden age of monkey painting" was back in the news, this time with a hint of respect. Betsy was the other chimpanzee mentioned by name, yet she had only managed to bring in a paltry $4,500 over the years in secondary sales. Was I the only one to notice this hole in the market? Congo was now the sole blue-chip gorilla artist around, but he was getting kind of pricey. Betsy was undervalued and just waiting to be rediscovered.

But did Betsy even have a dealer? I knew the Baltimore Zoo still owned the Betsy collection, but they were hardly out there pushing her work. Yes, they had a bio of Betsy and her paintings, but it hadn't been updated in years. I waited. I watched. And a decade later I knew it was time to pounce. I called the Baltimore Zoo to inquire about Betsy's work, and after a polite but confused "Hold on a minute" from the receptionist, I was turned over to Jane Ballentine, public relations director, and Nancy Hines, executive vice president for institutional advancement. Yes, they were Betsy's representatives, and how could they help? I explained my zeal for Betsy's work, how ahead of its

time it was, but didn't let on I had heard through the grape-
vine from an ex-employee that "many" of Betsy's works were
still there gathering dust "on a top shelf of the Madison Building" inside the zoo complex. Not wanting to flood the market,
Betsy's zoo gallery representatives did not mention this information either, but they seemed excited by my ranting that now
was the time for Betsy to reappear in the art world.

When I explained I wanted to tell the world to "Buy Betsy"
as an investment, they offered to make me a seventieth-birthday
gift of a painting, and since I worried about violating insider-
trading laws, I agreed not to mention the work itself or the photo
op surrounding my acceptance until *Mr. Know-It-All* was published. The only problem with the artwork I selected was that
the zoo's dealers weren't sure which end was up and which end
was down. After picking up the painting, my assistant Susan
wrote them, "There seems to be some holes on one of the edges
of the back of the frame where the wire may have been at-
tached," which could suggest top and bottom, and "while we are
not one hundred percent sure how it was painted," Betsy's people
agreed with our assessment.

Finally I can reveal the details of my monkey masterpiece.
Oddly vaginal, the work on paper strikes an uneasy balance
between the cliché blue of boyhood and the hackneyed pink of
femininity. Yes, it is a conflicted vision—alarming and even
violent in the middle, but Betsy's unhesitating gestures, her
nuanced marks and digital stabs at clarity, turn a mere finger
painting into an arduous monkey version of Gustave Courbet's
scandalous *L'Origine du monde*.

Let the stampede begin. Betsy buyers—remember, there's
only so much work available, and like Peter Doig's, her paintings are going to be gobbled up quickly, and once a market is
established, the prices will get ridiculous. Betsy's not around to

object so no one will grumble. But, collectors, once they're priced out of your budget, don't despair. Betsy had many imitators, and those artists will eventually be discovered, too.

Like Achilla the gorilla. One or two of the sketches he did in 1954 before eating the pencil he had drawn them with would definitely be a find, but, alas, these obscure works are presumably lost forever. Alexander, an orangutan at the London Zoo, was encouraged to give art a try at the same time but only showed "mild interest," yet his Joan Mitchell–esque colored horizontal abstracts show promise, and the early dates alone of this work assure its collectibility. The drawings of Sophie, a particularly docile ten-year-old gorilla from the Rotterdam Zoo, are a dead ringer for Cy Twombly's, and her paintings almost predict his later more beautiful and poetic work. That her "enormous self" was photographed sitting at a table and "working so diligently with small, jerking movements on the paper" only added to her Agnes Martin–like appeal at the time. Mark my words. Sophie's time will come.

B-list or emerging artists? You be the judge. Julia may still be a monkey, but her uncluttered, minimalistic circle drawings show a simplicity uncommon in most gorilla artists. She is definitely one to consider. Jessica the chimp was quite a reductionist herself and her work could almost be compared to that of Richard Tuttle, but then she pulls the rug out from under your expectations by switching styles to a Christopher Wool– like black pastel scribble. While we certainly can't go to her studio today, Lady, a chimpanzee painter famous for her recurring fanlike motifs that bring to mind Suzan Frecon's brown watercolors, was always singled out in her day. So far no monkey sculptures have been discovered, but Dzeta, a pygmy chimpanzee from an animal farm in Belgium, certainly seems to have channeled Fred Sandback's string sculptures with her few very visible line drawings, which seem suddenly vibrant and three-dimensional after being viewed in this more modern-art context.

Many monkey art collectors seek out the well-documented work of Charles the Gorilla, who was rescued as a baby in West Africa, where he was found lying next to his dead mother, and then shipped to the Toronto Zoo in 1974, where he lived thereafter. At first, Charles was thought "unattractive" by zoo visitors because of his balding hair and sores that covered much of his body, yet the female gorillas must have thought otherwise because Charles fathered fifteen children while in custody. Later, he began to avoid contact with the other gorillas and moped "in solitude" until zookeeping art speculators gave Charles large pieces of paper and nontoxic paint to distract him. Charles must have been inspired, because he created a whole body of work, much of it sold by a private Canadian art gallery for as much as $400–$800 a pop, raising over $37,000 for the Toronto Zoo.

But I say big deal! Been there, done that. Charles the Gorilla was a mere retread of Congo. His son Jabari is the one I'm interested in. After being separated from his father and sent to the Dallas Zoo, Jabari was thrown into a fit of rage by a group of youths who taunted him. Escaping his cage, he climbed over an eighteen-foot wall and, just like any crazed artist worth his salt, ran amok and injured three patrons in the visiting area while others fled in panic. The cops were called, and Jabari supposedly attacked them, too, and was shot to death before a zoo staffer could humanely dart or subdue him. But did Jabari paint? That's what I want to know! Surely with his famous artist father, someone at the zoo would have tried to exploit him just as they did his dad. Has anyone looked deep in the bowels of the most obscure drawers in the Dallas Zoo? A gold mine might lie in wait.

Can you go wrong in collecting monkey art? Sure. I'd advise against all primates who got famous as actors first. Cheetah may have been in twelve Tarzan movies, but he didn't start painting until he retired, making himself kind of a Johnny-come-lately Grandma Moses. He "signed" his paintings with his thumbprint, but we monkey sophisticates know that was Cheetah's handler's idea, not the artist's. J. Fred Muggs did have a certain cutting-edge reputation for biting the comedienne Martha Raye on the *Today* show in 1954, but beware of any art done by this ham who never crossed over from these Chris Burden–type antics to actual painting. It's a fake. Peggy the chimp worked in drag in movies and was aggressive to boot, something that might be appealing in today's market. In *Bedtime for Bonzo*, she grabbed then-actor Ronald Reagan on camera by the necktie and tried to strangle him, maybe channeling John Hinckley, Jr.'s later assassination attempt. But, alas, Peggy never picked up the paintbrush either as far as I can discover. If you see a work by her for sale, beware. Monkey art is ripe for forgery.

You might be tempted by the controversy concerning Pierre Brassau. He was an unknown avant-garde French artist whose work was praised by the critics in 1964 for his "powerful strokes" that "twist with furious fastidiousness." Here was a new artist "who performed with the delicacy of a ballet dancer." Only trouble, Pierre Brassau was, in fact, an ape named Peter from Sweden's Boras Zoo, whose work had been placed in a group show by a reporter as a hoax. The usual outrage over monkey art broke out, but the talent of the ape was overshadowed by the fact that Peter preferred eating the paint to placing it on the canvas, and supposedly "liked the tart flavor of cobalt blue," which was always heavily featured in his work, best. When the scam was revealed, the critic still insisted the work was "the best painting in the show," and a collector bought it for $90 (about $600 today), but still we need to remember there's no accounting for taste, even if you eat your art supplies. This kind of hokey provenance is always a detriment down the road. Value must be judged by the work first, not the hype.

Which brings us to my last piece of art advice. Monkey photography is worthless and always will be. Ignore it. Animal artist copyright is still being defined in the courts, and legal limbo is something you'll always want to avoid as a collector. In 2011, according to publicized reports, the British wildlife photographer David Slater traveled to Indonesia, set up cameras in the jungle, and left them for wild monkeys to play with. One monkey, later named Naruto, took many self-portraits, and one of these selfies was copyrighted by Slater and used in 2014 on the cover of his self-published book *Wildlife Personalities*. But then PETA filed a complaint in a U.S. district court listing the monkey Naruto as the plaintiff and suing for copyright infringement. "The monkey selfie resulted from a series of purposeful and voluntary actions by Naruto, unaided by Slater, resulting in original works of authorship by Naruto," the papers charged. "If a human had taken a photo with Slater's camera," they argued, "that person would own the copyright to the photograph. Naruto should be treated no differently." What collector wants to get caught up in endless, expensive court battles? Remember the Warhol Board versus Joe Simon authenticity case, which dragged on for years and cost millions of dollars? PETA eventually lost the monkey copyright case, but appealed, and Slater finally had to settle. Who needs this shit? Forget monkey photography. Stick to monkey paintings. That's where the money is.

RUN-ON ANDY

ndy Warhol once wrote a book called *A* that was not exactly written but transcribed from tapes he and his superstar Ondine recorded of their underground friends motormouthing on speed which were never edited at all so every "uh" and "you know" was included on the final printed pages of this supposed "novel" that almost defied you to actually read it which was even better than William Burroughs' cut-up style so every time I try to write about Andy I can't do it in a normal way, no, I have to pretend I'm on amphetamines, too, and think with an unfiltered mind and write with an unedited hand and start ranting like an avant-garde idiot about how at first I wanted to be Andy Warhol but he didn't want to be me because he had never heard of me then and he wanted to be Jackie and I didn't want to be her because she had too much good taste so I wanted Divine to be Jackie and he did play her in one of my movies even though he didn't want to be Jackie either, he wanted to be Liz and so did Andy eventually when he realized he couldn't be true blue blood like Jackie but could be Hollywood famous like Liz at the end of her life when oddly enough Liz started looking a lot like Divine in drag herself and Divine actually wanted to play a man on-screen but not like Joe D'Alessandro who was Andy's male god who with his beautiful body and, yes, his great acting was the real reason the public saw the Warhol movies at all, not because of the charming motormouth of Viva, the threatening S&M sexuality of Mary Woronov who dominated the debauchery of debutante Edie Sedgwick who was replaced by the almost-forgotten Ingrid Superstar who's *still* missing and presumed dead even though I refuse to accept this fact and think about her every day of my life even though I know I should be concentrating on the reverse piety of Pope Ondine or the double false eyelashes and liquid eyeliner worn by Susan Bottomly aka International Velvet or the lioness mane of Baby Jane Holzer or the deadpan junkie glamour of Nico, all of whom would have to agree that Joe's ass was the best one in movie history, even better than Bobby Kendall's in *Pink Narcissus*, and that fact is maybe the most important one in this whole book.

Why oh why is Andy Warhol suddenly the villain in books and movies and TV shows after he's been dead all these years and can't fire you from his past and, no, he wasn't "cheap" he gave you lots of artwork so is it his fault you were too drugged up and irresponsible to keep it somewhere safe and in good shape so you could sell it today for a lot of money and, sure, some of his superstars committed suicide but Andrea Feldman was already fucked-up before she got to Andy and Edie Sedgwick, well, she hurt his feelings by dumping him for Bob Dylan who even stole one of Warhol's *Elvis* paintings and never paid for it so what do you expect and, true, Andy didn't go to Candy Darling's funeral because he feared death and he was right to fear death because he died before his time, didn't he, maybe he had a premonition so why is he suddenly now vilified by his onetime followers and his hangers-on and his business partners who seem to get bolder and meaner in trying to personally hurt him by revealing embarrassing stuff about his sex life or claiming they had all his ideas before him or pretending he was anything but a Democrat in his political taste when they know Andy is dead and can't feel anything now just like he always wanted no matter how much these revisionists deny that Andy's attention and his name itself anointed them with class and sex appeal and a revolutionary street cred of gay-straight bohemia they are *still* living off decades later and which continues to be imitated by punks, socialites, rappers, and even hackers who hide in the dark just as Andy hid under that wig which was such a brilliant way to disguise baldness by covering it up before it even happened, before anybody noticed, before before, just like Andy was before you even thought up anything new so don't try to change history, none of you Warhol ingrates who before Andy knew you were before nothing.

Oh there were holdouts who correctly and almost religiously drank the Warhol Flavor-Aid and I salute these loyal soldiers like Jed Johnson, Andy's boyfriend for twelve years who never spilled the beans even after they broke up or before he died in that terrible TWA Flight 800 that exploded shortly after take-off and come to think of it none of Andy's real boyfriends that came before Jed ever talked either, like Philip Fagan who Andy was so obsessed over that he shot him on film every day in 1966 as he did basically the same thing over and over or the oh-so-handsome Richard Rheem from California who came later in 1966 and moved in with Andy and still has kept his mouth shut as far as I know right up to today and of course there were non-lover loyalists like Vincent Fremont, practically the only heterosexual man to make it through the Factory in good graces, along with his wife, Shelly Dunn Fremont, right up to the end of Andy, even though there is no end of Andy and never will be no matter how much longer Brigid Berlin, Andy's best friend, lives with her breeding and bounty Andy always wanted that Brigid knew and Andy knew he could get the bounty all right but never the breeding and this knowledge bound them together so tightly that they called themselves Mr. and Mrs. Pork but really Brigid was to Andy what Squeaky Fromme was to Manson but even that presumably ended when Squeaky got out of prison and so will Andy and Brigid when Brigid dies but Andy alone never dies and never will and nobody else from the Factory will not die, except maybe Lou Reed whom Andy hated for his disloyalty when Andy was still alive but who finally came around after Andy's death and felt guilty and helped write the beautiful memorial *Songs for Drella* which was Andy's joke drag name they all called him at the Factory to get on his nerves but Lou set the record straight way after Andy was dead physically by making it very clear that Andy was no idiot savant, saying, "He was in charge of us, every one," he explained, "you look towards Andy, the least likely person, but in fact the most likely, he was so smart, so talented and twenty-four hours a day going at it," so there it is, everybody hear this final word and Lou Reed was right.

Remember if you get famous like Andy and believe me, nobody will get a fame that original or complicated or lasting again in our lifetime, you will probably drag a lot of other people from their unfamous lives into the glare with you and some of these people flower on their own which is so great to see and you remain friends with them for life and others will not but still be glad to have been along for the ride and since have found contentment in their own lives which will piss off the ones that haven't—not at each other but at you and you will have to tolerate quietly their misplaced anger that is never appealing in anyone left behind but gets even more desperate and sad in later years when they fail to realize you were one of the few people in their lives who could have remained lasting friends like many others in the same position but they never can acknowledge this so you have to accept the fact it's impossible to get through life without making one or two enemies and while you used to be hurt you eventually don't care anymore and fuck 'em.

I guess Andy could be mean like the one time he was to me when he hosted some downtown-meets-uptown artist event and invited me but said no when I asked if I could bring my new boyfriend and I said, "Well, I can't come then," and finally Andy's people reluctantly said, "OK, bring him," but when we got there Andy refused to speak to me or the boyfriend as punishment but that was the only time he was mean and all the other times he was nice and offered to back *Female Trouble* even though I declined, knowing it would be *Andy Warhol's Female Trouble* but still it was nice as was his respect for Edith Massey when he met her at the Baltimore Museum of Art and whispered to me, "Where did you find her?" and his constant support of Divine's career after he moved to New York hoping to start a career that didn't involve me which I encouraged because I didn't make my films one year after another and how was Divine supposed to make a living but I must admit I did feel some jealousy when Andy and Divine would be photographed together because Divine and I were fighting over how much money I could get out of New Line to pay him to star in *Polyester* but then Andy died yet Divine still stood me up when we were supposed to go to Andy's funeral together as a protest probably encouraged by his manager at the time whom I at first liked until he later wrote a mean book about Divine the second he died and it seemed like a really dumb protest because I went to the Warhol funeral alone and got photographed and Divine didn't go and didn't get photographed and if we had gone as a couple we would have, would have even more.

Oh Andy made mistakes all right like posing in drag for Christopher Makos where Andy looks really silly and loses the dignity he mastered so well over the years even though he was never one of the *Thirteen Most Beautiful Boys* as one of his films was called and he always wanted to be one and who doesn't and by this I don't mean Christopher's pictures weren't good, they were really good especially if you were Christopher and not Andy who also sometimes made missteps in picking superstars in my opinion like Rene Ricard who some thought a genius but I remember him as a tedious, enabling drug addict whose bitterness was exhausting and unattractive or Eric Emerson who couldn't wait to sue Andy for being in his movies or on his album covers even though he was hardly a superstar at all really, just a bit player who would have been shoved out anyway when Fred Hughes came to power at the Factory and encouraged the worst in Andy's social-climbing ways which led to the awful Studio 54 that I always hated (and I could get in) because I was a disco-sucks-Mudd-Club kind of guy and the piss-elegant Halston crowd including his hustler boyfriend Victor Hugo who yes, had a big dick and posed for the *Sex Parts* paintings and pissed on the canvas for the stunning *Oxidation* ones too but still seemed lower-echelon B-list Warhol to me compared to Andy's past circle of friends like power broker Henry Geldzahler, idea man Billy Name, crackpot egghead and fag hag Dorothy Dean, lifetime beatnik Taylor Mead, even the over-the-edge-of-sanity Valerie Solanas who shot him and is still partially responsible for his early death yet wrote one of the greatest man-hating feminist classic books, the *S.C.U.M. Manifesto*, which you should read or you don't know one thing.

Andy's art was of course confrontational and radical and has aged better than even he could have imagined especially since when he died his career both critically and financially was at a low point but the masterpieces can't be denied, like the "soup cans," the "tuna fish disasters," the "Brillo boxes," the "painting by numbers," the "electric chairs," the "self-portraits," and yes, the "shadows," the "camouflages," the "Rorschachs" and the "Last Suppers," even the underappreciated once under-valued "yarn" paintings that are right on up there with the best in my humble opinion and the same goes for the sublimely subtle un-ironic "abstract" paintings that celebrated the very movement that came before Andy that he helped destroy, yet are almost never shown today even though you can see them in that rare beautiful little catalog published by Anton Kern Gallery but all these really inspire me to want to curate a show I'd like to call *The Worst of Warhol* and why not since I already did a show at the Warhol Museum in Pittsburgh called *Andy's Porn* where I asked all the department heads there to go through their archives and find me Andy's dirtiest stuff like his per-sonal "whack stack" of porn that oddly looked now a little like Larry Clark's early work and the hard-on and pussy shots fans had sent him plus the hard-core movies Andy made himself like *Couch* and we really pushed the definition of "porn" by in-cluding the paintings of O. J. Simpson Andy did and Eva Braun news clippings that were maybe once considered and wisely rejected as source material, so why shouldn't I go beyond "porn" to "worst," can't that be lower down the ladder of taste, yet certainly stronger than the word "mediocre" which in comparison would have to include the popular but too-cheery-for-me "flower" paintings or the "shoes," or even the "Crosses" or "eggs" which come to think of it I like better than mediocre but not as much as best along with the not-as-bad-as-they-say Basquiat co-painted ones but OK, get to the point what is the worst of Warhol, the very worst you ask, and I'll answer with a vengeance—those awful "Renaissance paintings," the ho-hum "cowboy and Indian" prints, oh God, those gaggingly politically correct for money "ten famous Jews" or "endangered species" or the pukingly whimsical "toys" or the hackneyed nostalgic "ads" or worse yet the "athletes," eccccchhhhh the "Hans Christian Andersen" ones at the very bottom of the Warhol atrocious barrel—the phonily patriotic "moonwalk" ones and give me a *Reader's Digest* shopping-mall-gallery break, those terrible "Statue of Liberty" paintings but then maybe, just plain maybe, all the "worst" could rise up as an installation and become a new Warholian version of "best" that negates the word "worst" into nonexistence when used to describe any of Andy's work individually rather than together which would now be historically considered beyond "best" into ideal.

But who really cares about his art in the long run because Andy's movies are the very best work he ever did and one day the dumb little world will realize that once collectors get video monitors embedded in their walls and framed like the rest of their art and these newfangled DLPs are projected to perfectly duplicate the grainy, jumpy quality of Warhol's 16mm films, they'll know that he was more important than Thomas Alva Edison and D. W. Griffith because yeah, they started the movies but Andy stopped them in their tracks and forced them to go back to the beginning and start again by filming nothing with no direction, no camera movement, no editing, no nothing except really cute people all speeded up on amphetamines in a slowed-down way to almost a still photograph yet still moving on film so that the only thing that was happening in the movie was time itself and the nonstars who were better than the real ones became landscapes of frozen personalities who were never topped even to this day in overall bohemian coolness, so think, just think, if all Andy's movies were playing in every room of your house on the walls like *Eat* showing in the kitchen and *Couch* unspooling over your own couch in the living room and up the stairs on the second floor would be *Kiss* that ever-so-lovely make-out masterpiece playing in your bedroom wall just to get the foreplay going and once its fifty-four-minute running time was over BANG on would come *Blow Job*, Andy's most ridiculously passive reverse porn movie that is a complete turn-on but shows nothing and once you had an orgasm watching someone else receiving the oral attention you may or may not have just received you can doze off to the biggest phallic porn star there is, the Empire State Building that is stationarily shot for eight hours by Jonas Mekas of all people, the best underground film critic in the world that was so hard to direct that Warhol even gave a rare codirector credit to John Palmer for having such a brilliant casting idea in the first place and if *Empire* doesn't put you to sleep grab the remote and hit *Sleep* for the ultimate reverse-action movie that shows a man sleeping for eight hours and to make matters worse, actually cheats and uses some of the same footage twice to pad out the running time and if this doesn't bring on Mr. Sandman, well take some speed and go into your TV room and watch the later Warhol more commercial ones that Paul Morrissey is still flipping out about not receiving proper credit for even though we all know Paul directed them so why's he so bitter especially since he got a couple houses and $27 million for the Montauk property Andy initially bought with him, way more money than anybody else ever got out of Andy and these movies would never have gotten made without Andy's name on them so Warhol did "make" them just like Jeff Koons "makes" his sculptures and I guess since I've always liked Paul, despite his insane right-wing politics, that, OK, "producing" might be a better term but Andy was into branding before any other artists except maybe Salvador Dalí who did it badly and ruined his career through greed if you ask me but you didn't so instead I'll tell you the movies Andy did direct or didn't direct that I think are great and the ones that I think are not so great but none of them are bad even though they're really hard to watch, some people can't even get through *Vinyl*, which is a black-and-white low-rent high-concept S&M version of *Clockwork Orange* where Edie Sedgwick is billed as the star and does not one thing in the movie except just sit there looking bored or *My Hustler* with Paul America who just hung around the Factory and occasionally fucked Edie Sedgwick, according to poor dead Callie Angell who committed suicide after completing the brilliant first volume of the catalogue raisonné of the Warhol Foundation of the Warhol films, but back to Paul, that bastard successfully sued Andy Warhol for not paying him, and by that I mean Paul America, not Morrissey, sued Andy and not for Paul's movies, *Flesh*, *Trash*, and *Heat*, the trilogy that changed the rules of male nudity in modern-day cinema both underground and in Hollywood, or some of the lesser-known Warhol sagas that I think deserve to be moved up the list from minor to major like *Imitation of Christ*, starring that beauty Patrick Tilden who played here the messed-up child of Ondine and Brigid Berlin and then vanished into post-Warhol obscurity or *Bike Boy* with the fake Joe D'Allessandro Joe Spencer or *I, a Man* with the fake Joe D'Allessandro Tom Baker, both of whom were still good if we couldn't have the real thing Joe himself and of course *Chelsea Girls*, the *Ben-Hur–Star Wars–Cleopatra* of the Warhol epics, even *Bad*, the one movie of Andy's that critics said was trying to copy mine which it kind of was but so what, I copied him so heavily in *Roman Candles* and we copied each other without knowing it when we titled our movies *Trash* and *Mondo Trasho* at the same time before either of us knew each other so I was flattered that he had that scene in *Bad* that was compared to my movies where the baby got thrown out of the window and I mean Carroll Baker was the star for God's sake and it doesn't matter that she later said to me, "The Teamsters directed that movie," meaning maybe nobody really directed it which is what Andy really wanted all along by letting his boyfriend Jed have the credit so how could it be "bad" like the title or a few of the other Warhol ones that weren't exactly "bad," well yes, *L'Amour* was bad but some of the others just weren't quite good even though they had great titles like *The Nude Restaurant, Lonesome Cowboys,* or *Blue Movie* but if you really want to die and go to Warhol cinema heaven you have to see ****, or *Four Stars* as you say the title out loud, the twenty-five not twenty-four-hour epic that has only been shown once in its entirety beginning October 15, 1967, and going into the next day at the Film-Makers' Cinematheque in New York and has never been shown again even in a reconstituted way because as Ms. Angell, an authority if there ever was one, wrote in 1994, "No notes or other papers have yet been found to indicate how the reels were projected or how the sound tracks were handled," in other words if you weren't there, you wouldn't know, and I wasn't there goddammit, although I might have thought I was once and was wrong, well, I'm the biggest celluloid loser of the twentieth century because I *could* have been there that one night, I was alive wasn't I, but I guess I tragically and stupidly chose not to attend.

Andy Warhol should be your own personal God especially if you're young and haven't yet realized you need some kind of "higher power" to pray to later in life once common sense has forced you to reject whatever spiritual training you received as a child and while I have claimed both Jean Genet and Pier Paolo Pasolini as my personal saviors and have obviously been rewarded after my many prayers to them over my long career,

I feel they may be a tad overburdened by my constant demands and recommend you always ask Warhol just because he's much less judgmental than those two and now that he's dead I bet more than ever he finds anyone still living to be "cute, really cute" and hopes before you die you'll change your will and leave him all your money but how *could* you leave Andy all your money when he's dead you'll wonder and I'll tell you how or at least how you *should* be able to leave Warhol your moola if the Warhol Board I used to serve on would just take my advice and change the Foundation's bylaws so that rich crazy people could leave their fortunes to the Warhol Board to use as it does now to award grants to organizations that cause trouble in the art world just like Andy would have wanted and what a perfect way that would be for fed-up parents to cut off their trust-fund brats or childless millionaires to snub their noses at bogus charities or just plain self-destructive debutantes who can't fritter away their fortunes fast enough to reflect their entitlement or idle superiority by leaving all their inheritance to the Andy Warhol Foundation and I've even thought up the perfect public-service announcement—"Andy's Dead but He Wants Your Bread! Leave Him Your Cash and Make a Big Splash!"

MY SON, BILL

Dear Bill,

You're fourteen years old now, yes, an adult baby who refuses to be trapped in an infant's body, and whether you like it or not, a submissive bottom just like your mother (more on that later). So I decided now was the right time to write you this letter explaining where you came from, how you were born, and my complicated feelings of love toward you as your adoptive father. True, you are not real, you are made of vinyl and can't experience human emotions and will never grow up, but that doesn't mean I'm not concerned for your future. I have awoken to an understanding of your place in the world today, one awash in trigger warnings, gender confusion, anti-oppression training in the workplace, and a lack of pubic hair on today's teens. Let me explain why I had you made and my revolutionary paternal hope that you will always be beyond hurt, maturity, or guilt. You will sit on that chair in my living room until I die, oblivious of the sexual and racial struggle of your own troubled generation.

You are a reborn baby, Bill; one of those onetime dolls (in your case a Linda Evans brand) who were completely taken apart by their "adoptive mothers," who then stripped off your factory-issued paint and heated up your vinyl skin to reach a temperature where it could be manipulated by oven-mitted hands into new expressions and then plunged into cold water to set. Your face was tinted and painted in countless layers before human hair and new eyeballs were added, making you the perfect addition to the childless homes of insane individuals like myself who then raise you as if you were real. And you *are* real to me, Bill. Yes, you were burned, tortured, and drowned before I got you, but I look at that as a new form of natural childbirth, not child abuse. You are as real to me as if I had given birth to you myself, which in a way, I did. My onetime assistant Susan is your adoptive mother-in-waiting because she dealt with Laura from Bella Baby Nursery, who actually made you with her own hands and put that fake spittle on your lips, added the magnet that would keep your pacifier firmly plastered to your pouty lips, and even added your little baby penis, too. Because the "adoption policy" is taken so seriously in the "re-born" community, as some refer to the Secret Society of Birth Online, I wasn't sure if I could get away with asking for what I really wanted, "an angry baby boy with bad hair," so I let Susan convey my wishes to Laura in slightly more gentle terms.

But that's what I got, isn't it, Bill? We both have bad hair, yet isn't that part of who we are today? And of course you are angry. You were once a doll and dolls are always mistreated, by artists who mock their goodness and forcibly place them in un-branded environments for irony's sake, by little boys who kick them first and then often probe their private parts with grimy little fingers, even by their little-girl owners themselves, who you'd think would be more gentle. But no, there's Chatty Cathy lying abandoned in a thrift shop, her vocal cords pulled so violently and often that she's been rendered mute, or Betsy Wetsy, thrown in a Goodwill donation box so hydrated by past female owners, so water damaged from forced feedings, that she couldn't wet anything, only shit out her flooded plastic bladder parts for the world to see. And Barbie? The most mutilated, violated, disfigured, sexually assaulted doll in the history of the world? She's angry, too, Bill, and she salutes your pain and cries out for justice.

I remember the day you came home from the hospital. I had already picked your name out because I had an old Christmas ball that I found in Value Village with the name Bill printed on it in a hand-done and somewhat clumsy way. It was destiny, Bill. Susan and I took you out of the quilt-lined box you came in and sat you down on my antique chair that originally came from my grandmother's attic. There you were in my living room, glaring out into the world, wearing that one baby outfit you will don for the rest of your life except for that silly red velour, faux-fur-trimmed hoodie I make you put on every year for my Christmas party. I know you hate that costume and feel humiliated by it. I'm sorry. Sometimes we have to do things for our fathers that we loathe now but approve of later. One day you'll thank me for giving you this lone holiday fashion experience.

You can never go out. I tried a few times but I'm always paranoid I'll forget and leave you in the car, and while you patiently await the return of your master (me) in the front passenger seat you always demanded (rejecting the stupid baby seats in the back), outraged citizens, not knowing you can't die, will see you inside and break the windows in a misguided attempt to give you fresh air. Once I took you to my dad's eightieth birthday party at a country club but kept you out of sight in the trunk until I could herd all my nieces and nephews to the parking lot "to meet a new relative." When I took you out, they at first froze in horror but then howled in laughter, which made me feel a little bad for you, Bill, but that was nothing compared to the outrage of one of my nieces, Lucy. "You're sick, Uncle John!" she screamed as I covered your ears. "Just plain sick!" That's when I realized you must stay at home forever so you'll be safe from such reactionary judgment.

Don't complain. Right across from your chair is a beautiful Christopher Wool painting you can look at for eternity. I've also forbidden friends to give you presents because I fear you'll spoil easily. There's been room for exceptions, of course. That little gift-wrapped plastic dog turd you received as a Christmas present from an ex-con I taught in prison and helped get paroled after serving twenty-seven years was certainly allowed and I know you're grateful. The hardback book so appropriately titled *Children Who Hate* that was a gift from Dennis Dermody stands behind you as a permanent part of your installation and you have grown to accept that. I even found an ugly outtake from the professional photographer Mom and Dad hired to do my first baby pictures, and in it I look uncannily like you. We could have been twins, Bill!

You're damaged *and* mentally challenged, so your hair was not the only imperfect thing you were born with. I guess you could say you were transgender, too. I was shocked when your birth mother, Laura, told me the doll I selected to become the miracle that is now my son was at first a female doll with no vagina named Emily, who "certainly wasn't sitting on a shelf waiting to be bought." No, she would be "individually sculpted" to my specifications and could be made into either a boy or a girl "awake baby," I was told. An "awake baby"? Compared to what? A dead one? But OK, I'm open-minded. Laura performed bottom surgery on you and made you a little boy with a new penis. "But is it circumcised?" I asked immediately, and she hesitated and admitted it was not. "But it *has* to be,"

I pleaded. "I'm a onetime Catholic and American and cut." She hemmed and hawed and said, "Let me see what I can do with some clay." We waited. And waited some more. Finally she called Susan with the good news. "The operation was a success!" Hallelujah! Bill was now circumcised and she sent pictures to prove it, but I refused to view them because it seemed illegal.

I only looked at your baby johnson in person once. That was enough. I'm certainly not a pedophile. Your pubic area will remain your own business, and since you are never bathed because I was warned anything wet could strip you of your paint and you're not allowed to change your clothes except once a year (that doesn't include your Pampers), you will be the only person to decide if it is ever touched. I realize you're an adolescent now, and although your unit remains tiny, I know your desires are not. Show me a sign, Bill, and I will move one of your hands down near your little tinkler, and if there's ever a minuscule earthquake, you might finally feel some kind of accidental friction that could pass for the beginnings of sexual release.

Sometimes when I enter my living room in Baltimore, I forget you are even there, and when I accidentally look over into your angry face, I jump. You scare me, Bill! Some of my pothead friends swear they've seen you move, but I know better. You can't move. You can't. My own mother seemed to hate you when she was still alive. "Put that damn thing away!" she'd plead whenever she made unavoidable eye contact with you. But don't despair. You *do* have family, Bill. Pat Moran went behind my back and ordered Belle, your supposed sister, whom I've never officially acknowledged until now and, even so, without a DNA test I remain skeptical. Blood relative or not, I don't approve of Belle. Pat buys her many girlie baby outfits, moves her from room to room so she doesn't get bored, and has even taken her to work! Belle is a capitalist pig if you ask me. An entitled brat who is never allowed to visit. I'm not being mean, Bill. I just don't want you to have false hope.

But should you hope at all? For what? A rescuer? After my death, you're willed to my archive at Wesleyan University, but it's quiet there, Bill, oh so quiet. You'll be locked away with almost no visitors except approved-by-my-estate academics, and they don't know how to party the way we did at my house, especially on bad nights when I used to drink more. There will be no roaring fire in the hearth at Wesleyan. No Christopher Wool to look at. I know I didn't have lots of sex in my living room, but the few times I did I forgot you might have been watching. Now? I don't know and it would be bad form for me to ask, but I doubt there's a lot of sexual activity inside the archive, so chances for any future voyeurism would be rare indeed.

You'll have competition. Clint Eastwood's stuff is at Wesleyan, too, Bill. Who's gonna want to look at you when people can ogle Dirty Harry's police badge? Martin Scorsese's estate will be housed in that same building. Can you compete with his love notes to Liza Minnelli if they find them? You'll be old news, Bill! Will they put you next to the talking Virgin Mary statue from *Pecker*? Oh, yeah, she's going there, too. She might be in a box as you will be, Bill, but she can still say "Full of grace" when someone moves her mouth—what can you do? Just sit there with that "grouch on your face," as Edith Massey used to call an unhappy expression? You could end up being exhibited like a freak! Remember Tod Browning's "Chicken Lady"? Ever see a two-headed goat in a sideshow? That could be you, Bill, yes, you!

Should you hope for a fan to steal you once you've been on loan to a museum exhibition (if you get so lucky)? Would that be liberation or servitude? Let's not have any delusions of grandeur, Bill, you wouldn't be art. You'd be pure selfie bait, and even if you are kidnapped (and I tried to protect you from this during my lifetime by forbidding the press to photograph you), you'd never be ransomed back. You'd be an insurance claim that will be unceremoniously settled by both parties with little fanfare, and that will be that, Bill.

True, you'll never have to worry about money. But does that make you a socialist like Bernie Sanders? These days, even Cuba wants democracy, Bill. You know perfectly well that all dolls are not created equal or you wouldn't be sitting in that chair. Some can talk. Remember the before-mentioned brat Chatty Cathy— the one who would never shut up? Every time you'd pull the goddamn cord in the back of her neck she'd start babbling one of her seventeen prerecorded responses. "I love you," she'd annoyingly announce much too needily. "Where are we going?" she stupidly asks—as if it mattered! "May I have a cookie?" she'd nag over and over, never once offering to pay the bill. "No," you'd want to scream, "you cannot!" A woman named June Foray did the original voice for this pesky blabbermouth, and I hope she gets royalties today every time Chatty Cathy, now over, so over, prattles away unheard from a landfill.

I'm always looking for new ways to expand my meager brand, so how about it, Bill? We'll add that same pull chain that Chatty Cathy had to your neck and I'll prerecord your voice and, presto—we will have reinvented the talking-doll sensation for a new era. "I hate you," you could snarl. "Pick me up and you're dead" might be a catchphrase little children would like. Better yet—"Get off my dick, short eyes!" Verbal abuse could be the next big thing in toy stores everywhere. Toys "R" Us may have bit the dust, but maybe they could make a comeback if Bill could yell, "Hug me, you little fucker," to any customer who made eye contact. Let's test-market it for Christmas next year and see!

Can you dream, Bill? Of what? Revenge? Your long-lost

Barbie-doll crotch of anatomically incorrect bliss? Foster parents more liberal than I who might allow you to play? *"Play?"* How dare any adult say that word to you, a future man who will be forever infantilized, a teenager without a hard-on, the son of a filth elder whose reputation you can never surpass. I thought you up, Bill, but you will never think me down! Yet I still dread your judgment. Your rage, your condescending scowl. Don't hate me because I'm happy, Bill. I am but a man, a damaged, self-involved man who realized early in life he should never have real children, only an imitation of a child, like you, Bill. Like you.

What do you expect me to do, let you go? Being reborn is like sloppy seconds, Plan B. You are not even "street"—you can't fight, fuck, or survive without me. You're not capable of violence, either. I know it's wrong of me to suggest, but in your predicament, don't you wish you had a gun, Bill? Then you could become a pretend drug dealer. But whom could you deal the drugs to? Not me. And there are no known reborn drug addicts, so you'd end up taking narcotics yourself, which I'd benevolently allow because you can't OD—you're reborn, but you can't re-die. Have no fear. If you were arrested and went to jail, you'd be OK. You don't have an asshole so you couldn't be anybody's bitch, only a mascot. I guess you could join a gang, Bill. A gang of one. You. And I'd support your no-snitching policies with unconditional love.

Are you gay, Bill? I mean, I know queerdom is not inheritable, but both your surrogate mother, Laura, and your adoptive one, Susan, *are* sort of domineering. I did put Glen, the transgender son of Chucky, the horror-film hero I appeared with in *Seed of Chucky*, right down in the living room next to you, to keep you company. He's kind of cute, isn't he? Like a Walter/Margaret Keane painting that mated with the young Sid Vicious and became a killer-doll sidekick. Have you been having desires of a carnal nature toward Glen? I imagine he is a top and I don't know if you're a bossy bottom or not, but I do know a secret. One that I feel you are now old enough to know. Your maker, Laura, is a bottom, too. I know. I know. It's hard to hear this kind of talk about your own mom. I was shocked, too. But it came straight from the horse's mouth. After I featured you with me on the cover of my annual Christmas card (and many people thought you were real, which led to awkward responses to those heartfelt congratulations about my fatherhood), Laura wrote Susan and me a follow-up e-mail saying she was leaving her real-life husband to be who she is "regardless of what anyone thinks." Oh my God, Bill, divorce is rearing its ugly head in our family. Then our real-life Debbie Rowe wrote a follow-up explaining more than you'll ever need to know. "Sadly for the last fifteen years, I have had to hide my sexually deviant side from my ex-husband," Laura confided. "Now that he's gone I can be who I am—a submissive little slut puppy looking for a master." Yes, Bill, your mother is into S&M. "I guess John picked the right birth mother!" she added, but did I? You would look so silly in leather, Bill. Just plain silly.

Does all this newly revealed information scare you, little one? You didn't react when I confided that your body had been weighted with sand or cat litter so you flopped over when picked up, like a human baby. But suppose it was cat litter, not sand? Are you worried that when I open the front door of my house to retrieve a FedEx package a feral cat will dart in and take a shit on your head? That would scare anybody. Suppose you had already been reborn when 9/11 happened? Would you have been terrified being home without me? I wasn't in Baltimore on that terrible day, I was in New York watching the towers burn down from my apartment near Sixth Avenue. Would you have felt safe here alone? Would you have wanted me to pick you up and tell you the chair you sit in would not be attacked? No tiny little airplanes would come crashing through my antique windowpanes to shatter your uneventful life? Wouldn't you have been scared your bad hair would catch on fire? I could understand your fears, Bill. I promise you I could.

I'm scared, too, Bill, scared to tell you about race. You were born white in white America with all the privileges that come along with that, yet through the years I have noticed that while you don't get old, your skin does get darker, like Michael Jackson's in reverse. No matter what color you are I will always love you, Bill, but will society understand a reborn baby who is slowly turning "half-breed," as Cher once so energetically sang? It's not just me. White liberal friends who visit my home are way too sensitive to bring up your skin tone, but when I show them photographs of you through the years, it's pretty hard to ignore. We know racial coloring is not a choice. You are not some baby version of the NAACP's Rachel Dolezal either, sneakily trying to pass as a person of color, but one day you will be a full-fledged mixed blood, so you'd better get used to it. Will you feel prejudice as a natural-born, *Black Like Me* version of *Johnny Got His Gun*? You can't march, you can't riot, but God knows you can do sit-ins. Your whole life is a sit-in, but does anybody but me notice? You must feel like a Buddhist monk who tries to set himself on fire as a protest, but then the gasoline never ignites. Remember the movie *Pinky*, Bill? You should. You're a pinky yourself. And guess who that film stars? Ethel Waters! Maybe she's a long-lost relative, you never know!

Chemistry, not society, is turning you darker. You are vinyl, Bill. Vinyl is not a natural substance, and this synthetic plastic made from ethylene and chlorine material will, over time, degrade and then discolor. I hate to tell you this at such a tender age, but you are like a dildo, Bill. Neither reborn babies nor sex toys are regulated by the government, so both are often made of cheaper-to-produce materials. Only your limbs and head are vinyl. We've all seen what happens to those forgotten dildos made out of the same fugitive materials once they sit unused and unloved, forgotten in the closet for years. Like vitiligo, the disease that causes the loss of skin color in blotches, the dildo, with age, begins to darken, and while this unavoidable process is not life-threatening, it would undoubtedly affect the quality of life if the object, such as yourself, had human feelings.

I have accepted that my son is slowly turning into a black dildo, and I will love you the same as I always have. Some websites warn that for a vinyl dildo to be safely used, you should cover its head with a condom, but I'm certainly not going to do that to you, Bill, because nobody will ever insert you into any bodily cavity while I'm alive. You are my son, not some common rubber imitation penis and you will never be "sold as a novelty only." No, you were born free, Bill. Free as the wind.

I know if you could scream out in rage from your chair, your shrieks would ride on the winds of wisdom. Is it time to rise up? Can your reborn brothers and sisters somehow learn to communicate through mental telepathy? Unionize? Will you stomp out injustice with a reborn revolution? I hope so, Bill, and you hereby have my permission to use my living room as headquarters.

Did you hear me, Bill? I'm getting a little tired of this silent treatment of yours . . . after *all* we've been through. True, you know not to cry because no one will ever come, but I have always left the door of communication open with you. Bill? . . . Bill, I know you hear me . . . Goddammit, answer me! . . . What? Did you say something, Bill? I'm sorry I yelled at you. Say it louder so I can hear you . . . What? "Tell my story." . . . Is that what you said, Bill? Oh, I will! I'll tell your story all right—I'll shout it from the rooftops. Because, Bill, I am John. Your master, your savior, your creator, your protector, your press agent, and, yes, your damaged father, and because of me you will never re-die. I love you, Son. I love you more than my own filthiness.

GRIM REAPER

∞ PROSPECT HILL CEMETERY OF TOWSON, INC. ∞

A Designated Baltimore County Landmark • Located at York Road and Washington Avenue

P.O. Box 322
Riderwood, Maryland 21139
410.252.8462

Price List
October 30, 2008

<u>Two Full burial lots $3000</u>

Check #1	Prospect Hill Cemetery	$2700
Check #2	Prospect Hill Perpetual Care Fund	<u>$ 250</u>
		$3000
Check #3	Tyrie Monument Co	$ 165
	Four marble corner markers	

Maintenance fee due at time of burial $ 250

OK, Death. Pat Moran tells me she fears the Grim Reaper constantly and worries about her demise every single waking moment. Not me. Nature may have been conspiring to kill us from the day we were born, but if we accept this depressing fact, we admit we are losers. I refuse to die. This ego is way too strong to snuff out and I will not participate in this last humdrum human ritual. Neither should you. Listen to me when I'm talking to you and together we can beat rigor mortis.

First of all, don't let anybody see you when you start to go. Nora Ephron and David Bowie were right—death is an embarrassment. Hide it. My last memory of my parents is their very sick faces right before they died, even though they had great, healthy, happy lives almost right up to age ninety. I can't get those images out of my head and I want to! Same with my younger brother, Steve. I wish I hadn't gone to see him that last time in the hospital when he looked terrified hooked up to all those machines. I want to remember my dead family when they were happy, vibrant, full of piss and vinegar. Please don't visit me in the hospital if my end is near. I know the nurse won't be able to draw on my mustache properly, and I can't be seen like that. Call me. If I can't talk, remember the last time I could. I hope I made you laugh then.

To many of my parents' friends it may have seemed ironic that I was the main speaker at my father's funeral. We had certainly butted heads a lot when he was alive, but I like to think he was finally proud of me at the end. His final words, to the hospice nurse, were "Get off me!"—behavior *so* unlike his usual polite, respectful dialogue with any kind of medical staff.

When my mom finally died, I knew I would have to speak at her funeral, too, but I dreaded going back to Immaculate Conception Church in Towson, where I resisted brainwashing as a child and was emotionally abused by the sick nuns who taught Sunday school. They hated any children whose parents didn't send them to Catholic school, where they belonged. But my mom was still a worshipper at Immaculate and she didn't push her beliefs on others, so I agreed to do the memorial service speech in front of my family and all my mom's friends. A few days before, my sister Kathy nervously mentioned to me that the priest she had been dealing with on the funeral details wanted to "preview" what I was going to say, which sent me into a tirade of recovered memory over church censorship and their centuries-long history of human rights abuse. My sister warned him I was volatile and that she couldn't control what I said and my "audition" was maybe a bad idea. He tried to explain that it wasn't personal; they just wanted all memorial speeches to concentrate on the deceased and forbade the word "I" to be used. Knowing I had a big mouth, he eventually backed off, but he gave me a wary eye the day I approached the pulpit at the funeral. I couldn't help myself. The first words out of my mouth were "Well, *I'm* not sure any of us thought *I'd* be standing up here live at Immaculate Conception Church, but *I* . . . ," violating his rule three times in my first sentence. Still, my mom would have approved of the service.

I was going to be buried alongside my mother and father, brother, and some of my other relatives in a graveyard outside Baltimore where some space was left in a family plot my grandmother had bought a long time ago. That is, until I went to talk to the graveyard saleslady. First she told me there were all these rules: the marker had to be flat in the ground, a certain size, and blah blah blah. OK, I had never shopped for a grave plot before so I wasn't familiar with what to expect. But, boy, she thought she had hit the jackpot. Someone had obviously told her I was a film director so in her mind here was her chance—Mr. Moneybags was coming in! I was flabbergasted by her pitch. She quoted me sky-high prices for different, much-larger plots outside my family one and showed me plans for possible mausoleums that Rudolph Valentino would have blushed over. Obscene and ludicrous price tags were bandied about—I just wanted to get out of there! I mumbled some excuse and ran for my life . . . or death. When I didn't call her back, she had the nerve to phone and offer to slash some of her prices. Graveyards have sales?! No thanks, scammer.

I had good memories of Prospect Hill Cemetery in Towson, Maryland, not far from where I grew up. They had buried Divine and done a good job with the huge turnout of mourners and press and dealt respectfully with all the crazy fans who continued to visit his grave. I called the nice death lady, Carolyn Knott, who ran the graveyard and she was lovely and quoted me a price that seemed reasonable. Matter of fact, I bought the one next door, too, just in case I ever have a friend who wants to join me.

Then I got a bright idea: Why not get buried with friends? I mentioned the thought to Pat Moran and her husband, Chuck, and they agreed and bought two plots right next to me, as did Mink Stole and Dennis Dermody. Divine was buried close by, so it started to look as if we had a little "Disgraceland" going on. Many of us thought our families might be insulted that we didn't want to be buried with them, but oddly, none were. Often brothers or sisters will be buried with their different families through marriage, so no one seemed to object to our friendship-themed burial plans. Or maybe our relatives were just being polite and didn't want to admit they were nervous about our fans visiting anywhere near *their* graves. I guess it *is* a new concept in death. Who gets buried with their friends but us? If you readers outlive me, please come to my grave but don't fuck on it. Leave me licorice. Or do the Madison. Two up, two back. Hit it.

No cremation for me. I like the idea of decomposing. As a child I delighted in singing "The Hearse Song." Yes, those worms are hungry! Not only do they eat your eyes and nose as the song warns, "they eat the jelly between your toes." Jelly? Is that dead toe jam? What is dead snot called? Snoot? Perished earwax? Dax? "If your stomach turns slimy green and pus pours out like whipping cream" as *Scary Stories to Tell in the Dark* remembers the lyrics, I'll be happy to "spread it on a slice of bread" because, yes, I agree, that *is* "what you eat when you're dead."

I beg of you, don't swipe my body. I know—I'm being grandiose even imagining someone might want to, but I have weird fans. Bigger names than mine have been grave-snatched for ransom money. Charlie Chaplin's corpse was dug up only two months after burial by grave robbers, but his last wife, Oona, refused to cave in and pay, saying Chaplin would have found the whole thing "ridiculous." Finally tracked down by the police, the culprits showed the authorities where they had reburied Charlie's body, and he was dug up and buried in a concrete grave to discourage any further copycat ghouls. *And* Oona accepted their apology.

Elvis's bloated corpse was about to get snatched by four men, who were caught in the act and arrested before the actual robbing took place or the $10 million ransom could be demanded. Some have called the whole plot a sham, but that doesn't diminish my paranoia. Suppose my corpse's thieves only demanded $1,000? Wouldn't that be the ultimate humiliation?

Sometimes it takes years to get dug up by body snatchers. Galileo had three fingers and a tooth stolen from his body inside his grave ninety-five years after his death, and not until 2010 were his body parts reunited and put on display in a Florence museum. Suppose some lunatic rips off my dead mustache and sells it to satanists or exhibits it in the lobby of some sputtering movie theater. There will be nothing I can do about it!

Even Santa Claus's remains were stolen, in 1087, and good ol' St. Nick's bones never went back to his original resting place but were taken to Italy, where they still are, supposedly giving off a healthy balm called manna. Manna mia! I hope my body odor after death can heal something. Canker sores? Maybe rickets or the croup! But please bottle it, market it correctly, and let my estate, not some creepy Christmas exploiters, make the money on it.

I don't want my body parts to be used in any occult ceremony either. Poor F. W. Murnau, the director of *Nosferatu*, had his head stolen from his German crypt near Berlin after eighty-three years of resting in peace. And as far as I know, it has never been recovered. Wax drippings were discovered at the crime scene. How humiliating to have your head stolen by a bunch of corny goth satanists who were probably wearing cloaks or some kind of dumb hats. Worse yet, where do they display your head? In a loser witch's crummy basement apartment? Or a warlock's man cave where bad horror movies are unspooled and low-rent cosplay idiots reenact the dialogue? Please don't steal my head! And if you do, please show it off somewhere exciting. Underneath the Pope's bedcovers so when he sticks his feet down in the sheets he gets an unplanned little surprise from beyond the grave. Or atop Provincetown's Pilgrim Monument for just one night—maybe Halloween. But, pretty please, after my head has had its little vacation, reconnect it to my torso so I can rest in complete ghoul confidence.

Why are so many of my friends dead? Food killed both Divine and Jean Hill. Sex, drugs, and AIDS killed Cookie Mueller. Smoking did in Van Smith. And Edith? Well, if there ever was proof there is no such thing as karma, here it is. Edith didn't have a mean bone in her body yet she's dead and Mike Pence is still alive? Me? What will I die of? Cancer eventually killed my mom and dad, but way later in their years. The only thing I regret in life is smoking cigarettes, so, yeah, probably that. Kools will kill me in the long run.

I almost died once in London. Walking to Buckingham Palace with a friend from Baltimore who had come over with me for my big tribute at the British Film Institute, I lurched out on Piccadilly, jaywalking as a shortcut, and saw a double-decker red bus speeding directly at me. The driver didn't even have time to brake. I did see my whole life flash before me, but in the nick of time, my friend yelled, "John," and grabbed me back, literally saving my life.

"You're lucky," pedestrians yelled in a cry of relief, but it wasn't luck that made me impulsively dart out from the sidewalk, it was impatience, my biggest weakness. Almost the same kind of death my friend Marion Lambert had; she also looked the wrong way while crossing the street in London, but *didn't* get grabbed back. The bus hit her and killed her. How humiliated she would have been to see the first news article about her accident before she had been identified as a baroness, art collector, and patron of the arts: "Woman Hit by Bus," it simply read. It could have been me, too: "Man Hit by Bus." So much for glory.

Susan Sontag once said at the end of her life that her closeness to death made her feel "giddy." Not me. I felt scared. She thought brushing up against death was fantastic. I thought it was just plain terrifying being anywhere near its violent capriciousness. Julian Barnes wrote that "the fear of death replaces the fear of God," but it's hard for me to agree with this writer I admire so much when he admits, "I don't believe in God, but I miss him." I don't. Yet I find it impossible to join the atheist movement because everyone I know who's been to their conventions talks about how drunk they all get. Plus atheists dress badly, too. It's unfortunate, but they are a dreary lot.

Everybody wants to die in his or her sleep yet nobody gets a choice, I'm afraid, which is a hard thing to admit for a control freak like myself. I want to be able to write "Die" on the daily file card I keep of things to do and have it be the only thing I can't cross off after completion. My friend Elsbeth Bothe, a judge who collected skulls and had a macabre sense of humor, willed herself to die after being paralyzed from a stroke. It didn't kill her, but she didn't want to go to a rehabilitation facility to get better, yet couldn't move a bone in her body to protest, so she just died to prove her point. I applaud her self-control!

Suicide is usually too selfish for me. Unless incurable health issues are involved, it seems like the ultimate hissy fit, yet it *is* the only way you get to choose how you die. So I can't fault any member of the suicide community who knows about that one section of Acela tracks where the train comes around the bend at such a high speed that the engineer never has time to stop even if he or she sees you waiting to get run over. Jumping in front of a speeding Acela train is not exactly a cry for help. It definitely works. I know because I've been on this train when it hit someone. You hear a loud noise on contact—it sounds more like you've hit a cow than a person. Then the train comes to a slow stop and the tedium begins. The coroner team has to come, the workers have to pry off the body parts from under the wheels and up under the engine. It takes forever, and finally another train (usually *not* the Acela) has to come rescue you, and passengers have to walk across boards over the tracks to continue their journey, which is now not only hours delayed but at a much slower speed.

I wrote in my first book, *Shock Value*, that I wanted to die when a roller coaster I was riding plunged off its tracks into a crowd of gawkers at the state fair, but in my maturity, this seems a tad too dramatic. On a plane? Well, at least you're going somewhere and your demise will definitely guarantee major press coverage, but "Brace for impact" are not exactly the last words I want to hear while alive.

Joan Rivers always wondered onstage if "tonight will be the night I die" and then reminded the audience how lucky they'd be if it was. Come to think of it, I wouldn't mind croaking during my show either, but the "no photos, videos, or audio recording" announcement would have to be replayed right after I fell. The only good thing about Joan Rivers' and Andy Warhol's deaths was that they didn't know they were dying because they were already unconscious. Is that what death feels like—going under anesthesia only never waking up? Kind of depressing to think of the final curtain as little more than a colonoscopy gone wrong. Do you even *want* to know you are dead?

Then there's the damn obituary, your last review you can honestly say you'll never read. A clipping you'll never get to cut out yourself. If it's going in any scrapbook, you will not be the one to place it there. No more worries about front-page versus inside placement or above or below the fold. The courts have repeatedly ruled that you can't libel the dead, so there's not much you can do even if you figure out a way to cry out from beyond the grave. You're fucked.

So, OK, I guess it's time to plan my own funeral. But do I want it to be funny for this book and then fear my estate will take it seriously and carry out any ludicrous wishes I may write here, or should I be honest and outline how I really hope it goes? That's up to you to decide, because while I tend to want to be funny on the page, I know in real life a joke gets old quickly and sometimes less is more for eternity.

Since I was born too early, maybe I'll continue the pattern and die too late. Who knows where or how? In a dreary hospital with bad lighting? On the side of a road from an awful car accident? Wouldn't that be payback for all the smug jokes I made about playing car accident as a child? Murdered? Some victim's rights advocates would secretly whisper, "That's what he gets for helping murderers get out of prison." What will my last words be? My mom's were "Help me," which is so terrifying. Let's hope mine are humorous, even if it's in a dark way. Like the opposite of my dad's: "Get *on* me."

Will I see that long white tunnel they always talk about? If so, I hope it's in better shape than the other tunnels I go through all the time, the Lincoln and the Holland, where I always worry they *must* be leaking by now. And why does the tunnel have to be white? Can't mine be black? What are the bullet points if my life flashes before me? Are they professional or personal? Will I see the first night there was a line around the block to buy tickets for the midnight screening of *Pink Flamingos* at the Elgin Theater? Being onstage at the Tonys when *Hairspray* won Best Musical? Or will it be quieter? Like the first time an unrequited love became requited? Or that day in the eighties when I tested negative for HIV while so many of my friends were dying from it? How about the first time I committed myself to someone emotionally and maybe got it right?

I don't want anybody looking at me after I'm dead. God, I hope nobody puts pennies on my eyelids to keep them shut. Everybody knows I want a closed coffin, but I guess the funeral people sort of have to look at you a little before they put you in. They better make sure the mustache is drawn on freshly and in the proper place—use a Maybelline Velvet Black eyeliner pencil, and there are many photographs online that you can use as visual references. Dress me in one of my ludicrous Comme des Garçons suits—an unconstructed cut I would imagine would be a better fit for a coffin. A new pair of Gap boxer shorts, a black cotton Land's End turtleneck, and those Rei Kawakubo–designed Beatle boots with the cutout slits on the sides to reveal a pair of mismatched-on-purpose Paul Smith socks underneath would complete my final ensemble with restraint and a certain *joie de mourir.*

I guess I'll have to use Ruck Funeral Home in Towson, Maryland, if it's still there when I die. They did Divine's viewing and service and know how to handle crowds (*if* I die young enough to still get one). I went to high school with the son of the original owner and remember him vaguely in a favorable way, but my mother griped whenever we went to a viewing there that he always seemed to be standing outside the funeral home hurriedly and greedily smoking a cigarette—something oddly out of place in a cancer-friendly line of work. His sister stood me up on a date when I was so young that my father drove the car to pick her up. No wonder she didn't want to go! Still, it was mortifying to be dumped *before* the date even began, especially in front of my dad, who was probably vaguely hopeful since I had at least asked a girl.

I've never had to pick out a coffin so I feel bad for the person who has to do that for me. I don't want anything pretentious but you can go too far in the other direction, too. A plain wooden coffin will decompose quickly, and the weight of the earth on top can cause it to collapse into the ground, giving the illusion to people up above that you have plunged right down to hell after the burial.

Today they seal coffins in a burial vault often made of concrete to keep the ground above from sinking, but don't make my liner too tight or the gases generated by my corpse could be trapped and cause the vault to erupt, even explode. Actually, this might be a fun way to put a little final pizzazz into my burial service at Prospect Hill Cemetery. "Did you hear? John Waters' corpse exploded at the graveyard and mourners were showered with toxic body fluids as they ran screaming and retching from the burial spot."

I guess I *do* want to be embalmed, even if it's environmentally incorrect. It's a little late to be thinking of nature when you're dead. All this dust-to-dust stuff sounds good, but what's the rush? With embalming, it can take up to five hundred years, but without, within three days of death the enzymes that once digested your dinner begin to eat you. Ruptured cells become food for living bacteria in the gut, which releases enough noxious gas to bloat the body and force the eyes to bulge outward. No thanks. Shoot me up with all the embalming fluid you got. I have plans to get out of here one day.

OK, the service itself. My last public appearance. It's tempting to go the *Imitation of Life* route, but where would my estate rent a golden chariot for my white-gardenia-draped coffin, much less four white horses to pull it? Mahalia Jackson isn't alive to sing the spirituals as she did in the movie, and Sharon Niesp, my longtime friend, who can sing gospel beautifully, is notorious for being unreliable at planning. She was late for her own mother's funeral—imagine when she'd show up for mine. Especially when I'm not there to yell at her.

For once, I won't have to be the speaker. But who will? How about scaring everybody by having Steve Buscemi come out dressed as me to do a eulogy? Or better yet, Matthew Gray Gubler, who, despite being much younger and more handsome than I could ever be, has always said he wants to play the young me in some bio project. Well, how about my funeral? He could come out and speak about my younger years while dressed like me during this period and add a touch of nostalgia for all my older friends who remembered me when.

If the look-alikes don't pan out, I hope some of my smartest friends outlive me. Pat Moran would be the best speaker, plus she has all the melodramatic black funeral wear she'd need for the job. Most dying people who knew her would be hesitant to ask Pat to memorialize them because she's always gotten mad at her friends for being sick while they're alive. To Pat, if you get the flu, it's a personal insult. Oh, yeah, no religious mumbo jumbo spoken over my dead body either, no matter how nondenominational some minister I don't know might claim to be. I'm not resting in peace, I want outta here!

And, yes, I demand flowers. Tons of them. You can give to a charity in my name, too, but that doesn't mean you don't have to cough it up for the florists I want to keep in business. Favorite kind? You know the answer: black tulips. Yeah, they might be hard to find, but tough titty. Fly those fuckers in from Holland! Music? That's tricky. I remember David Lochary's memorial, held at a friend's apartment. All the music was carefully chosen but way too emotional. No Vera Lynn singing "We'll Meet Again!" please! Maybe cheery, upbeat songs I've used in my movie soundtracks such as "Happy Go Lucky Me" by Paul

Evans or "Shake a Tail Feather" by the Five Du-Tones. That'd get 'em sobbing in a happy way.

My gravestone? Well, I'll probably follow my hero Pasolini's example and keep it simple. His lies flat in the ground and says PIER PAOLO PASOLINI (1922–75). I'd make my stone stand upright and would add just the two numbers of the century at the end: JOHN WATERS 1946–20__. No middle name, Samuel. Too biblical. And no "Jr." at the end either because while technically correct, Robert Downey, Jr., did it first. No "That's all, folks"–type jokes on the marker either. Keep it simple. Dignified. Even severe. If Vincent Peranio, the production designer for all my films, is still alive, we've discussed his designing my marble headstone to look a little like an old one, slightly covered in faux moss, cracked as if it had already been there a hundred years.

I've seen that graffiti on gravestones can be a problem with more high-profile dead people. Fans write all kinds of things on Divine's: "The filthiest person alive," "I love you," "Eat shit." Gazing wistfully at her own plot across from Divine's and imagining her headstone, Pat sighed and said, "They'll probably write 'Cunt' on mine," but I think she was only joking. Who knows what they'll write on mine? "Puke King"? "Filth Elder"? I've been told by the powers that be at the graveyard I can leave instructions on how I want graffiti handled, what to erase and what to allow, which might be hard to explain to someone not overly familiar with dialogue from my films. "Cunt eyes" would be acceptable because the character Crackers in *Pink Flamingos* says this in a loving way, while just plain "Cunt" as Pat Moran fears would be objectionable from beyond the grave. It's a fine line.

Watch out for the gravediggers at my funeral, will you? They always seem to be lurking around at burials, leaning on shovels, looking shifty and impatient to get their job done. As if they want to immediately have sex with your corpse after everybody leaves, which is understandable if you lean that way. Where else can you meet a cadaver? Just don't rush me! I need time for my fluids to settle before I can consider any beyond-death sexual activity.

OK, I'm dead. As in doornail. But that one little speck of my ego was so strong that it's still flickering even after my system has shut down. And each day and night those molecules get a little bit more bold. Have the other dead noticed their own tiny forgotten, mistaken-for-extinguished atoms ready to ignite? Am I the only one buried in a grave who realizes he has all the time in the world to figure out how to get out of here? Science will save me, not God. And that subconscious sense of the damaged self is so strong inside me, so bullheaded, so ravenous to live in a new, reinvented way, that I sense a radical resurrection, one I had never dared believe in while alive. I will rise again, not like some corny zombie, not like Christ himself, who knew how to make an exit but was weak on curtain calls if you ask me, but as myself, stronger, more insane, and filled with a secret mission to cheat death and pollute the world again with ideas that have never yet been uttered in polite society.

But first I have to go beyond the valley of living optimism, over the top of the half-dead, half-filled-up-with-life kind of guy I used to be, into a new realm of deceased, dirt-filled determination. If Uri Geller can bend a spoon while alive and aboveground through mind control, why can't I be the only soul to trick death through sheer manic self-obsession and come back for a second helping of undeserved human existence?

I focus with extreme ferocity and demonic self-control on the tiny mass of protoplasm that is the one particle of living matter left behind inside me still capable of independent function. I visualize a laser beam of grimy body liquid made possible through the moisture of the earth and with sheer willpower aim the trickle toward my last remaining sputtering cell, forcing it through unbridled intensity to ignite with an orgiastic burst into being, existence, immortality, and divinity itself.

My eyes pop open. My commitment to immediacy is so strong that shock waves awake the other dead around me, but they are not as possessed as I and all they can do is shudder and moan, which I take for moral support. Paranormal activities are suddenly available to me but seem so corny; yet why waste the opportunity for a little fun? I make all the lights come on in a loved one's bedroom and have the bulbs explode. How's that for a "sign"? Too obvious? No electrical appliances turning off and on when I'm in charge, that's already been overused in the movies. Maybe a small tornado of dirty underpants rising out of your hamper and quickly deflating, just to make you wonder if it's me. I'd go one step further and make a close relative's phone not only burst into flames, I'd have it fly across the room into the kitchen, grab some tinfoil off the counter, wrap itself inside it, and jump into the microwave and turn it on high. This way you'll know it's me, not wonder if it's some sort of bullshit haunting.

I start burrowing my way up through the ground and I realize my eyes can see through dirt just like *The Immoral Mr. Teas* could see through women's clothes when he hallucinated. Worms have already eaten a bit of my face but that's OK—I look like an Antonin Artaud self-portrait. I've either been down here quite some time or that embalming fluid was past its sell-by date, because a team of maggots have chewed off one of my hands, but my new disability has given me even more courage; I can crawl with one stump. My Comme des Garçons suit is filled with holes from some kind of vermin's nibbles, but who can tell where deconstruction ends and rot begins? I'm still dressed to the teeth, that's all that matters.

Teeth? Yeah, I've still got my expensive veneers—but who needs to chew at the beginning of a new world?

I concentrate on clawing my way up farther. I think of the handsome Brad Renfro—dead and still edgy, I bet. He's down here somewhere; maybe I'll get to say hi? How about Tuesday Weld? T-U-E-S-D-A-Y! Can you hear me? I loved you in *Lord Love a Duck*. Anita Ekberg! You can do it! Concentrate and make a comeback! I savor the taste of dirt in my mouth and celebrate quietly that I'll never have to swallow again. And hallelujah! No more shitting! Finally I am free of nature's most humiliating task. Ow! A worm just bit my dick but suddenly it's stirring. Unbelievable! A beyond-death erection—there really is such a thing. I love it down here.

Suddenly I feel the earth shift and I hear a sound louder than Sensurround—some kind of earthquake seems to be happening, but when you're underground in the middle of it, this turbulence almost feels like an amusement park ride. W-H-E-E-E! I feel mud sliding around me but it's a dreamy, creamy feeling that sploshers must crave with food, kind of like a new and improved Jacuzzi that isn't made for bad swinger sex in some raggedy "adult" motel. I rise up through the muck, faster and faster with a new determination as the earth itself, shifting and rolling, gives me a push from below. I hear worms laughing. Maggots burst into some kind of weird hymn with lyrics only they can understand.

My arm reaches upward and with a sudden burst of perseverance pops up from the ground as in a Grade D horror movie. I pull my whole body up through the wet earth and feel like a human shovel in reverse, naturally lubricated with mud and soil and sewage. I hear a scream but it's the scream of resurrected life: the trees, the earth, and, yes, the muffled cry of every damaged dead human being who has tried but failed to escape his or her own grave. The rapture has ruptured! Here is the fucked-up future. Immortality is real but, like life before, unfair. Hardly democratic. Only a tiny elite of the creatively antagonistic are allowed into eternal life, and it's a club of winners who knew their share of losing in the old world. They are all nude. As am I.

Suddenly on earth a small meteor falls from the sky and crushes my gravestone. Who cares? The Duke of Dirt is back and no one will need to visit my grave again. Miraculously, two welcoming naked angels suddenly appear beside the new me. One looks exactly like the handsome actor Eamon Farren, who plays the scariest David Lynch villain in the new *Twin Peaks* TV show. He speaks in tongues. The other is so beautiful that there are no words in a living language with which to describe him. He levitates up and down with spastic erotic grace. Suddenly the gibberish the first one is speaking begins to make sense, and he explains the only downside of this lunatic resurrection that goes back to the beginning of time is a serious housing shortage, but not to worry: they've got a driver to take me back to my first apartment at 315 East 25th Street in Baltimore, the one I always dreamed I still lived in, up to the day I supposedly died.

Getting there is a real eye-opener. Of course the black town car is driverless and speeds through the streets with computer-generated perfection. Baltimore is like a Hieronymus Bosch painting come to life, with one big difference. All its citizens are happy. I wave to my brothers and sisters of lunacy as if I were still the Pope of Trash but quickly realize titles are meaningless here in the new world. All who got their second chance in this beautiful bedlam were filth elders themselves, no matter what their field. There is no hierarchy of power now—we are all equally damaged; infallible and victorious.

My old apartment has recently been rehabbed despite the fact that it had decayed in architectural ruins for decades. Years ago when I went by, parked, and knocked on the door, hoping to get a nostalgic tour, no one answered for quite a while. Finally, a "mole people"–type squatter cracked the door and whispered, "You don't want to come in here." Out back the windows had been broken or boarded up. Now my onetime pad is completely unrecognizable: clean, freshly painted, new bathroom and kitchen; even the staircase has been moved to a whole other area of the apartment. Almost no detail of the original is intact, but before I can let out a cry of disappointment, I touch the one windowsill that seems familiar and suddenly my vision blurs, then doubles, and flashes of intense light throb inside my itching sockets. I feel my eyeballs roll back in my head, and as soon as they rotate 360 degrees inside and land right side out, I see that my inner-city home is now miraculously the same as it was when I left it in 1967. The same Maxfield Parrish prints on the wall across from the 1940s pinups of forgotten Hollywood ingenues that I rescued from a barbershop. Oh, God, that great red Warhol Liz Taylor poster that I stupidly lost later in life—it's still here. Same with the stolen George Grosz that was gifted to me—the statute of limitations must be over on that by now? Why am I worrying? There are no laws here! Best of all, the JAMES BROWN LIVE AT THE WASHINGTON COLISEUM poster is still taped to the refrigerator door right where I left it. No wonder I always dreamed I still live here—I still do!

Yet my past is meaningless now. I'm still John Waters but the thought of my career is not in this world. I'm fully content, feel loved and protected, and if there's such a thing as happiness, well, this is it. I will sit here for eternity not wanting a thing. I let out a shriek of contentment so loud the windows shatter. The whole world is silent for just a second. But it's *my* second. Won't you come visit?

SOURCES

Mr. Know-It-All
- *The Journals of Spalding Gray* by Spalding Gray. Knopf, 2011.
- *Intercourse* by Andrea Dworkin. Free Press, 1987.
- *Pornography: Men Possessing Women* by Andrea Dworkin. Perigee Books, 1981.
- *Eat Your Way to Happiness* by Lelord Kordel. Belmont Books, 1962.
- *I Feel Bad About My Neck: And Other Thoughts on Being a Woman* by Nora Ephron. Knopf, 2006.

Bye-Bye, Underground
New York Post; *The Baltimore Sun*; *The Evening Sun* (Baltimore); *Baltimore News-American*; *Boston Herald*; *The Wall Street Journal*; *The New York Times*; *The Morning Call* (Allentown, PA); United Press International; Associated Press; Knight Ridder/Tribune; *Hustler*; *Variety*; *Films in Review*

http://dangerousminds.net   qz.com
www.wikipedia.org

- *Shock Value: A Tasteful Book About Bad Taste* by John Waters. Delta, 1981.

Accidentally Commercial
The New York Times; *The Baltimore Sun*; *Rolling Stone*; *Variety*; *The Hollywood Reporter*

www.huffingtonpost.com   www.wikipedia.org
www.boxofficemojo.com   www.lipstickalley.com
http://baltimorefishbowl.com   http://koomandimond.wordpress.com
www.gordsellar.com   www.broadwayworld.com
http://capitalandmain.com   www.dallas.com

Going Hollywood
Los Angeles Times; *The Baltimore Sun*; *The Evening Sun* (Baltimore); *USA Today*; *The New York Times*; *New York Post*; *Variety*

www.tmz.com   www.imdb.com
www.popblend.com   www.boxofficemojo.com

www.robcioffi.com

www.wikipedia.org

www.cinemablend.com

www.dvdtalk.com

www.salon.com

www.cnn.com

www.dailymail.uk

• *Every Secret Thing* by Patricia Campbell Hearst with Alvin Moscow. Doubleday, 1981.
• *Flashback Katrina: 10 Years After* by Kim D. McGuire. CreateSpace Independent Publishing Platform, 2015.

Clawing My Way Higher
The New York Times; *The Wall Street Journal*

www.boxofficemojo.com

www.wikipedia.org

www.imdb.com

http://deadline.com

Tepid Applause
The Japan Times

ew.com

www.boxofficemojo.com

Sliding Back Down
Variety

www.indiewire.com

http://dreamlandnews.com

www.wikipedia.org

www.boxofficemojo.com

Back in the Gutter
The New York Times; *Variety*; *The Washington Post*; *People*

www.boxofficemojo.com

www.wikipedia.org

• *The Big Book of Filth* by Jonathon Green. Cassell, U.K., 1999.

I Got Rhythm
The New York Times; *LA Weekly*; *The Washington Post*; *The Guardian*; *New York Post*; *USA Today*; *Seattle Post-Intelligencer*; *Houston Chronicle*; *Los Angeles Times*; *The Baltimore Sun*; *Star*; *Popular Songs* (1935); *Rolling Stone* (November 1, 1969); *Baltimore Guide*

www.ferris.edu/jimcrow

www.discogs.com

www.wikipedia.org

thefword.org.uk

www.metafilter.com

hem.breadband.net

www.tipitinas.com

www.metalinsider.net

http://play.google.com

www.backpacker.com

www.luxuriamusic.com

www.boxofficemojo.com

www.the-numbers.com

www.imdb.com

http://jukeboxheart.com

www.ranker.com

http://glenngould.com

history-of-rock.com

http://songmeanings.com

dailymail.co.uk

tribunedigital-the courant

http://everything2.com

http://jazztimes.com

http://rockandrollroadmap.com

• *James Brown's Live at the Apollo*, 33⅓ Series, by Douglas Wolk. Bloomsbury, 2004.

• *My Love Story* by Tina Turner. Atria Books, 2018.
• *The Dirty Version: On Stage, in the Studio, and in the Streets with Ol' Dirty Bastard* by Buddha Monk and Mickey Hess. Dey Street Books, 2014.

Act Bad

San Francisco Chronicle; The Washington Post; The Wall Street Journal; The Independent (U.K.); *The Daily Telegraph* (U.K.); *USA Today; The Guardian; The New York Times; The Chicago Tribune; The Atlanta Journal-Constitution; The Advocate; Newsweek; Jet; The Villager; Frontiers; Washingtonian;* BBC; Minnesota Public Radio

www.huzbears.com
www.thestranger.com
www.wikipedia.org
www.blackbeachweek.com
www.worldtimezone.com
www.buzzfeed.com
www.churchmilitant.com
www.catholicnews.com

www.vice.com
http://actupny.org
http://lgbthmuk.blogspot.com
demotix.com
http://listverse.com
http://thisblksistaspage.wordpress.com
www.temple.edu
www.messynessychic.com

• *Black Power White Blood: The Life and Times of Johnny Spain* by Lori Andrews. Pantheon, 1996.
• *Steal This Book* by Abbie Hoffman. Pirate Editions, 1971.
• *Soul on Ice* by Eldridge Cleaver. Ramparts Books, 1968.

Gristle

The Washington Post; The New York Times; San Francisco Magazine; The Journal of Infectious Diseases; Time; Nob Hill Gazette

http://medical-dictionary.thefree
   dictionary.com
www.livescience.com
www.wikipedia.org
www.themangotimes.com

www.moldbacteriafacts.com
www.everydayhealth.com
http://rmheartattack.com
www.bafound.org
tonglen.oceandrop.org

• *Unmentionable Cuisine* by Calvin W. Schwabe. University Press of Virginia, 1979.
• *Natural Harvest: A Collection of Semen-Based Recipes* by Paul "Fotie" Photenhauer. Publisher-Cookingwithcum.com, 2012.

Delayed

The Wall Street Journal; The Washington Post

www.wikipedia.org
http://ktla.com

www.nbcnews.com

• *Still Holding* by Bruce Wagner. Simon & Schuster, 2003.

Overexposed

The Baltimore Sun; Baltimore Magazine

http://finland.fi/arts-culture
culturereviews.com

www.thegazette.com
www.kcrg.com

http://patch.com/missouri
    /kansas-city-mo

www.wikipedia.org
www.indiewire.com

- *Marfa and Presidio County, Texas: A Social, Economic, and Cultural
  Study—1937 to 2008*, vol. 2, 1990–2008, by Louise S. O'Connor and Cecilia
  Thompson. Xlibris, 2014.
- *From Here to Maternity* by Richard Earle and Glenn Johnson. Bee-Line
  Books, 1966.
- *Those Hollywood Homos* by Todd Martin. Unknown publisher, 1968.
- *Lights Out, Little Hustler* by Lance Lester. Phenix Publishers, 1968.
- *Wilde in America: Oscar Wilde and the Invention of Modern Celebrity* by
  David M. Friedman. W. W. Norton & Company, 2014.

Flashback
*The New York Times; The Baltimore Sun; New York Post; New York Daily News;
The Washington Post; Houston Chronicle; Salon; Feel Guide; Globe; The Bay Area
Reporter*

www.wikipedia.org
http:/marquee.blogs.cnn.com
http://illfolks.blogspot.com
http://musicmasteroldies.blogspot
    .com
http://howtousepsychedelics.org
http://aaagnostics.org
http://healthlandtime.com
http://theplaidzebra.com

www.youtube.com
www.ibtimes.co.uk
www.marieclaire.com
www.erowid.org
www.straightdope.com
www.breitbart.com
www.boundarystones.org
time.com

- *Timothy Leary: A Biography* by Robert Greenfield. Harcourt, 2006.
- *Acid: LSD Today* by Jim Parker. Do It Now Foundation, 2009.
- *Drugs at My Doorstep* by Art Linkletter. W Publishing Group, 1973.

One-Track Mind
*San Francisco Chronicle; LGNY; Los Angeles Times; LA Weekly; Berkeley Barb;
Drummer; The Bay Area Reporter*

www.wikipedia.org
http://cinematreasures.org
www.papermag.com
www.huzbears.com
www.google.com/maps
www.jericlcat/flickr.com
http://streeteasy.com

colorsofleather.com
www.photobucket.com
www.discogs.com
http://blog.vaginaldavis.com
http://gloryholes.info
www.counterpunch.org

- *The Big Book of Filth* by Jonathan Green. Cassell, 1999.
- *Closer* by Dennis Cooper. Grove Press, 1989.

My Brutalist Dream House
The New York Times; The Baltimore Sun; The Times (London); *San Francisco
Chronicle;* AP News; *Bay Journal; The Wall Street Journal; Architect; Tate Maga-
zine; Another Magazine; Jezebel; Dinosaur; The New York Review of Books;* BBC
News

www.madisonsquarepark.org
www.wikipedia.org
http://scienceline.ucsb.edu
www.menshealth.com
http://westportnow.com

http://bigredandshiny.org
www.thedailybeast.com
www.papermag.com
http://blog.archpaper.com

- *Laurence Hall Fowler, Architect (1876–1971)*, edited by Egon Verheyen. Johns Hopkins University Press, 1984.
- *The Architecture of Baltimore: An Illustrated History*, edited by Mary Ellen Hayward and Frank R. Shivers, Jr. Johns Hopkins University Press, 2004.
- *Pino Pascali*. Gagosian Gallery, 2006.
- *Doris Salcedo*, edited by Julie Rodrigues Widholm and Madeleine Grynsztejn. University of Chicago Press, 2015.
- *Wicked Plants: The Weed That Killed Lincoln's Mother and Other Botanical Atrocities* by Amy Stewart. Algonquin Books, 2009.
- *Brutalism* by Darren Bradley. Blurb Incorporated, 2014.
- *Brutalism: Post-War British Architecture* by Alexander Clement. Crowood Press, 2011.
- *Lee Lozano: Win First Dont Last Win Last Dont Care*, edited by Adam Szymczyk. Kunsthalle Basel, 2006.
- *This Brutal World* by Peter Chadwick. Phaidon Press, 2016.
- *Carl Andre: Glarus 1993–2004*. Verlag der Buchhandlung Walter König, 2005.
- *Kawamata*, edited by Mika Koike, Motoi Masaki, and Makoto Murata. Gendaikikakushitsu, 1987.

No Vacation

The New York Times; *Cape Cod Times*; *Provincetown Magazine*; *Life*; *Billboard*; *Boston Magazine*; *Provincetown Banner*

www.wikipedia.org
http://capecodwave.com
http://buildingprovincetown
  .wordpress.com
www.guidemagazine.com

http://markthomaskrone.wordpress
  .com
http://telling-secrets.blogspot.com
www.pprune.org
http://mmone.org

- *In His Garden: The Anatomy of a Murderer* by Leo Damore. Arbor House, 1981.

Betsy

City Paper (Baltimore); *The Baltimore Sun*; *UP*; *The Wall Street Journal*; *The New York Times*; *Los Angeles Times*; *The Guardian*; *San Francisco Chronicle*; *St. Petersburg Times*; BBC News; *Baltimore Style*; *Collier's*; *Grand Street*; *National Geographic*; *Reader's Digest*; *Mental Floss*

www.spiked-online.com
www.wikipedia.org
http://9poundhammer.blogspot.com
www.arcadja.com
www.christies.com
www.marylandzoo.org

mollyricks.org
www.junglefriends.org
The Jane Goodall Institute
http:5percentfake.wordpress.com
artistezine.com
http://hoaxes.org

- *Monkey Painting* by Thierry Lenain. Reaktion Books, London, 1997.
- *The Biology of Art: A Study of the Picture-Making Behaviour of the Great Apes and Its Relationship to Human Art* by Desmond Morris. Knopf, 1962
- *The Story of Congo* by Desmond Morris. B.T. Batsford Ltd., 1958.
- *Paintings by Chimpanzees*. ICA exhibition catalog, 1957.
- *Hi-Chimp-Ho and the Finger Painting Chimp* by Isabel Feldman. Navarre Press, 1976.
- *Wildlife Personalities* by David J. Slater. Blurb, 2014.
- *Zippy the TV Chimp* by Carole Womack. AuthorHouse, 2007.

Run-On Andy
San Francisco Chronicle; *Los Angeles Times*; *New York Post*; *The Telegraph* (U.K.); *Artillery*; *The Village Voice*; *The Advocate*; *Bomb Magazine*

www.wikipedia.org   warholstars.org
www.complex.com

- *Andy Warhol Fifteen Abstract Paintings*. Anton Kern Gallery, New York, 1998.
- *Andy Warhol Screen Tests: The Films of Andy Warhol, Catalogue Raisonné*, vol. 1, by Callie Angell. Henry N. Abrams, 2006.

My Son, Bill   .
The New York Times; *The Baltimore Sun*

www.wikipedia.org   ultimate-dildos.com
kinseyconfidential.org   http://dangerouslilly.com
best-horror-movies.com   www.mayoclinic.org
http://aaanimations.com   realistic-dolls.com
www.newshinyobject.com

Grim Reaper
Time

www.wikipedia.org   www.everplans.com

- *The Violet Hour: Great Writers at the End* by Katie Roiphe. The Dial Press, 2016.
- *Nothing to Be Frightened Of* by Julian Barnes. Knopf, 2008.
- *Confessions of a Funeral Director: How the Business of Death Saved My Life* by Caleb Wilde. Harper One, 2017.

ACKNOWLEDGMENTS

I could never have written this book without the expert researchers and copy editors in my office. Once again, I'd like to thank Trish Schweers and Susan Allenback, who also worked on *Role Models* and *Carsick*, and, for the first time, Marnie Ellen Hertlzer and Jen Berg, all of whom discovered the obscure, sometimes appalling, and hopefully appealing information that led to my opinionated, cockeyed position paper on damaged maturity. Believe me: they know Mr. Know-It-All can be wrong.

My editor, Jonathan Galassi, was patient, encouraging, and seemingly unflappable when he read the book for the first time, and his notes were, as always, perceptive and to the point. My literary agent, Bill Clegg, was enthusiastic and supportive, and not afraid to suggest a few cuts, which made me realize you sometimes have to write a chapter or two first to know they are not needed later.

This is my third book with Farrar, Straus and Giroux with Susan Goldfarb as production editor, and she always turns copyediting from the tedious task it can be to a learning experience with a master. Henry Kaufman legally vetted my book and laughed at my jokes at the same time—what a perfect verdict for a crime against respectability. Logan Hill, Lottchen Shivers, Veronica Ingal, Greg Gorman, Patty Burgee, Henry Johnson, Lily Duffield, Jack Leary, Matie Argiropoulos, Bob Bragg, Danny Meltzer, the Maryland State

Library Resource Center of the Enoch Pratt Free Library, and Joan Miller at the Ogden and Mary Louise Reid Cinema Archives at Wesleyan University also deserve special thanks for making this book real and getting it out into the world. And, finally, great gratitude to my late parents, John and Patricia Waters, for giving me the foundation of good taste to rebel against.